Contents

Alone Together

Alone Together

HOW MARRIAGE IN AMERICA IS CHANGING

Paul R. Amato

Alan Booth

David R. Johnson

Stacy J. Rogers

HARVARD UNIVERSITY PRESS

Cambridge, Massachusetts

London, England

First Harvard University Press paperback edition, 2009.

Library of Congress Cataloging-in-Publication Data

Alone together : how marriage in America is changing / Paul R. Amato . . .
[et al.].
      p.   cm.
   Includes bibliographical references and index.
   ISBN 978-0-674-02281-2 (cloth)
   ISBN 978-0-674-03217-0 (pbk.)
   1. Marriage—United States.   I. Amato, Paul R.
HQ536A538 2007
306.810973'09045—dc22   2006043728

Figures

Acknowledgments

We thank Norval Glenn, Susan Welch, and the anonymous reviewers for assistance and advice with various aspects of this book. We also thank Glenn Firebaugh for guidance on data analysis. We are grateful to numerous students with whom we have discussed our findings and interpretations. In addition, we are indebted to the respondents who participated so generously in the study. The data set described in this book is based on the efforts of many people. John Edwards, Gay Kitson, F. Ivan Nye, and Lynn White helped to design the original study, and the staff of the Bureau of Sociological Research at the University of Nebraska–Lincoln carried out the interviews and prepared the computer files for data analysis. The study was supported by the Pennsylvania State University Population Research Institute, the University of Nebraska–Lincoln Research Council, grant number 5R01 AG04146 from the National Institute on Aging, and grant number R24 HD41025 from the National Institute of Child Health and Human Development. We are grateful to Ann Twombly for her excellent copyediting: not too little and not too much. Finally, we greatly appreciate the support of Michael Aronson and Donna Bouvier of Harvard University Press, who guided our book to completion.

Alone Together

𝒮 1

The Continuing Transformation
of Marriage in America

𝒯HROUGHOUT MOST of American history, marriage has
been the social arrangement that, more than any other, provided structure and meaning in people's lives. Matrimony served as a marker for
leaving the parental home, forming one's own household, becoming
economically independent of parents, initiating regular sexual activity,
and having children. Moreover, the roles of husband and wife provided
scripts that guided and organized everyday activities such as breadwinning, household labor, and child rearing. Spousal roles also were
core features of people's identities. Many people did not feel that they
had reached adulthood until they accepted the responsibilities of marriage and parenthood. Because matrimony was a central feature of
adult life, the great majority of people in the United States married,
married relatively early in life, and stayed continuously married until the death of one spouse. And remarriage following the death of a
spouse (or the occasional divorce) was the norm.

But times have changed. The growing popularity of nonmarital cohabitation, the increase in the percentage of children born outside
marriage, the rise in age at first marriage, the continuing high divorce
rate, and the declining remarriage rate indicate that marriage has become a more voluntary and less permanent part of adult life now than
in the past. Changes in public attitudes—involving more positive evaluations of single lifestyles and other alternatives to marriage, such as

1

nonmarital cohabitation—also reflect a decline in the centrality of marriage. After centuries of being the bedrock of the American family system, marriage is losing its privileged status and is becoming one lifestyle choice among many.

Despite these changes, the great majority of young adults in the United States have positive views of marriage and wish to marry one day (Glenn, 1996; Thornton and Young-DeMarco, 2001). These positive views and expectations exist across all racial and ethnic groups (Tucker, 2000). Moreover, demographers project that most young adults eventually will marry (Casper and Bianchi, 2002). Marriage may have lost much of its former status, but it still has much to offer. Married couples have a higher standard of living than do single individuals (Hirschl, Altobelli, and Rank, 2003; Nock, 1998), and positive marital relationships promote the physical health and psychological well-being of women and men (Burman and Margolin, 1992; Marks and Lambert, 1998; Schoenborn, 2004; Stack and Eshleman, 1998; Williams, 2003). Moreover, children are most likely to thrive when they grow up with two happily married parents (Amato and Booth, 1997; McLanahan and Sandefur, 1994).

Stable and harmonious marriages, however, are in short supply these days. Norval Glenn (1998), using data from the General Social Survey (GSS), found that only one-third of all marriages were both happy and intact after 16 years. In another study based on repeated cross sections from the GSS, Glenn (2001) showed that the percentage of people who were "very happy" with their marriages declined significantly between the mid-1970s and the mid-1980s. Moreover, longitudinal research demonstrates that marital happiness tends to decline continuously throughout the years of marriage. This decline is steepest in the early years of marriage and slows down in the later years, but most couples never recover the happiness they experienced when their unions were young (VanLaningham, Johnson, and Amato, 2001).

Concern over the apparently declining state of marriage has stimulated a good deal of debate, which we review below. Our goal is to inform this debate by providing new information on how marriage in the United States changed during the last two decades of the twentieth century. We approach this task in four steps.

1. We describe how the aggregate level of marital quality in the U.S. population changed between 1980 and 2000. We focus on

multiple dimensions of marital quality, including the extent to which people are happy with their spouses, the amount of positive interaction between spouses, the level of conflict in the relationship, the number of perceived problems in the marriage, and people's thoughts about ending their marriages.

2. We describe changes in the organization and functioning of marriages between 1980 and 2000. In particular, we focus on changes in (a) the demographic composition of the married population, (b) husbands' and wives' employment patterns, (c) the economic well-being of married couples, (d) gender equity within marriage, (e) the integration of spouses into supportive networks of friends, relatives, and community organizations, (f) religiosity and attendance at religious services, and (g) spouses' attitudes toward marriage and divorce.

3. We relate changes in marital quality to changes in the organization and functioning of marriage between 1980 and 2000. We address a number of questions; for example: Have recent shifts in husbands' and wives' economic roles improved marital happiness by increasing equality and financial security? Or have these changes created more tension between spouses by increasing normative ambiguity and work-family conflict?

4. We determine whether changes in marriage between 1980 and 2000 had different consequences for the marital quality of husbands and wives. For example, increases in wives' share of family income and husbands' performance of household chores may have benefited wives more than husbands, or vice versa.

To achieve these aims, we rely on two national surveys of married individuals, one completed in 1980 and the other completed in 2000. These two studies—which used identical sampling methods and interview schedules—provide the most complete picture currently available of how marriage has changed in recent decades. Reviewing the evidence from these two studies makes it possible to assess whether marriage has become a more troubled arrangement in recent times or is adapting successfully to the changing social and economic conditions of American society. Moreover, understanding how marriage is changing allows us to make informed projections about the future of marriage—an issue of great interest to scholars, policy makers, and the general public.

In 2003 we published a journal article that provided a preliminary look at the evidence from our two surveys (Amato, Johnson, Booth, and Rogers, 2003). In that article we reported that interaction between husbands and wives (such as eating the main meal of the day together or going out together for leisure activities) declined significantly between 1980 and 2000. In contrast, levels of marital happiness and divorce proneness (thinking about divorce and raising the topic of divorce with one's spouse) did not change. Although these initial findings were intriguing, they raised many questions that could not be answered in a short article. We examine similar issues in this book but with a wider lens that incorporates more dimensions of marital quality, more aspects of marriage, and a deeper consideration of the conceptual, methodological, and policy implications of our findings.

Background

The Marital-Decline Perspective

Some scholars view the retreat from marriage and the corresponding spread of single-parent families as a cause for concern (Blankenhorn, 1990; Glenn, 1996; Popenoe, 1988, 1993, 1996; Waite and Gallagher, 2000; Whitehead, 1993, 1996; Wilson, 2002). These scholars do not agree on all issues, and their political orientations range from conservative to liberal. But despite their differences, they share four basic assumptions that we refer to as a *marital-decline perspective.*

1. The institution of marriage is weaker now than in the past.
2. The most important cause of this change is the growing and excessive individualism of American culture.
3. The declining status of marriage has had negative consequences for adults, children, and society in general.
4. We should initiate steps to strengthen the institution of marriage.

This perspective recognizes that individualism has always played a prominent role in American culture. Individualism, however, became especially pronounced during the 1960s and 1970s. Since then people have become inordinately preoccupied with the unrestricted pursuit of personal happiness. Because people no longer wish to be hampered with obligations to others, commitment to traditional institutions that require these obligations, such as marriage, has eroded. For example, David Popenoe (1996) argued: "Traditionally, marriage has been understood as a social obligation—an institution designed mainly for economic security and procreation. Today, marriage is understood mainly as a path toward self-fulfillment . . . No longer comprising a set of norms and social obligations that are widely enforced, marriage today is a voluntary relationship that individuals can make and break at will" (p. 533). According to Popenoe, people are no longer willing to remain married through the difficult times, "for better or worse, until death do us part." Instead, marital commitment lasts only as long as people are happy and feel that their needs are being met.

Similarly, Norval Glenn (1996) argued that the relentless pursuit of personal gratification has eroded moral and legal support for the ideal of marital permanence. Although people expect a high level of personal satisfaction from marriage these days, many are unwilling to make the long-term commitments and sacrifices that are necessary to ensure marital stability. Glenn noted:

> The progressives who believed that lowering the barriers to divorce . . . would necessarily enhance the quality of marriages and contribute to personal happiness ignored what the most astute social philosophers have always known, namely, that a completely unfettered pursuit of self-interest by individuals does not lead to the maximization of the well-being of the population as a whole. They ignored the fact that freedom of one spouse to leave the marriage at will is the other spouse's insecurity, and that without a reasonable degree of security, it is unlikely that a spouse will commit fully to the marriage and make the sacrifices and investments needed to make it succeed. (p. 31)

Most advocates of the marital decline perspective have emphasized the negative consequences of recent family change. According to this view, the decline in lifelong marriage, and the corresponding increase in single-parent families, has contributed to a variety of social problems, including poverty, delinquency, violence, substance abuse, declining academic standards, and the erosion of neighborhoods and communities. Barbara Whitehead (1993) stated:

Family disruption would be a serious problem even if it affected only individual children and families. But its impact is far broader. Indeed, it is not an exaggeration to characterize it as a central cause of many of our most vexing social problems . . . Disrupted families threaten the psychological well-being of children and diminish the investment of adult time and money in them. Family diversity in the form of increasing numbers of single-parent and stepparent families does not strengthen the social fabric. It dramatically weakens and undermines society, placing new burdens on schools, courts, prisons, and the welfare system. (p. 77)

The cure for this problem, according to advocates of this perspective, is to create a culture that is more supportive of marriage—a culture that values commitment and encourages people to accept responsibility for others, including their spouses and children. In terms of specific policies, advocates of this view have called for public education programs focusing on the value of marriage, the introduction of courses on relationship skills and conflict resolution in school programs, and greater government funding for marriage counseling and premarital education services.

The Marital-Resilience Perspective

Other family scholars reject the marital-decline perspective (Bengtson, Biblarz, and Roberts, 2002, Coontz, 1992, 2000; Demo, 1992; Hackstaff, 1999; Scanzoni, 2001; Skolnick, 1991; Stacey, 1996). Although these scholars hold a variety of views, they share several basic assumptions that we refer to as a *marital-resilience perspective.*

1. The institution of marriage is changing, but it is not necessarily in a state of decline.
2. Americans have not become excessively individualistic and selfish during the last few decades.
3. Recent changes in marriage and family life have had few negative consequences for adults, children, or the wider society.
4. We should support all types of families, not just married heterosexual couples with children.

Most of these scholars question the belief that the proportion of unsuccessful marriages has increased in recent decades. According to this perspective, marriages were as likely to be troubled in the past as they are today. But obtaining a divorce was time-consuming and expensive. Moreover, divorced individuals were stigmatized, and wives were economically dependent on their husbands. For these reasons, most of these troubled marriages remained "intact." These scholars also point out that earlier generations of children were raised in a variety of family forms and not exclusively in households with two biological parents. Stephanie Coontz (2000) argued that many observers are unwilling to acknowledge the extent to which family diversity *always* has existed in American society. She stated:

> Most of the contemporary debate over family forms and values is not occasioned by the existence of diversity but by its increasing legitimation. Historical studies of family life . . . make it clear that families have always differed. Many different family forms and values have worked (or not worked) for various groups at different times. There is no reason to assume that family forms and practices that differ from those of the dominant ideal are necessarily destructive. (p. 28)

Rather than view the rise in marital instability with alarm, advocates of this perspective point out that divorce provides a second chance at happiness for adults and an escape from a dysfunctional home environment for many children. And because children are adaptable and can develop successfully in a variety of family structures, the spread of alternatives to mandatory lifelong marriage poses few problems for the next generation. For example, Vern Bengtson and his colleagues (2002), after describing the results of their longitudinal study of three generations, concluded: "Our findings challenge the myths that . . . families are declining in function and influence, and that nontraditional or 'alternative' family structures spell the downfall of American youth. While rapid social change has presented families with many challenges, we find that most families are resilient and adaptive, and that American families continue to perform their socialization functions in the face of rapid social change and varied family structures" (p. 157).

Feminist scholars, in particular, have argued that changes in family life during the last several decades have strengthened, rather than undermined, the quality of intimate relationships. For example, Judith

Stacey (1996) stated that "changes in work, family, and sexual opportunities for women and men . . . open the prospect of introducing greater democracy, equality and choice than ever before into our most intimate relationships, especially for women and members of sexual minorities" (p. 9). According to Stacey, an increased level of marital instability is a necessary consequence of the decline in patriarchal authority and the rising economic independence of women. But rather than being harmful, the freedom to leave unequal relationships allows people (especially women) to find more equal and, ultimately, more satisfying relationships.

According to a marital-resilience perspective, poverty, unemployment, poorly funded schools, and lack of government services represent more serious threats to the well-being of children than do the growth of individualism and the corresponding decline in two-parent families. Consequently, advocates of this view do not support policies that would promote marriage. Instead, these scholars argue that social policies should provide greater support to adults and children in all types of families and not privilege one form (lifelong, heterosexual marriage) over other arrangements. In this context Judith Stacey (1996) argued:

> We have only two real choices. Either we can come to grips with the postmodern family condition by accepting the end of a singular ideal family and begin to promote better living and spiritual conditions for the diverse array of real families we actually inhabit and desire. Or we can continue to engage in denial, resistance, displacement, and bad faith, by cleaving to a moralistic ideology of *the family* at the same time that we fail to provide social and economic conditions that make life for the modern family or any other kind of family viable, let alone dignified and secure. (p. 11)

Marital Decline, Marital Resilience, and Marital Quality

The marital-decline and marital-resilience perspectives are useful for thinking about recent changes in marital quality and stability. In doing so, however, it is necessary to distinguish between two possibilities. The first is that marital instability became more common during the second half of the twentieth century because people's expectations for

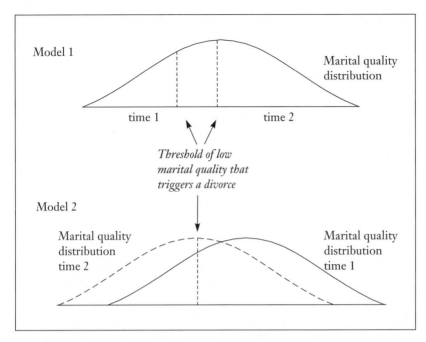

Figure 1.1   Changes in marital quality and divorce: two models

marriage increased and the barriers to leaving an unhappy marriage became weaker. Another way of stating this assumption is that the minimum level of marital quality necessary for spouses to stay married is higher now than in the past. This model is illustrated in the top half of Figure 1.1. Marital quality takes the form of an approximately normal distribution, with a small proportion of marriages (on the left) being of poor quality, a small proportion of marriages (on the right) being of high quality, and a large proportion of marriages (in the middle) being of moderate quality. Model 1 assumes that the distribution of marital quality in the population has been stable, but the threshold of low marital quality sufficient to trigger a divorce has increased. The vertical lines running through the marital quality distribution represent these thresholds. Because the threshold increased (that is, shifted to the right) between time 1 and time 2, a larger proportion of marriages of moderate quality ended in divorce. In other words, as people's expectations for marriage increased, and as the barriers to divorce declined, the proportion of marriages that did not live up to people's expectations—and hence ended in divorce—also increased.

If these assumptions are correct, then the mean level of marital quality among surviving marriages should be *higher* today than in the past. Nevertheless, from a marital-decline perspective, this trend is problematic, because it means that a large number of divorces are occurring in marriages that are not seriously troubled. Moreover, policy interventions, such as improving access to premarital education and marital counseling, could shift the quality of some of these moderately unhappy marriages above the divorce threshold, which would benefit spouses as well as children.

The lower half of Figure 1.1 illustrates an alternative model implicit in the marital-decline perspective. In the second model, the time 2 marital quality distribution is shifted toward the left of the time 1 distribution, which indicates a decline in marital quality in the population. The threshold of low marital quality sufficient to trigger a divorce, however, did not change. If this version is correct, then the mean level of marital quality declined, even among marriages that did not end in divorce. This model is consistent with the notion that excessive individualism has undermined spouses' willingness to make short-term sacrifices for the long-term viability of their marriages, thus eroding relationship quality. It also is possible that an increase in disagreements between spouses over gender roles, declines in social support for married couples, and other social changes have made marriage a more difficult and less satisfying arrangement today than in the past.

Most marital-resilience scholars would not dispute the first model in Figure 1.1 and would agree that the increase in marital instability largely reflects a rise in people's expectations for marriage and a decline in the barriers to divorce. Unlike marital-decline scholars, however, marital-resilience scholars would not see this trend as being problematic. Instead, they would argue that the shift toward more liberal divorce laws during the 1970s, combined with the growing economic independence of wives, allowed more couples to abandon relationships of moderate quality and seek out greater happiness with alternative partners. Few marital-resilience scholars, however, would agree with model 2; as we noted above, they assume that recent social and cultural changes have improved rather than eroded the quality of intimate relationships.

Of course, it is likely that changes occurred in average levels of marital quality in the population (model 2) *and* in the threshold of marital quality at which people seek divorces (model 1). Indeed, if people's expectations for a satisfactory marriage increased over time, then average levels of marital quality in the population almost certainly declined. Spouses who do not feel that their expectations are being met are likely to become increasingly unhappy, view more aspects of their relationships as problematic, argue more frequently with their partners, and think more often about ending their marriages.

It is difficult to test these models empirically, mainly because appropriate data are not available. Only a few studies have attempted to assess changes in aggregate levels of marital quality over time. As we noted above, Glenn (1991) found that the percentage of people reporting that their marriages were "very happy" declined gradually from 1973 to 1988. Another study (Rogers and Amato, 2000) found that couples in the late 1990s reported more marital problems, more conflict, and less interaction than did couples in 1980. These findings are the opposite of what one would expect if the rise in divorce were due only to the increased ending of unhappy marriages. Instead, these studies appear to support the second version of the marital-decline perspective, that is, that mean levels of marital quality declined in the recent past.

Our study is not able to address the marital decline and resilience perspectives in their full complexity, but we can determine whether marital quality is declining or improving. As we describe later in this chapter, our data come from 1980 and 2000—two decades in which the divorce rate in the United States was relatively stable. Consequently, we are able to compare measures of marital quality across this 20-year interval without having to account for changes in the rate of marital disruption. As we see it, overall declines in marital quality between 1980 and 2000 would support a marital-decline perspective, whereas overall improvements in marital quality would support a marital-resilience perspective.

From Institutional to Individualistic Marriage

Although advocates of the decline and resilience perspectives agree that marriage and family life in the United States changed dramatically during the second half of the twentieth century, they disagree on whether these changes should be condemned (and reversed) or embraced (and supported). Of course, marriage always has been in a state of flux, to a degree that our collective memory often fails to recognize. Although many contemporary observers are troubled by changes that occurred in marriage during the second half of the twentieth century, changes in marriage during the first half of the century also generated a great deal of concern. Early sociologists feared that one of the fundamental institutions of society—marriage—was breaking down, and in the 1920s and 1930s social scientists published books with titles such as *The Marriage Crisis* (Groves, 1928), *Family Disorganization* (Mowrer, 1927), and *Marriage at the Crossroads* (Stekel, 1931). Concern about the status of marriage and family life has been a recurring theme in American social science.

In trying to make sense of marital change, we refer to the work of Ernest Burgess, a sociologist who wrote extensively on marriage and family life in the first part of the twentieth century (Burgess and Cottrell, 1939; Burgess, Locke, and Thomes, 1963; Burgess and Wallin, 1954). Burgess argued that marriage was in a process of transition from a social institution to a relationship based on companionship. Burgess used the term *institutional marriage*, by which he meant a fundamental unit of social organization—a formal status regulated by social norms, public opinion, law, and religion. In contrast, the emerging form of marriage was based primarily on emotional bonds between two partners. We believe that Burgess's views help to clarify our understanding of marital change at the end of the twentieth century.

According to Burgess, the industrialization and urbanization of the United States weakened the institutional basis of marriage. Before the last few decades of the nineteenth century, the United States was predominantly a rural society, and most adults and children lived and worked on family farms. During this era marriage was essential to the welfare of individual family members and the larger community. Before the development of specialized services and institutions, family members relied on each other to meet a wide range of needs, including child care, economic production, job training, and elder care. Because cohesive families were necessary for survival, the entire community had an interest in ensuring marital stability (Goode, 1963). Although arranged marriages were never common in the United States, parents and kin monitored older children's interactions with members of the other sex, and parental approval was expected before young adults married (Coontz, 2005). Once married, spouses were expected not only to conform to traditional standards of behavior, but also to sacrifice their personal goals, if necessary, for the sake of the marriage. Because marriages were patriarchal, wives had less power than did husbands. Nevertheless, through marriage men and women participated in an institution that was larger and more significant than themselves. For these reasons, divorce was frowned on and was allowed only if one partner had seriously violated the marriage contract by, for example, engaging in serious physical abuse, infidelity, or desertion.

By 1900 the United States had become industrialized, and two-parent breadwinner-homemaker families replaced farm families as the dominant family form (Hernandez, 1993). Burgess believed that through industrialization and urbanization, individuals came to have more control over their marriages. This change was brought about by several related factors, including the greater geographical mobility of youth (which freed young adults from the domination of parents and the larger kin group), the rise of democratic institutions (which increased the status and power of women), and a decline in religious control (which resulted in more freedom to adopt unconventional views and behaviors). Moreover, during the twentieth century the growth of economic opportunities for women gave adult daughters more economic independence from their parents and gave wives more economic independence from their husbands. As parents, religion, community expectations, and patriarchal traditions exerted less control over individuals, marriage was based increasingly on mutual affection between spouses.

Steven Mintz and Susan Kellogg (1988), two family historians, described the shift from institutional marriage in the following manner:

> By the beginning of the twentieth century, middle-class families had been shorn of many traditional economic, educational, and welfare functions. The family's role in education, in health care, and in the care of the aged, poor and mentally ill had increasingly been assumed by specialists and institutions outside the family. At the same time, however, the family had acquired new burdens and expectations. The middle-class family was assigned primary responsibilities for fulfilling the emotional and psychological needs of its members. Along with providing economic security and a sta-

ble environment for children, family life was now expected to provide romance, sexual fulfillment, companionship, and emotional satisfaction. (pp. 107–108)

Burgess referred to the new model (and ideal) of marriage as *companionate marriage*. According to Burgess, companionate marriage is characterized by egalitarian rather than patriarchal relationships between spouses. Companionate marriage is held together not by bonds of social obligation but by ties of love, friendship, and common interest. And unlike institutional marriage, which emphasizes conformity to social norms, companionate marriage allows for an ample degree of self-expression and personal satisfaction.

Burgess further argued that in an urbanized society in which interaction takes place largely within the context of impersonal, secondary relationships, companionate marriage is the central source of social and emotional support in most people's lives. Although the nuclear family household was dominant throughout the nineteenth century, it was common for households to contain a variety of other individuals, including adult children, aging parents, other relatives, boarders, lodgers, apprentices, and servants. During the twentieth century, however, privacy became an ideal of family life, especially among the middle class, and boundaries around the nuclear family household became more distinct (Hareven, 1978). As the nuclear family became increasingly segregated from kin, nonrelatives, and the rest of society, spouses became more reliant on each other for companionship, assistance, and affection.

Of course, people in the United States have always expected marriage to be a source of love and emotional support. But the notion that marriage should be based *primarily* on relationship quality is relatively recent. According to Stephanie Coontz (2005), the belief that love is the reason for marriage emerged in the late eighteenth century, and it became increasingly popular during the following century. By the early decades of the twentieth century, the free choice of spouses based on love was widely accepted. Psychologists, educators, and social service providers applied these ideas in their professional practice, and it was in this context that marital counseling emerged as a discipline, with its goal being to help couples achieve emotional closeness and sexual satisfaction through improved communication and conflict management.

By the 1950s almost all Americans, irrespective of social class, accepted the companionate model of marriage as the cultural ideal (Mintz and Kellogg, 1988).

Burgess believed that by the middle of the twentieth century (the time in which he wrote), marriage had adopted many companionate characteristics but still retained some institutional features. This transformation appears to be ongoing. For example, before the 1960s interracial marriages were not allowed in some states. The removal of this legal restriction by the U.S. Supreme Court in 1967 gave people more freedom to select spouses from a broad marriage market. Similarly, although the legal grounds for divorce were relaxed during the first half of the twentieth century, the shift to no-fault divorce in the 1970s reflected a sharp break with the past. Unlike the earlier fault regime, which allowed marital dissolution only if one spouse could prove that the other was guilty of violating the marriage contract, no-fault divorce had only one ground for divorce: The marriage was irretrievably broken because of irreconcilable differences. Moreover, most states adopted unilateral versions of no-fault divorce in which one spouse could obtain a divorce, even if the other spouse wanted the marriage to continue. (See Glendon, 1989, for a discussion of changes in the legal regulation of divorce.) Changes in state law and court rulings also undermined the patriarchal nature of marriage during the second half of the century. For example, in the 1970s and 1980s state courts ruled that husbands did not "own" their wives' sexuality and, hence, could be prosecuted for marital rape. All these changes reflected growing individual autonomy and a corresponding deinstitutionalization of marriage (Ooms, 2001).

Other evidence for the continuing shift from institutional to companionate marriage comes from attitude surveys of university students. One study, based on data from 1939 to the 1990s, found changes in college students' rankings of the most important characteristics of a future spouse (Buss, Shackelford, Kirkpatrick, and Larsen, 2001). In 1939, of 18 characteristics, women ranked love in fifth place. But by the 1970s (and continuing through the 1990s) women ranked love as the most important characteristic. Similarly, men's rankings of love rose from fourth place to first place during this period. For both genders, mutual attraction, education, intelligence, sociability, and good looks also increased in importance. Correspondingly, men attached less importance to their wives' being good housekeepers and cooks, and women attached less importance to their husbands' being ambitious or industrious. The rise in the importance of love (and the decline in the importance of strictly instrumental qualities) is consistent with the notion of a movement away from traditional social roles and toward a more companionate ideal.

Another study of college students' expectations for marriage yielded comparable results (Barich and Bielby, 1996). Between 1967 and 1994 students' expectations for "healthy and happy children," "moral and religious unity," and "maintenance of a home" declined in importance. In contrast, students' expectations of "companionship," "personality development," and "emotional security" increased in importance. This trend suggests that young adults today, compared with young adults in the recent past, attach less importance to the structural aspects of marriage (children, religion, and home) and more importance to the personal rewards and individual development that marriage makes possible.

Recently, Andrew Cherlin (2004) argued that contemporary marriages are more individualistic than Burgess or other observers of his time ever envisioned. According to Cherlin, the companionate ideal reached its zenith in the relatively stable breadwinner-homemaker marriages of the 1950s. Although these marriages were held together by mutual bonds of friendship and affection, spouses also obtained satisfaction from the fulfillment of complementary marital roles, such as breadwinner, homemaker, and parent. But during the second half of the twentieth century, especially during the 1960s and 1970s, American culture shifted toward an ethic of "expressive individualism" (Bellah, Madsen, Sullivan, Swidler, and Tipton, 1985). This ethic assumes that people have an intrinsic need to express their innermost feelings, and that close relationships exist primarily to enhance individual satisfaction and maximize psychological growth. As these ideas grew in popularity, self-development and personal fulfillment came to replace mutual satisfaction and successful team effort as the basis of marriage. In *individualistic marriage,* love is necessary to form a union, but these unions are successful only to the extent that they meet each partner's innermost psychological needs. If these needs are not met, then spouses will jettison the union to seek happiness with alternative partners. The ascendance of individualistic marriage was accompanied by other dramatic demographic changes, such as an acceleration in the divorce rate, the rise of nonmarital cohabitation, the delay of first marriage, and the increase in the proportion of children born outside marriage. These changes were so rapid and pervasive that some demographers have referred to them, collectively, as a fundamental demographic transition in Western societies (Lesthaeghe, 1995; Lesthaeghe and Neels, 2002).

The distinction between institutional and individualistic marriage casts light on the marital-decline and marital-resilience perspectives that we described earlier. Advocates of the decline perspective emphasize the institutional dimension of marriage and focus on the extent to which marriage meets the needs of society. According to these individuals, the deinstitutionalization of marriage has gone too far. The unrestricted pursuit of self-interest has undermined family solidarity, and the dwindling supply of well-functioning married-couple families has made the maintenance of social order more difficult. What is required is a strengthening of the cultural values of commitment, obligation, and sacrifice in marriage. In other words, we need to reinstitutionalize marriage. The recent introduction of covenant marriage in several states represents an effort in this direction (Sanchez, Nock, Wright, and Gager, 2002).

Advocates of the marital-resilience perspective, in contrast, emphasize individual rights and free choice over social obligations and tradition. Consequently, they value the enhanced freedom, possibilities for self-development, and potential for egalitarian relationships that contemporary marriage provides. Some of these individuals might welcome the complete privatization of marriage (which would occur, for example, if the state stopped performing and registering marriages), whereas others might see some balance of institutional and individual elements as optimal. It is clear, however, that these individuals would resist turning back the clock and surrendering the individual liberties that contemporary marriages provide.

We believe that the transition from institutional to companionate to individualistic marriage provides a useful framework for thinking about recent social change. Although marriage has lost most of its institutional features, it continues to be regulated by social norms, legal requirements, and religious traditions (Nock, 1998). Almost all spouses these days, however, expect marriage to provide a high level of personal fulfillment. These two dimensions of marriage—the institutional and the individual—pull in different directions and underlie much of the tension found in current marital relationships. For example, when parents wonder if they should divorce or stay together for the sake of the children, they confront the basic dilemma of pursuing personal happiness versus meeting obligations to others.

Although the debate over marriage provides a general background to our research, it is beyond the scope of this book to resolve fundamental disagreements about the meaning and desirability of recent social trends. Our goal, instead, is to inform this debate by providing new information on recent changes in the nature and quality of marriage. People may hold clashing interpretations of events, but it is essential that the basic facts about which people disagree are clear.

Recent Changes in Marriage

Two broad sociological assumptions underlie our research. First, we assume that macro-level social change has the potential to affect the quality of people's private lives—including their marriages. Moreover, social change often involves a mixture of positive and negative elements. For example, the deinstitutionalization of marriage during the twentieth century created opportunities for individuals to pursue intimate relationships and personal happiness with few constraints from traditional expectations. But by making marriage a more private arrangement, this shift reduced the amount of support that couples receive from parents, kin, the religious congregation, and the wider community. During any historical era, some elements of social change have the potential to make marriage a more satisfying and stable arrangement, whereas other elements have the potential to make it a more troubled and less stable arrangement. At any given time, therefore, the average level of marital quality and stability in the population reflects a balance between these positive and negative forces.

Second, we assume that the average level of marital quality in a population is a product of a large number of forces, each having a relatively modest effect. Given the complexity of marital relationships, it is unlikely that any single explanatory factor can account for more than a small proportion of any observed aggregate-level shifts in marital quality. For this reason, understanding broad changes in marital quality at the societal level requires the investigation of a large number of factors that may have complementary or offsetting effects.

Our focus is on the last two decades of the twentieth century. During this period a variety of demographic, economic, social, and cultural changes in the United States had the potential to affect people's marriages either positively or negatively. Some of these shifts reflected the ongoing transformation of marriage to a more private relationship. Other changes, such as the increase in immigration from Latino cultures, reflected unique historical trends. Although the 20-year period between 1980 and 2000 may not seem like a long time, the social and economic contexts of marriage and family life shifted in fundamental ways during these years. In the following section we review changes in the married population that are likely to have had implications for mean levels of marital quality and stability.

Demographic Trends

Race and ethnicity. Compared with whites, African Americans tend to be less satisfied with their marriages (Broman, 1993) and are more likely to divorce (Bramlett and Mosher, 2002; Heaton, 2002). The proportion of all married individuals who are African American, however, changed little between 1980 and 2000 (U.S. Census Bureau, 2001, Table 49). The percentage of Latino married couples, in contrast, nearly doubled during this period (ibid.). Few studies are available on marital quality in this population, but rates of divorce vary considerably between Latino groups. Compared with non-Hispanic whites, Puerto Ricans have a higher rate of divorce, Cubans have a lower rate of divorce, and Mexicans have a comparable rate of divorce (Sweet and Bumpass, 1987). Given heterogeneity within this group, the implications of the increase in the Latino population for aggregate levels of marital quality and stability are unclear.

Education. During the last two decades of the twentieth century, the educational level of the U.S. population rose substantially. In 1980 fewer than two-thirds of adults over the age of 25 were high school graduates, but by 2000 this figure had increased to 80%. Similarly, in 1980 only 16% of adults over the age of 25 were college graduates, but by 2000 the corresponding figure was 24% (Bauman and Graf, 2003, Figure 3). By the close of the century, men and women were bringing higher levels of education and human capital to their marriages than at any time in U.S. history.

The rise in educational attainment may have strengthened people's marriages. Well-educated individuals, compared with poorly educated ones, possess more effective communication and problem-solving skills, are happier with their lives, and have better mental and physical health (Amato and Booth, 1997; Kessler, 1982; Ross and Wu, 1995). Education also is positively associated with earnings and occupational status (Farley, 1996; White and Rogers, 2000). By lowering the risk of economic distress, education promotes positive interaction between spouses (Conger and Elder, 1994; Fox and Chancey, 1998). Given these benefits, it is not surprising that education is associated with a lower risk of divorce (Bramlett and Mosher, 2002; Heaton, 2002).

Age at marriage. The marriage rate—defined as the number of marriages per 1,000 unmarried women 15 years or older—began to decline in the 1950s, and this trend continued during the last two decades of the twentieth century (U.S. Census Bureau, 2000, Table 144). This decline occurred largely because young adults were postponing matrimony until later ages (Casper and Bianchi, 2002). In 1980 the median age at first marriage was 22 for women and 24 for men, but by 1990 it had increased to 24 for women and 26 for men (U.S. Census Bureau, 1998, Table 159). These figures indicate that young adults have retreated from early marriage but not from marriage itself.

How has the increase in age at marriage affected the quality of marriage? People who marry at young ages, compared with those who marry at older ages, spend less time searching for suitable partners, have fewer financial resources, and are less mature psychologically. Presumably for these reasons people who marry early report an elevated number of marital problems (Amato and Rogers, 1997; Booth and Edwards, 1985) and are more likely to see their marriages end in divorce (Bramlett and Mosher, 2002; Bumpass, Martin, and Sweet, 1991; Heaton, 2002). The trend for young adults to postpone marriage, therefore, may have improved the aggregate level of marital quality in the population. We cannot be certain of this conclusion, however, because many young adults who postpone marriage choose to cohabit instead, and cohabitation may have negative consequences for the quality of subsequent marriages.

Premarital cohabitation. Although young adults are postponing marriage, they are not postponing intimate residential unions. The number of unrelated adults of the opposite sex living together rose from 1.6 million in 1980 to 4.9 million in 2000 (U.S. Census Bureau, 2000, Table 57). This trend affected individuals in all racial and ethnic groups. Between 1987 and 1992 the percentage of couples who cohabited before marriage increased from 43% to 50% for African Americans, from 30% to 47% for whites, and from 30% to 38% for Mexican Americans. Currently, more than 40% of women between 15 and 44 have cohabited, and about half of all first marriages are preceded by cohabitation between partners (Casper and Bianchi, 2002).

The increasing popularity of cohabitation may have benefited or undermined the aggregate level of marital quality in the population. On the one hand, cohabitation may have improved marital quality by leading to the termination of undesirable unions before marriage could occur. On the other hand, people who live together before marriage are more likely to see their unions end in divorce than are people who do not live together before marriage (Booth and Johnson, 1988; Bramlett and Mosher, 2002; Bumpass, Martin, and Sweet, 1991; Teachman and Polonko, 1990). This difference may be due to selection; that is, people who hold unconventional attitudes or a weak commitment to the norm of lifelong marriage may be more likely to cohabit as well as to divorce (Bennett, Blanc, and Bloom, 1988; Booth and Johnson, 1988). If the selection explanation is correct, then the association between premarital cohabitation and divorce should have grown weaker as cohabitation became more common, because cohabitation became less selective of people with high-risk traits for divorce. Recent studies indicate, however, that the increased risk of divorce associated with premarital cohabitation has remained constant across recent decades (Dush, Cohan, and Amato, 2003; Teachman, 2002).

An alternative explanation is that the experience of cohabitation increases later marital instability. Longitudinal studies show that people become less religious and adopt more favorable attitudes toward divorce following cohabitation (Axinn and Thornton, 1992; Thornton, Axinn, and Hill, 1992). People who are low in religiosity and who hold attitudes favorable to divorce, in turn, are more likely to see their marriages end in dissolution. Moreover, people probably spend less time deliberating over the decision to cohabit than the decision to marry. Indeed, research suggests that cohabiting individuals are less concerned about the characteristics of their partners than are married individuals (Casper and Bianchi, 2002). Once couples begin living together, however, their chances of marrying increase. Some cohabiting couples may decide to marry because of pressure from parents, an unintended pregnancy, or the gradual buildup of investments in the relationship (such as jointly owned furniture, shared memories, children, and common friends)—despite the fact that they are not well suited for a long-term relationship. To the extent that cohabitation leads to marriages that would not have occurred otherwise, cohabitation may contribute to subsequent marital problems and instability.

Children. After the baby boom of 1946–1964, the fertility rate declined in the late 1960s, and this trend continued between 1980 and 2000. Specifically, there were 68.4 births per 1,000 women (ages 15–44) in 1980 compared with 65.9 in 2000 (U.S. Census Bureau, 2003, Table 85). Correspondingly, the proportion of married couples without children under the age of 18 increased from 49% in 1980 to 54% in 1999 (U.S. Census Bureau, 2003, Table 66). Studies typically show that couples with children report more disenchantment with their marriages, spend less time in positive interaction with each other, and have sex less often than do couples without children (Cowan and Cowan, 1992; Glenn and McLanahan, 1982). Observers disagree, however, about whether this association exists because having children lowers marital quality (Cowan and Cowan, 1992) or because having children reduces the likelihood that unhappily married couples divorce (White, Booth, and Edwards, 1986). Regardless of the explanation, the decline in the proportion of couples with children may have raised the mean level of marital quality in the population.

Although overall fertility has declined, the rise in the age at first marriage increased the number of years during which young women are at risk of having a nonmarital birth. For this reason, and because of a decline in marital fertility, the percentage of births to unmarried mothers increased from 18 in 1980 to 33 at the end of the 1990s (U.S. Census Bureau, 2000, Table 85). Correspondingly, the percentage of premaritally pregnant women who marry before the child's birth declined between 1980 and the mid-1990s (Bachu, 1999). Nevertheless, many unwed mothers eventually get married—either to the fathers of their children or to new partners. Entering marriage with a premarital birth, however, is associated with greater marital discord and instability

(Amato and Booth, 2001; Bramlett and Mosher, 2002). The increase in the proportion of children born outside wedlock, therefore, appears to be a destabilizing element in contemporary marriages.

Marital dissolution. The divorce rate increased dramatically in the United States in the 1960s and 1970s, then crested at a historically high level in the early 1980s (Cherlin, 1992). Since then the divorce rate has declined slightly, from 23 divorces per 1,000 married couples in 1980 to 20 per 1,000 married couples in 1996 (U.S. Census Bureau, 2000, Table 144). The rise in divorce (coupled with an increase in nonmarital births) led to a decline in the percentage of children growing up without both parents. In 1980, 77% of all children lived with their biological mothers and fathers, compared with 68% in 1998. During this same period, the percentage of children living with single parents increased from 20% to 27% (U.S. Census Bureau, 2000, Table 69).

The increasing instability of childbearing unions may have had detrimental consequences for recent marriages for two reasons. First, the proportion of young married adults who spent part of their childhoods in single-parent families was higher at the end of the twentieth century than in 1980 (the year in which the divorce rate reached its peak). Studies consistently show that individuals with divorced parents are more likely than individuals with continuously married parents to see their own marriages end in divorce (Amato, 1996; Bumpass, Martin, and Sweet, 1991; Feng, Giarrusso, Bengtson, and Frye, 1999; Glenn and Kramer, 1987; Wolfinger, 1999). Similarly, studies show that individuals with divorced parents report less marital happiness, more marital problems, and greater marital conflict (Glenn and Kramer, 1987; McLeod, 1991; Tallman, Gray, Kullberg, and Henderson, 1999). These findings suggest that increased exposure to parental divorce during recent decades may have had long-term detrimental consequences for the quality and stability of adult offspring's marriages.

Second, despite the fact that remarriage rates following divorce have declined, the majority of divorced individuals eventually marry again (Cherlin, 1992). In fact, nearly half of all marriages these days represent a second (or higher-order) marriage for one or both partners (U.S. Census Bureau, 2000, Table 145). The risk of a marriage ending in divorce, however, is greater for people in higher-order marriages than for people in first marriages (Booth and Edwards, 1992; White, 1990). The continuing high level of marital instability has resulted in a large pool of single people on the marriage market with an elevated risk of subsequent marital dissolution. In this sense, marital instability breeds more marital instability.

Heterogamy. People tend to chose spouses much like themselves with respect to age, education, religion, and race—a tendency that family sociologists refer to as homogamy. The inclination to seek out similar partners, however, has receded in recent years. For example, the proportion of marriages that were interracial increased from 1.3% in 1980 to 2.6% in 2000 (U.S. Census Bureau, 2001, Table 50). The increase in interracial (and interethnic) marriage held for most groups, including European Americans, blacks, Latinos, Asians, and Native Americans (Rosenfeld, 2002). Religious intermarriage also increased during this time, as did marriages in which wives were older than their husbands (Heaton, 2002; Lehrer, 1998). The increase in heterogamy (marrying someone with different characteristics) probably reflects a relaxation of prohibitive attitudes toward intermarriage, along with the greater geographical mobility of youth, which allows them to date and experiment with relationships without the close watch of their parents (Rosenfeld and Kim, 2005). Despite a more supportive social climate these days, however, recent studies indicate that spouses in heterogamous marriages report less happiness, quarrel more frequently, spend less time in positive interaction, and divorce more often than do individuals in homogamous marriages (Booth and Edwards, 1992; Curtis and Ellison, 2002; Heaton, 2002; Heaton and Pratt, 1990). The increase in marital heterogamy during the last few decades, therefore, may have lowered the mean level of marital quality in the population.

Employment and Income

Employment. The long-term convergence in husbands' and wives' economic roles that began early in the twentieth century continued between 1980 and 2000. During these two decades the overall employment rate for married women under age 55 increased from 64% to 76% (White and Rogers, 2000). The employment rates for married mothers with children increased even more dramatically. In 1980, 45% of married mothers with children less than six years of age and 62% of married mothers with children between the ages of six and 17 were employed. By 2000 these figures had increased to 63% and 77%, respectively (U.S. Census Bureau, 2001, Table 577). Today most married women demonstrate a pattern of consistent attachment to the labor force: wives no longer leave the labor force during the prime years of childbearing (Spain and Bianchi, 1996). In contrast, employment among husbands declined slightly during the 1980s and 1990s (White and Rogers, 2000).

Most men today view women's employment and earnings in a positive light. Among recent cohorts of youth, women with high-paying jobs are more likely to marry in a given year than are women with low-paying jobs, which suggests that women's income-earning potential has become an asset on the marriage market (Sweeney, 2002). Some authors claim that similarity in the work roles of husbands and wives can facilitate intimacy and mutual support (Blumstein and Schwartz, 1983; Coltrane, 1996; Scanzoni, 1978). If this is true, then the trend toward greater sharing of breadwinning responsibilities between spouses may have increased the aggregate level of marital quality in the population.

The increase in wives' labor-force participation, however, also may have had negative consequences for marriage. For example, employed wives are more likely than wives without jobs to challenge men's traditional authority in the family, thus increasing the level of discord in some homes. In addition, the potential for work-family conflict has grown in recent decades, particularly among wives with young children. Numerous studies have documented the potential for the conflicting demands of work and family life to create stress for mothers—stress that often spills over and erodes the quality of marital relations (Booth, Johnson, White, and Edwards, 1984; Glass and Fugimoto, 1994; Hochschild, 1989, 1997; Perry-Jenkins, Repetti, and Crouter, 2000; Spain and Bianchi, 1996). Spending long hours on the job may decrease the time that spouses have available for positive interaction, increase both spouses' feelings of role overload, and raise women's awareness of inequities in the division of household labor and child care. For these reasons, increases in wives' employment during the last few decades may have lowered aggregate levels of marital quality in the population.

Income. Structural changes in the U.S. economy have had mixed consequences for the economic well-being of men and women. Since 1980 men—especially young men and men with relatively little education—have experienced deteriorating work opportunities because of declines in the manufacturing, mining, and construction sectors (Farley, 1996; Levy, 1995). In contrast, women—especially women with high levels of education—benefited from the burgeoning service sector of the economy and experienced increases in real income (Spain and Bianchi, 1996). These gender differences had implications for the financial well-being of families. The median family income (in constant 1998 dollars) for married couples with an employed wife increased from $53,940 in 1980 to $63,370 in 1998. In contrast, during the same period the median family income for married couples with a nonemployed wife declined from $37,580 to $35,670 (White and Rogers, 2000). These figures indicate that wives' employment contributed substantially to the financial security and advancement of married couples during the last few decades.

The rise in wives' employment and income presumably benefited many marriages by lowering the risk of economic hardship. Studies consistently show that financial distress increases the risk of marital discord (Conger et al., 1990), marital violence (Fox, Benson, DeMaris, and Van Wyk, 2002), and divorce (Bramlett and Mosher, 2002; Lehrer, 2003). Correspondingly, the decline in men's economic resources may have increased the level of strain in some marriages, especially in traditional families where husbands are (or expect to be) the sole providers. These considerations suggest that recent large-scale economic changes in American society improved marital satisfaction and harmony among dual-earner couples but had the opposite effect on single-earner couples.

Gender Relations in Marriage

Attitudes toward gender arrangements. Both women and men have become less traditional in their attitudes toward gender arrangements in marriage since the 1960s (Thornton and Young-DeMarco, 2001). Traditional views stress the distinctness of the husband as breadwinner and the wife as homemaker roles, the economic interdependence of husbands and wives, and the hierarchal power relations implicit in these specialized functions. In contrast, nontraditional views emphasize the common capacities of men and women for economic productivity and nurturance, the economic independence of wives, and the egalitarian power relations implied by these shared roles. Does this change in attitudes have implications for marital quality?

Many scholars maintain that a shift toward less traditional (and more egalitarian) attitudes and lifestyles improves marital quality (Blumstein and Schwartz, 1983; Coltrane, 1996; Hackstaff, 1999; Hood, 1983; Scanzoni, 1978). For example, Scanzoni (1978) argued that egalitarianism is an essential foundation for emotional closeness between spouses. According to this perspective, negotiation (and disagreement) between equal spouses tends to increase marital satisfaction and cohesion in the long run by allowing spouses to reach mutually acceptable (rather than one-sided) solutions. In addition, to the extent that nontraditional gender role attitudes lead to greater sharing of economic and domestic duties, marriage becomes more adaptable to a shifting economic climate (Danziger and Gottschalk, 1995). Oppenheimer (1997) noted that a marriage based on a sharing model, in which both spouses are capable of performing economic and household work competently, is better equipped to respond to problems—such as a spell of unemployment, a downturn in the economy, or the incapacitation of a spouse—than is a marriage based on strict gender specialization. The ability to respond to shifts in the economy is particularly important today, given that many husbands' economic fortunes have declined since the 1970s.

Despite these potential benefits, growing support for nontraditional gender arrangements in marriage is likely to clash with the existing gender-based division of labor and the patriarchal power relations that continue to underpin many marriages (Thompson and Walker, 1991). Thornton and Young-DeMarco (2001) found that women have embraced nontraditional views more quickly than men—a discrepancy that is likely to create conflicting expectations between husbands and wives. Amato and Booth (1995) found that wives who adopted less traditional (and more egalitarian) gender attitudes became less satisfied with their marriages and reported greater discord. Presumably, nontraditional wives seek to negotiate work and family responsibilities with their husbands that previous generations of spouses took for granted, thus raising the potential for disagreement and tension in the relationship. Given these mixed considerations, it is difficult to say whether the growing acceptance of nontraditional, egalitarian gender attitudes has improved or lowered the mean level of marital quality in the population.

Husbands' share of housework. Married women's increased commitment to paid work has been accompanied by a decline in household work among wives and a modest increase in housework among husbands (Casper and Bianchi, 2002; Coltrane, 2000; Robinson and Godbey, 1997). Some research suggests that marriages tend to be more harmonious and stable when husbands do a substantial share of housework (Kalmijn, 1999; Pleck and Masciadrelli, 2004). Wives' expectations for sharing housework and child care, however, appear to have risen faster than have husbands' willingness to meet these expectations. To the extent that this is true, wives' perceptions that the household division of labor is unfair may have increased in recent years, despite the fact that their husbands are doing more housework now than in the past. Of course, some men resist doing any housework at all, even if their wives are employed. Research indicates that perceptions of unfairness in the division of household labor contribute to arguments and feelings of resentment in many marriages (Greenstein, 1996; Hochschild, 1989; Pina and Bengtson, 1993). On the basis of these considerations, it is difficult to say whether the increase in men's share of housework has had positive implications for marital quality, or whether most wives view their husbands' modest contributions as "too little, too late."

Decision-making power. Economic resources are a basis for marital power, and wives often expect (and get) more decision-making power when they make substantial financial contributions to the marriage (Blumberg and Coleman, 1989). It is likely, therefore, that the decision-making power of wives has increased in recent decades. Observational research indicates that asymmetric power—when husbands have more influence than wives—is more common among dissatisfied than satisfied couples (Gottman, 1994, p. 57). Shared decision making, in contrast, has the potential to create more intimate marital relationships, as we noted earlier (e.g., Scanzoni, 1978). For these reasons, we expect that recent increases in wives' decision-making power were followed by improvements in marital quality for many couples.

Social Integration, Religiosity, and Attitudes toward Marriage

Social integration. The political scientist Robert Putnam (2000) documented a trend for Americans to be less involved in social networks and community institutions now than in the past. According to Putnam, people are less likely these days to participate in civic organizations, recreational groups, and religiously sponsored social events. In addition, as society has become increasingly urbanized, people are less likely to know their neighbors, and high levels of residential mobility mean that people often live great distances from their families of origin and extended kin (Fischer, 1982). These trends suggest that married couples are less integrated into supportive social networks today than they were in the recent past. Studies have shown that social integration and support from network members tend to stabilize marriage, but mainly during the first six years (Booth, Edwards, and Johnson, 1991). The early years of marriage constitute a period of change and adjustment, and friends, kin, and organizational affiliations can help to stabilize the relationship during times of stress. Members of support networks not only provide advice and encouragement to married couples experiencing problems, but also make salient the social norms that emphasize marital commitment. To the extent that the social integration of married couples has declined in recent decades, marital stability and quality are likely to have suffered.

Religiosity. The great majority of Americans report that religion is important in their lives. About 90% of adults claim some sort of religious preference—a figure that changed little between 1980 and 2000 (U.S. Census Bureau, 2001, Table 66). In addition, rates of attendance at religious services in the United States are higher than in most Western societies (Finke, 1992; Sherkat and Ellison, 1999). Nevertheless, the influence of religion declined somewhat during the second half of the twentieth century. Surveys reveal consistent decreases in the extent to which people have confidence in religious answers to important questions, place trust in religious authorities, and pray or read religious materials (Glenn, 1987; Greeley, 1976; Thornton, 1996). Contrary to this trend, however, is the fact that the percentage of people who reported attending a church or synagogue during the previous week increased from 40 to 44 between 1980 and 2000 (U.S. Census Bureau, 2001, Table 66). It is not clear, therefore, whether the influence of religion among married individuals declined or increased after 1980.

Good reasons exist for assuming that religiosity promotes marital quality and stability. Most religions emphasize the centrality of family life and the importance of strong marital bonds. Religious institutions also organize activities that bring families together into communities of like-minded believers. These communities not only reinforce religious norms, but also provide social support to married couples—including couples that may be experiencing relationship problems. And as this reasoning would lead us to expect, people with deep-rooted religious orientations tend to voice strong support for the norm of life-long marriage, have low rates of divorce, and report relatively high levels of marital commitment and happiness (Bramlett and Mosher, 2002; Dollahite, Marks, and Goodman, 2004; Heaton and Pratt, 1990). In addition, people who attend religious services frequently, especially evangelical Protestants, tend to view divorce as a serious social problem (Brooks, 2002). For these reasons, if religiosity among married couples declined in recent decades, then marital quality and stability are likely to have eroded as well.

The norm of lifelong marriage. Americans have adopted more accepting attitudes toward divorce since the 1960s (Thornton and Young-DeMarco, 2001). For example, the majority of people now believe that divorce is the best solution when a couple cannot get along. More dramatically, the percentage of individuals who believe that it is generally in children's best interest for parents to stay together, even if they do not get along, declined from about 50 in the 1960s to less than 20 in the 1990s. The increased acceptance of divorce, and the corresponding decline in support of the norm of lifelong marriage, may be related to a general rise in individualistic values favoring personal growth and self-fulfillment at the expense of commitment and obligation to others (Bellah et al., 1985; Glenn, 1996).

How might this shift in attitudes be related to marital quality? Amato and Rogers (1999) argued that individuals with a strong belief in marital permanence are likely to invest a good deal of time and effort in trying to resolve marital disagreements and problems. In contrast, individuals who are tolerant of divorce may prefer to jettison an existing marriage (rather than invest more effort in it) to find greater happiness with a new partner. Amato and Rogers (ibid.) thus found that individuals who adopted more favorable attitudes toward divorce tended to experience declines in marital happiness and increases in marital conflict. In contrast, shifts in marital quality did not appear to affect people's attitudes toward divorce. For this reason, decline in support for the norm of marital permanence may have lowered the aggregate level of marital quality in the population.

Summary of Recent Changes in Marriage

Our review reveals that the gradual, long-term transformation of marriage from a formal and public social contract to a private, more individualistic relationship continued during the latter part of the twentieth century. With affection, friendship, and personal growth now serving as the central goals of marriage, people are likely to end unsatisfying unions through divorce. The continuing high rate of divorce, in turn, has produced an increase in the number of second and higher-order marriages in the population. Because people have high expectations for self-fulfillment through marriage, they are taking longer to search for suitable spouses, which has resulted in an increase in the age at first marriage. Premarital cohabitation also has increased, as many people prefer to try out a residential union before marriage. The decline in the influence of parents, kin, and community members means that adults are freer now to marry whomever they please, including members of other races, the result being an increase in marital heterogamy. The growth in the labor-force participation of wives and the rise in women's wages may have facilitated egalitarian relations between husbands and wives. In short, most of the changes in marriage that occurred during the final decades of the 1900s were not discrete, unique historical events. Instead, these interconnected trends reflect an overarching, long-term structural transformation from institutional marriage to a more private and individualistic form of marriage—in essence the culmination of forces that have been active for more than two centuries. It is not clear, however, whether this general transformation has raised or lowered the average level of marital quality in the population.

A positive interpretation of these trends would emphasize the fact that couples today, compared with couples in the recent past, are older, more mature, and better educated at the time of marriage. Because premarital cohabitation prevents many high-risk marriages from occurring, and because divorce allows incompatible couples to exit the married population quickly, most married couples today are happy. Although many husbands saw their earnings decline in recent decades, many wives saw their earnings increase. Wives' growing economic contributions not only prevented many families from slipping into poverty, but also allowed dual-earner couples to achieve a higher standard of living, thus enhancing economic security. The adoption of less traditional gender attitudes and behavior may have contributed to more egalitarian power relations in marriage, with a corresponding strengthening of marital cohesion. As a result of these changes, marriages may be in better shape today than in earlier decades.

A negative interpretation of recent history, in contrast, would argue that people today, compared with people in the past, are more likely to enter marriage after having experienced a parental divorce, after a period of cohabitation, and following a previous marriage that ended in divorce. All these trends predict higher levels of marital discord and instability. Moreover, the continuing high rate of divorce reflects a culture that values personal happiness more than marital commitment and, hence, introduces an element of insecurity into all marital relationships. The decline in husbands' wages has forced many single-earner families to the brink of economic hardship. And the increase in maternal employment may have generated work-family conflict, uncertainty over gender arrangements, and tension between husbands and wives over housework and decision-making power. Finally, the declining social integration of married couples means that many must struggle with the inevitable ups and downs of married life without the support of kin, friends, neighbors, coworkers, and community organizations. As a result of these changes, marriage may have become a weaker and more vulnerable arrangement during the last several decades.

We suspect that the truth lies somewhere between these two extreme views. Owing to the number and complexity of these changes, however, their overall effect on marital quality is difficult to assess. It remains an open question whether marital quality has improved, declined, or remained constant in recent decades.

The 1980 and 2000 Marriage Surveys

To study change in marriage, it is necessary to have information from at least two points in time. During the last few decades, social scientists have conducted a number of longitudinal surveys of family life, such as the National Survey of Families and Households, the Longitudinal Study of Youth, and the National Study of Family Growth. Because these studies are based on interviews with the same respondents at each wave of data collection, it is possible to see how individual family members change over time. For example, with longitudinal data, one can study how people's attitudes toward marriage shift as they grow older, how marital satisfaction varies with marital duration, and how people's psychological well-being changes following events such as marriage, having children, or divorce. Longitudinal studies, however, are not useful for studying change at the societal level. Because these studies are restricted to people who participated in the first interview, subsequent waves lose people who exit the married population (through death or divorce) and omit people who enter the married population after the initial wave of data collection.

The best method to understand change at the societal level is to analyze repeated cross sections, that is, two or more surveys that are conducted at different points in time, focus on the same target population, use the same method to sample from the population, and ask identical questions (Firebaugh, 1997). In a properly designed study, the only factor that varies is the year during which the surveys are administered. Repeated cross sections are relatively rare in the family literature. Two of the best data sets of this type are the Decennial Census of the U.S. population and the annual Current Population Surveys, which are conducted by the U.S. Census Bureau. Both are excellent sources of information on changes in the composition of the married population. These data sets, however, contain little information on psychological variables, such as attitudes toward marriage, or information on family processes, such as marital interaction. Another data source is the General Social Survey (GSS), which has been conducted by the National Opinion Research Center in most years since 1972. This data set contains several items that measure attitudes toward marriage and family life (such as attitudes toward racial intermarriage and nonmarital births), along with a single-item measure of marital happiness. But because the GSS covers a wide range of topics of interest to many social scientists, its coverage of family variables is sparse.

To overcome the limitations of existing data, we use two national surveys, one conducted in 1980 and the other conducted in 2000, that focus exclusively on marriage. Because these two surveys were based on identical sampling procedures, methods of data collection, and interview schedules, it is possible to answer a range of questions about changes in people's experiences of marriage over this 20-year period.

Our 1980 data come from the first wave of what later became the Marital Instability over the Life Course study (Booth, Johnson, White, and Edwards, 1981). Our 2000 data come from the Survey of Marriage and Family Life. For detailed information on the two surveys, see Appendix 1.

Plan of the Book

In this chapter we described two sets of ideas that provide a background to our work. First, the marital-decline and marital-resilience perspectives make different assessments of changes in marriage during the last two decades. Decrements in marital quality during this period would support a decline perspective, whereas improvements in marital quality would support a resilience perspective. Second, we draw on the work of Ernest Burgess, who described the shift from institutional to companionate marriage, as well as Andrew Cherlin, who described the shift from companionate to individualistic marriage. Many of the variables what we examine in this book can be viewed as indicators of institutional, companionate, or individualistic marriage, and we examine not only how these indicators have changed over time, but also how they are related to aggregate shifts in marital quality.

In Chapter 2 we examine husbands' and wives' reports of marital quality in 1980 and 2000. We consider five dimensions of marital quality: marital happiness, marital interaction, marital conflict, marital problems, and divorce proneness. Because husbands and wives may experience marriage differently, we examine trends in marital quality separately by gender. Chapter 3 summarizes data on changes in the demographic composition of the married population between 1980 and 2000—especially changes that reflect greater individualism and personal choice in marriage. We also consider whether changes in these demographic characteristics had consequences for people's marital quality during this period.

Chapter 4 focuses on changes in employment between the two surveys, including spouses' hours of employment, spouses' job demands, and wives' reasons for employment. This chapter also examines aspects of economic well-being, including earned income, financial assets, perceptions of economic distress, and use of public assistance. Chapter 5 deals with gender relations in marriage, including attitudes toward gender roles, husbands' share of housework and child care, perceptions of unfairness in the household division of labor, and the balance of decision-making power between husbands and wives.

Chapter 6 looks at the extent to which married individuals are integrated into networks of friends, kin, and community organizations. For example, we examine the quality of relations with parents and in-laws.

We also explore the number of close friends that people have, the number of clubs and organizations to which they belong, and the extent to which people share these friends and organizational memberships with their spouses. This chapter also includes material on religiosity (religious affiliation, feelings, and attendance at services) and attitudes toward divorce and marriage.

In Chapter 7 we summarize the overall conclusions of our study. We also present an alternative way of looking at marital change— that is, a person-centered approach that clusters individuals into different types of marriages on the basis of their scores on a variety of explanatory variables. Chapter 8 presents some implications of our research. First, reflecting on our experiences in conducting this study, we include suggestions for future research on marital quality. Second, we discuss the implications of our research for general perspectives on family change. Our discussion focuses on the marital-decline and marital-resilience perspectives, as well as the transition from institutional to companionate to individualistic marriage. Third, strengthening healthy marriages has become a central focus of social policy in recent years—a focus that remains highly controversial. For this reason, we relate our findings to current debates about marriage and marriage policy in the United States. We conclude with some general thoughts about the possible future of marriage.

❧ 2

Stability and Change in
Marital Quality

𝒲HAT DO WE MEAN when we say that someone has a good marriage or a bad marriage? Although we use these terms frequently in everyday conversation, defining a good marriage or a bad marriage is not a straightforward task. Consider a husband and wife who have strong feelings of love for one another but fight frequently. How does this marriage compare with a marriage in which spouses no longer have strong feelings of love for one another, yet maintain a cooperative relationship, are committed to the stability of their union, and are determined to raise their children together? Is marital quality higher in the first or the second marriage? Marital quality means many different things, not only to married persons but also to the scholars who study families.

Although difficult to define and measure, martial quality has been the focus of thousands of studies by social scientists. This widespread interest exists for several reasons. First, a large number of studies show that happily married people have better physical and mental health than do unhappily married people or single individuals (Burman and Margolin, 1992; Marks and Lambert, 1998; Schoenborn, 2004; Stack and Eshleman 1998, Williams, 2003). In addition to promoting adult well-being, high-quality marriages benefit society by providing positive home environments for children's development and by discouraging delinquency and deviance among youth (Amato and Booth, 1997;

Laub, Nagin, and Sampson, 1998). Spouses' reports of marital quality also are good predictors of marital dissolution (Booth, Johnson, White, and Edwards, 1985; Rogge and Bradbury, 1999). Finally, research on marital quality provides a necessary foundation for designing effective premarital education programs and therapeutic interventions for troubled couples.

This chapter begins with a brief overview of how family scholars have defined and measured marital quality. We then discuss our own approach to measuring marital quality and provide information on the reliability, validity, and intercorrelations of our scales. We next describe how marital quality in the United States changed between 1980 and 2000. Because husbands and wives may differ in their perceptions of marital quality, we present this information separately by gender.

Measuring Marital Quality

Family researchers use three major methods to study marriage. Some scholars (typically family psychologists) observe marital interaction in laboratory or home settings. In a typical study, researchers ask couples to discuss a topic, such as a recurring marital problem, while a camera records the interaction. Teams of observers later code spouses' behavior (the content of the conversation along with facial expressions and other forms of nonverbal behavior) into a detailed set of categories for analysis. Some laboratory researchers also record physiological data, such as heart rate and respiration, during these sessions. (For a review of observational research on marital interaction, see Gottman and Notarius, 2000). In contrast to methods that rely on the observation of interaction, qualitative researchers from a number of fields (sociology, communication studies, clinical psychology) conduct informal, face-to-face interviews with married individuals. These interviews may be audio-recorded so that people's responses can be transcribed verbatim. Researchers then assemble the responses into coherent categories and themes, with an emphasis on the meaning of events to spouses (e.g., Rubin, 1983; Stacey, 1990). Finally, most quantitative sociologists rely on surveys of large, representative samples of married individuals. These interviews (which may be conducted in person or over the telephone) contain questions with precoded response options that are easy to manipulate statistically. Because we are survey researchers, the material in this book reflects the third approach. It is important to recognize, however, that all these methods yield valid and useful information, and that family scholars need to be familiar with findings generated within all three research traditions.

Family researchers have been developing quantitative, self-report measures to assess marital quality for more than seven decades. In one of the earliest attempts to measure marital quality, Hamilton (1929) transcribed people's responses to 13 open-ended questions about their marriages, and these responses were later scored to reflect marital adjustment. Interestingly, Hamilton reported symptoms of serious maladjustment in 45% of these marriages—a finding that probably reflects the clinical setting of the study (the author was a psychiatrist). A decade later Terman (1938) developed an 80-item index that assessed happiness with various facets of the marriage. Terman found that the majority of married people reported being either *extraordinarily happy* or *decidedly more happy than average*—a finding that persists in current research. In one of the first large-scale sociological surveys of marriage, Burgess and Cottrell (1939) assessed multiple dimensions of marital quality among 526 married individuals. Their survey instrument included 27 questions on the frequency of disagreements about different topics, common interests and activities, demonstrations of affection, and feelings of dissatisfaction with the relationship. Rather than examine these dimensions separately, Burgess combined people's responses into a single scale of "marital adjustment." Burgess found that people's marital adjustment scores were related to a variety of background characteristics, such as education, religiosity, closeness to parents, and recollections of parents' marital happiness.

Since this early research, literally hundreds of scales that measure some aspect of marital quality have appeared in the family literature (Touliatos, 2001). This proliferation of instruments reflects a lack of consensus among researchers about the meaning of marital quality. For example, researchers disagree about whether assessments of marital quality should include behavioral as well as evaluative components, and whether a single instrument or multiple instruments should be used. Amid a plethora of approaches and views, three general perspectives can be delineated: marital quality as adjustment, martial quality as a global evaluation of a marriage, and marital quality as a set of conceptually distinct but correlated dimensions.

The Marital-Adjustment Perspective

Proponents of the marital-adjustment perspective have adopted a pragmatic approach to measurement. A good measure of marital adjustment, according to this view, is one that distinguishes between poorly adjusted couples and well-adjusted couples, as defined by some external criterion. For example, a researcher may include one group of couples currently receiving marital therapy for a relationship problem and a second group of couples who have not received marital therapy and claim to be happily married. Alternatively, these groups may consist of couples who remained married for a certain number of years and couples who ended their marriages in divorce. Questionnaire items that successfully distinguish between these groups are included on the scale, and items that fail to distinguish between these groups are excluded. Because the goal of this approach is to differentiate between distressed and nondistressed marriages as accurately as possible, item content spans a wide range of domains, such as conflict, agreement, communication, satisfaction, and commitment. Although marital adjustment (or maladjustment) can take many forms, there is an explicit assumption that a single ordering of marriages—from poorly adjusted to well-adjusted—is possible.

One of the most commonly used marital adjustment measures is the Locke-Wallace Marital Adjustment Test (MAT; Locke and Wallace, 1959). These authors created a 15-item instrument by selecting items from longer tests administered in therapeutic settings, and this relatively short scale was found to discriminate well between maladjusted and well-adjusted marriages on the basis of clinical criteria. The MAT includes items about marital happiness, disagreements, marital interaction, and whether the respondent would marry the same person again. Graham Spanier's (1976) Dyadic Adjustment Scale (DAS) is another widely used measure of marital adjustment. To create the scale, Spanier pooled items from a variety of previously published marital assessment instruments. People in two groups responded to the pooled set of questions: married people who answered the questions with respect to their current marriage, and recently divorced individuals who answered the questions with respect to the last few months of their former marriages. Thirty-two items that discriminated successfully between these two groups were retained on the final scale. The DAS contains items that refer to global happiness (how happy spouses are with their relationship overall), agreement about different areas of the relationship, quarrels, marital interaction, and displays of affection. Although the items are multidimensional in content, the DAS, like the MAT, yields a single adjustment score.

One of the limitations of the marital adjustment perspective is that collapsing different marital dimensions into a single score restricts the use of the scale for research purposes. For example, researchers who wish to test a model in which communication and consensus are seen as causes of marital happiness would find the MAT and the DAS to be inappropriate. Moreover, because items are included on these scales for pragmatic reasons (that is, the ability of items to distinguish empirically between well-adjusted couples and poorly adjusted couples), there is relatively little attempt to develop theoretically coherent marital quality components. For these reasons, marital-adjustment measures, although useful as quick screening guides to identify distressed couples, are of limited usefulness in the development of theoretical models of marital relations and in the empirical testing of these models.

The Subjective Evaluation Perspective

Some researchers (Fincham and Bradbury, 1987; Glenn, 1990; Norton, 1983) have recommended that the term *marital quality* be restricted to individuals' global evaluations of their marriages, as reflected in overall happiness or satisfaction. According to this view, interpersonal behaviors such as communication, consensus, and conflict are causes of marital quality rather than forms of marital quality. For this reason, researchers interested in the extent to which positive communication affects marital quality would make a serious methodological mistake by using a summary measure of marital adjustment as the outcome. Because positive communication (the independent variable) is included as a component of marital adjustment (the dependent variable), shared item content will inflate the correlation between communication and marital quality. Moreover, advocates of this perspective point out that factors such as marital satisfaction, the quality of marital communication, and the amount of conflict in a marriage tend to yield different patterns of correlations with external variables (such as age at marriage or education). Combining these dimensions into a single score, therefore, tends to obscure or distort these correlations.

The Kansas Marital Satisfaction Scale (Schumm et al., 1986) is an example of a unidimensional instrument that measures people's subjective evaluations of their marriages. Although this instrument is relatively short (consisting of only three items) it has good reliability and validity. Single-item measures of marital happiness, such as the item that appears in most years of the General Social Survey and the item on the 1987–1988 National Survey of Families and Households, also fall into this category.

Measuring marital happiness (or satisfaction) is important for two reasons. First, longitudinal studies show that marital unhappiness is a good predictor of divorce (Booth, Johnson, White, and Edwards, 1985). Second, marital unhappiness is linked to a variety of problematic outcomes, including inept parenting (Hetherington and Kelly, 2002), psychological distress (Bradbury, Fincham, and Beach, 2000), and poor physical health—especially among wives (Kiecolt-Glaser and Newton, 2001). Nevertheless, measures of marital happiness provide only a partial understanding of how people subjectively evaluate their marriages. Moreover, knowing that people are happy or unhappy with their marriages tells us little about the patterns of interaction that accompany these subjective evaluations.

Marital Quality as a Set of Conceptually Distinct but Empirically Correlated Dimensions

This third approach treats marital quality as a general concept that encompasses several specific marital behaviors and evaluations, as each component is assessed by a separate instrument. Like the subjective evaluation perspective, this approach includes a scale that taps people's happiness or satisfaction with marriage. And like the marital-adjustment perspective, this approach includes measures of other dimensions, such as conflict, interaction, and perceived problems. This approach differs from the marital-adjustment perspective, however, in that the various dimensions are not combined into a single summary score. Although various dimensions of marriage are assumed to be correlated, individuals can exhibit a variety of profiles. For example, at the aggregate level, happiness and conflict are negatively correlated. But in a particular marriage, spouses might be low on happiness as well as conflict or, alternatively, high on happiness as well as conflict.

In this book we view marital quality as a set of conceptually distinct but empirically correlated dimensions. Recognizing that marital quality is a broadly subjective evaluation, we employ a scale that measures people's overall happiness with their marriages. Because we also are interested in interpersonal aspects of marriage, we include scales that assess the frequency of shared activities, the amount of conflict in the relationship, the number of perceived problems in the relationship, and the extent to which the marriage is prone to divorce. Unlike some authors, we consider all these constructs to be aspects of marital quality. We are careful, however, not to combine these five dimensions into a single marital quality score, because this strategy would result in conceptual and empirical confusion.

Earlier work with our scales supports the usefulness of viewing marital quality as multidimensional. In previous analyses, for example, we found that marital happiness (a measure of positive marital quality) and divorce proneness (a measure of negative marital quality) both tend to decline with marital duration (Booth, Johnson, and Edwards, 1983; VanLaningham, Johnson, and Amato, 2001). Because marriages tend to become less happy but more stable over time, combining happiness and divorce proneness into a single score would lead to the incorrect conclusion that marital quality does not vary with marital duration. (For other examples, see Amato and Booth, 1997; Johnson, White, Edwards, and Booth, 1986.) In this book, assessing multiple dimensions of marital quality allows us to construct a detailed picture of how the quality of marriage has changed in recent decades.

Our Measures of Marital Quality

As part of a national panel study of married individuals, Alan Booth, David Johnson, Lynn White, and John Edwards (1981) devised a set of scales to measure five distinct dimensions of marital quality that were assumed to be good predictors of divorce or permanent separation. Scale items were selected on the basis of a review of previously published instruments, and a pretest on a national sample of 300 individuals resulted in the elimination of some items and the rewording of other items. The final versions of the scales appeared in the first wave of the Marital Instability over the Life Course study in 1980, as well as the new cross section of married individuals interviewed in 2000.

Description of the Scales

Marital happiness. Marital happiness is one of the most frequently studied dimensions of marital quality. Most investigators view marital happiness as an individual property reflecting positive feelings about the marriage. Typical measures have included global assessments of the marriage as well as assessments of specific aspects of the relationship. To develop our measure of happiness, we began with 15 interview items. We eliminated five items after conducting a reliability analysis, which resulted in a ten-item scale. A factor analysis indicated that the scale was unidimensional, with a single factor accounting for 50% of the variance in the items. The overall alpha reliability coefficient for the scale was .88. Husbands' and wives' alpha coefficients were similar, as were the alpha coefficients for respondents in 1980 and 2000.

Seven items asked respondents to state whether they were (1) not too happy, (2) pretty happy, or (3) very happy with

- The amount of understanding received from your spouse
- The amount of love and affection received from your spouse
- The extent to which you and your spouse agree about things
- Your sexual relationship with your spouse
- Your spouse as someone who takes care of things around the home
- Your spouse as someone to do things with
- Your spouse's faithfulness.

We supplemented these specific items with three global items:

- "Overall, how happy is your marriage?" (1 = not too happy, 2 = pretty happy, 3 = very happy)
- "Compared to other marriages you know about, do you think your marriage is better than most, about the same as most, or not as good as most?" (1 = not as good, 2 = about the same, 3 = better than most)
- "Would you say the feeling of love you have for your spouse is extremely strong, very strong, pretty strong, not too strong, or not strong at all?" (1 = not strong at all, 5 = extremely strong).

We equally weighted and added these items to produce the scale score.

Marital interaction. Marital interaction refers to the extent to which people share day-to-day activities with their spouses. The interaction scale is based on respondents' reports of how often they and their spouses jointly engage in five different activities:

1. Eating the main meal of the day together
2. Shopping
3. Visiting friends
4. Working on projects around the house
5. Going out for recreation (e.g., playing cards, movies, bowling).

Items were coded so that high scores indicated more interaction (1 = never, 2 = occasionally, 3 = usually, 4 = almost always). A factor analysis revealed that the scale was unidimensional, and a single factor accounted for 42% of the variance in the items. We equally weighted and added the items to produce a marital interaction score. The alpha coefficient for the scale was .65, and this coefficient did not vary with the gender of the respondent or the year of the survey. Because the alpha coefficient is partly a product of the number of items (Carmines and Zeller, 1979), the reliability of this scale was reasonable for a short, survey-based instrument.

Marital conflict. Marital conflict is frequently studied in the research literature on marriage. Conflict occurs in all marriages, including marriages that are relatively happy and stable. For this reason, the study of conflict is a useful complement to the study of marital happiness and interaction. Our scale included the following items:

- "Do you and your spouse have arguments or disagreements about whether one of you is doing your share of the housework?" (0 = no, 1 = yes)
- "In general, how often do you disagree with your spouse?" (1 = never, 2 = rarely, 3 = sometimes, 4 = often, 5 = very often)
- "How many serious quarrels have you had with your spouse in the last two months?" (coded as 0 through 6 or more)
- "In many households bad feelings and arguments occur from time to time. In some cases people get so angry that they slap, hit, punch, kick, or throw things at one another. Has this ever happened between you and your spouse?" (0 = no, 1 = yes)

- "How many times has this [physical aggression] happened over the last three years?" (coded as 0 through 6 or more).

These items were equally weighted and added to produce the conflict score.

The conflict scale was unidimensional, and a single factor accounted for 37% of the total item variance. The overall alpha reliability coefficient was .62, and this coefficient did not vary with the gender of the respondent or the year of the survey. The interviews also contained a question about arguments or disagreements about children, but because many of the couples in our study did not have children, we omitted this item from the scale. We present data on this particular item, however, later in this chapter.

Marital problems. We also were interested in the extent that the behaviors and traits of either spouse led to perceptions of problems in the marriage. The marital problems scale was derived by asking respondents about 13 potential problems: Have you had a problem in your marriage because one of you . . .

- gets angry easily?
- has feelings that are easily hurt?
- is jealous?
- is domineering?
- is critical?
- is moody?
- won't talk to the other?
- has had a sexual relationship with someone else?
- has irritating habits?
- is not at home enough?
- spends money foolishly?
- drinks or uses drugs?
- has been in trouble with the law?

If a problem existed in the marriage, respondents reported whether the problem was due to the husband, the wife, or both spouses. (For example, a problem might exist because the husband has difficulty controlling anger, the wife has difficulty controlling anger, or both spouses have difficulty controlling anger.) A study using this instrument found that people's reports of marital problems did not appear to be self-serving; that is, people generally did not attribute more problems to their spouses than to themselves (Amato and Rogers, 1997).

We constructed the marital problems scale score by adding the total number of problems, irrespective of which spouse caused the problem. The alpha reliability coefficient was .78, and this coefficient varied little with the gender of the respondent or the year of the survey. A factor analysis revealed that the scale contained two factors. The first factor (which accounted for 28% of the variance in the 13 items) represented interpersonal problems. Items with high loadings on this factor (defined as loadings of .4 or greater) included getting angry easily, being domineering, being critical, being jealous, having feelings that are easily hurt, being moody, and not talking to the spouse. Many of these items reflect behaviors that Gottman (1994) described as symptomatic of unstable marriages. The second factor (which accounted for 10% of the variance in the 13 items) represented antisocial characteristics. High-loading items included drinking too much or using drugs, having been in trouble with the law, having had extramarital sex, and spending money foolishly. The items dealing with irritating habits and not spending enough time at home did not load on either factor. The correlation between the two factors was .30—a modest but significant association. Most of the analyses in this book focus on the total marital problems scale, but because this scale contains two distinguishable factors, we describe the results for the separate factors when they yield different results.

Divorce proneness. Divorce proneness is the propensity to divorce and includes both a cognitive component (thinking that one would like to live apart from one's spouse, thinking that one's marriage is in trouble, considering the possibility of getting a divorce) and actions (talking with one' spouse about divorce, consulting with an attorney about divorce). The scale consists of 13 items that tapped both the frequency and the timing of indicators of relationship instability. For example, a question on thinking about divorce was scored 0 = never have thought about divorce, 1 = have thought about divorce but not within the last three years, 2 = have thought about divorce within the last three years but not recently, and 3 = thinking about divorce now. This scoring strategy is based on the assumption that marriages in which spouses are currently thinking about divorce are the most unstable, marriage in which spouses have thought about divorce in the past are moderately unstable, and marriages in which spouses have never thought about divorce are the most stable. (The same reasoning applies to the other items as well.) The overall alpha coefficient for the scale was .92, and this value did not vary with the respondents' gender or the year of the survey. A factor analysis revealed one underlying factor that accounted for 44% of the variance in the items. The items were:

- "Sometimes married people think they would enjoy living apart from their spouse. Have you ever felt this way?"
- "Even people who get along quite well with their spouse sometimes wonder whether their marriage is working out. Have you ever thought your marriage might be in trouble?"
- "Have you talked with your husband/wife about these problems?"
- "Have you ever talked with family members, friends, counselors, clergy, or social workers about problems in your marriage?"
- "As far as you know, has your husband/wife talked with family members, friends, or counselors about problems in your marriage?"
- "As far as you know, has your spouse ever thought your marriage is in trouble?"
- "Has the thought of getting a divorce or separation crossed your mind?"
- "As far as you know, has the thought of divorce or separation crossed your spouse's mind?"
- "Have you or your husband/wife seriously suggested the idea of divorce?"
- "Have you discussed a divorce or separation with family members or a close friend?"
- "Have you or your husband/wife consulted an attorney about a separation or divorce?"
- "Have you or your husband/wife filed a divorce or separation petition?"

• "Because of problems people are having with their marriage, they sometimes leave home either for a short time or as a trial separation. Has this ever happened in your marriage?"

Stability, Validity, and Correlations between Scales

Stability. To assess the stability of these scales over time, we used the first two waves of the Marital Instability over the Life Course study. The first survey was conducted in 1980, and a follow-up survey of the same respondents was conducted in 1983. Among continuously married respondents, stability was moderately high across the five measures of marital quality: marital happiness ($r = .62$), marital interaction ($r = .54$), marital conflict ($r = .56$), marital problems ($r = .62$), and divorce proneness ($r = .52$). After controlling for measurement error with structural equation methods, correlations between these variables ranged between .8 and .9 (Johnson, Amoloza, and Booth, 1992). The degree of stability was unaffected by the respondents' gender or the duration of marriage.

The high level of stability across time raises the question of whether marital quality (as assessed by our measures) is a product of the marital relationship or a product of stable individual characteristics (such as personality traits). We addressed this question by examining the marital quality of individuals who divorced and remarried between interviews. For individuals in different marriages, the cross-time correlations were weak and nonsignificant, in general. This finding suggests that marital quality is due mostly to dyadic properties of the marriage rather than to traits that people carry from one marriage to the next. The one exception involved marital problems—especially problems reflecting antisocial forms of behavior (such as drug use or heavy drinking). For this variable, the correlation for the same individuals in different marriages was positive and significant, although not as high as the cross-time correlation for individuals within the same marriages (Johnson and Booth, 1998).

Validity. Following the logic of construct validity, our five scales are correlated with other variables (both concurrently and predictively) in ways that are consistent with the assumption that the scales measure aspects of marital quality. For example, all five scales (happiness, interaction, conflict, problems, and divorce proneness) are correlated significantly with personal happiness. Similarly, all five scales are significant predictors of divorce. Of the five measures, divorce proneness is the best predictor, with the odds of divorcing being nine times higher for individuals who scored one standard deviation above the mean than for individuals who scored one standard deviation below the mean (Booth, Johnson, and Edwards, 1983; Booth, Johnson, White, and Edwards, 1985). Moreover, *parents'* ratings of the five dimensions of marital quality in 1980 are significant predictors of *children's* self-reports of psychological well-being in 1992 and 1997 (Amato and Booth, 1997; Booth and Amato, 2001), which is consistent with earlier research and theory. In general, previous research provides strong support for the construct validity of our measures of marital quality.

Correlations between scales. One might think that the five dimensions of marital quality are highly interrelated. The associations between the five measures, however, are moderate rather than large, with correlations ranging from .21 to .61. (See Table 1 in Appendix 2). The pattern of correlations was similar in the 1980 and 2000 surveys, and a general test of the difference in covariance matrices (Arbuckle, 1997) was not significant. Marital happiness has the most consistent set of associations with the other scales and yields correlations ranging from .44 to .53. Correlations of this magnitude suggest that the five scales are measuring conceptually distinct but empirically related constructs. The largest proportion of variance shared between any two scales is .37 ($.61^2$). Consequently, combining these scales into a summary measure would throw away potentially useful information. Moreover, as we show later, the five dimensions of marital quality exhibit different patterns of change over time.

How Did Marital Quality Change between 1980 and 2000?

Changes in Scale Means

In the first chapter we described two perspectives on marital change: the marital-decline perspective and the marital-resilience perspective. The first assumes that the institution of marriage is in a state of decline; the second stresses the adaptability of marriage to changing social and historical circumstances. Our surveys reveal that the overall pattern of change between 1980 and 2000 was not consistent with either of these perspectives.

Figure 2.1 shows the mean levels of marital quality in both decades.

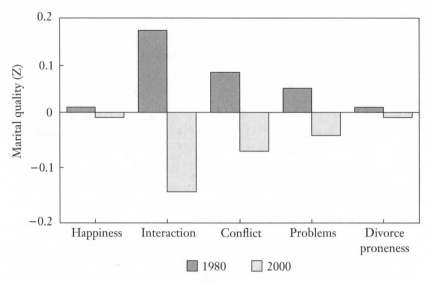

Figure 2.1   Mean scores on five dimensions of marital quality, 1980 and 2000

(In this chapter and in subsequent chapters, we standardized each measure of marital quality to have a mean of 0 and a standard deviation of 1.) There were no significant changes in the mean levels of marital happiness or divorce proneness between 1980 and 2000. In fact, the means for these variables were nearly identical in both years. Two aspects of marital quality, conflict and problems, decreased between surveys, which suggests improvements in marital quality. These differences were modest rather than large; the mean for marital conflict declined by .15 of a standard deviation, and the mean for marital problems declined by .10 of a standard deviation. In contrast, the mean for marital interaction decreased by about one-third of a standard deviation during this period, which indicates a moderate decline in this dimension of marital quality. Overall, two dimensions of marital quality improved (conflict and problems), one dimension of marital quality deteriorated (interaction), and two dimensions of marital quality were unchanged (happiness and divorce proneness).

It is tempting to speculate that the level of marital conflict declined because the level of marital interaction also declined. After all, if couples spend less time together, then they should have fewer opportunities to quarrel. This interpretation would not be correct, however, because interaction is negatively (not positively) associated with conflict.

Couples who spend a great deal of time together tend to report low rather than high levels of conflict. Indeed, if we control for the drop in interaction between 1980 and 2000, then the estimated decline in conflict becomes larger rather than smaller—a result that would not occur if the decline in conflict were due to the corresponding decline in interaction.

Table 2 in Appendix 2 shows the mean levels of marital quality in 1980 and 2000 for husbands and wives separately. Wives gave less positive responses than did husbands across all five measures, irrespective of the year of the survey. That is, wives reported less happiness, less interaction, more conflict, more problems, and greater divorce proneness than did husbands. This gender difference is consistent with earlier studies suggesting that wives, compared with husbands, are more critical of their marriages (Lewis and Spanier, 1979) and more likely to initiate divorce (Amato and Previti, 2003; Kitson, 1992). Some feminist authors have argued that this difference exists because marriage tends to benefit men more than women (Bernard, 1982). For example, many wives perform more than their fair share of housework and child care (Hochschild, 1989). Other research indicates that women tend to monitor the quality of their intimate relationships more closely than do men (Thompson and Walker, 1991). For this reason, wives may be critical of their marriages because they are more aware of relationship problems. Another possibility is that wives have higher expectations for marriage than do husbands (expectations that are less easily satisfied), although earlier research has not addressed this possibility.

Despite these gender differences, overall changes in marital quality between 1980 and 2000 were comparable for husbands and wives. Irrespective of the gender of the respondent, interaction, conflict, and problems declined to about the same degree, and divorce proneness changed little between decades. The one exception involved marital happiness, which produced a significant interaction between the respondents' gender and the decade of the survey. Husbands' happiness decreased slightly between surveys, whereas wives' happiness increased slightly. This gender difference, however, was not large enough to be of substantive importance. When we restricted the analysis to one gender at a time, neither the decrease in husbands' happiness nor the increase in wives' happiness was statistically significant.

In addition to comparing the means, we also compared the variances of the scales across decades. This analysis revealed that two dimensions of marital quality were dispersed differently in 2000 from the way they were in 1980. First, the variance of the marital conflict scale declined, although this probably reflects the decline in the mean for this scale. (In general, variables with smaller means tend to have smaller variances.) Second, the variance of the divorce proneness scale increased by about 10%. In other words, although the mean level of divorce proneness did not change, scores were more spread out around the mean in 2000 than in 1980. This result suggests an increase in the proportion of married people with either very low or very high levels of divorce proneness in the population. (We return to this point below.)

Changes in Individual Scale Items

Marital happiness. As we noted earlier, the mean level of marital happiness in the population did not change between surveys. Correspondingly, there was no change in people's responses to most of the individual items on the scale, including happiness with the amount of understanding received from the spouse, with the spouse's affection, with the spouse as someone who takes care of things around the home, with the spouse as a companion, with the spouse's faithfulness, and overall with the marriage. The lack of change in happiness with the spouse as a companion is of interest. Although levels of marital interaction decreased substantially between surveys (as we noted earlier), people were as happy with their spouses as companions. This finding may reflect a tendency for spouses to focus on the quality of time spent together, rather than the amount of time spent together. This focus would allow couples to be just as happy with their spouses as companions in 2000 as in 1980, even though they engaged in fewer shared activities.

A few of the individual items on the marital happiness scale shifted during this period, but the direction of change was not consistent. Two shifted upward (indicating greater happiness) and two shifted downward (indicating less happiness). Figure 2.2 shows the percentage of people in both survey years who gave the most positive responses to these questions. The percentage of people who were "very happy" with the extent of agreement with their spouses increased from 42 to 49, and the percentage of people who described their feelings of love for their

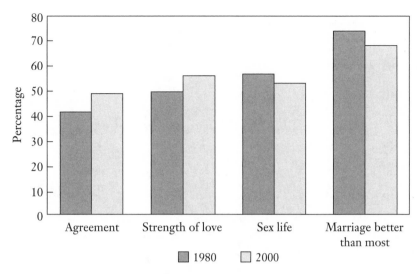

Figure 2.2 Percentage of people giving the most positive responses to questions on marital happiness, 1980 and 2000

spouses as "extremely strong" increased from 50 to 56. The increase in happiness with the extent of agreement may reflect the fact that men's and women's views about marriage became more similar between 1980 and 2000 (see Chapter 5). The increase in feelings of love may reflect a strengthening of the belief that love is the central defining characteristic of a good marriage, as we noted earlier (Buss, Shackelford, Kirkpatrick, and Larsen, 2001).

In contrast to these upward trends, the percentage of people who were "very happy" with their sex lives decreased slightly from 57 to 53. Although we can only speculate about the reason, this decline may reflect the continuing sexualization of the American media (music, movies, television, magazines) during the last few decades. If increased exposure to sexual imagery increased people's expectations for sexual satisfaction, then it is not surprising that happiness with marital sex declined slightly. Finally, the percentage of people who thought that their marriages were "better than most" declined from 74 to 68. The explanation for the decline is not clear. To the extent that this change reflects the adoption of a more realistic view of marriage on the part of some spouses, however, this change may be constructive. Despite this decline, it is worth noting that the substantial majority of spouses in 2000 continued to view their marriages as better than average.

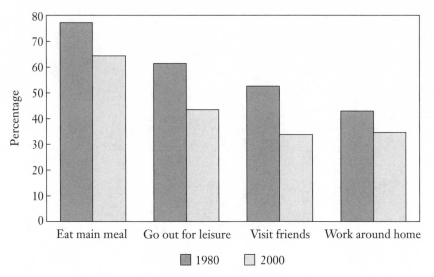

Figure 2.3   Percentage of respondents who "almost always" shared activities with their spouses, 1980 and 2000

Marital interaction. Reports of interaction declined between 1980 and 2000 across all five items on the marital interaction scale. Figure 2.3 illustrates these differences by focusing on the percentage of people who reported "almost always" engaging in activities with their spouses. The largest decline occurred for visiting friends together. In 1980, 53% of people reported that their spouses almost always accompanied them while visiting friends, but by 2000 this figure had declined to 34% (a drop of 19 percentage points). Similarly, people's reports that they almost always went out with their spouses for leisure activities dropped from 62% to 44% (a drop of 18 percentage points). The figure also shows declines in eating the main meal of the day together (78% to 66%) and working together on projects around the house (43% to 34%). Although not shown in the figure, reports of shopping together also dropped modestly. These results indicate that the decline in marital interaction was pervasive, encompassing leisure activities as well as task-oriented activities.

Marital conflict. Of the five items on the marital conflict scale, three declined significantly between 1980 and 2000. Reports of disagreeing with one's spouse "often" or "very often" declined from 12% to 8%. More remarkably, reports of violence ever occurring in the marriage (slapping, hitting, kicking, or throwing things) declined from 21% to

12%. Similarly, reports of marital violence within the previous three years declined by one-half, from 12% to 6%. These last two items suggest a major decline in marital violence during the last two decades of the twentieth century. People were no less (or more) likely to report arguments over the household division of labor in 2000 than in 1980. Similarly, responses to the question dealing with the number of serious quarrels in the previous two months did not change. And although not included as part of the scale, the item on arguments about taking care of the children also did not change between decades. In general, most of the change in our measure of conflict was due to a decline in marital violence. Following Michael Johnson and Janel Leone (2005), we assume that most of the decline in aggression reflected "common couple violence," that is, a tendency for couple's arguments to escalate to the point of aggression, but without engaging in serious forms of physical abuse.

What might account for such a dramatic change? Since 1980 the American public has become more aware of domestic violence as a serious social problem. And contrary to the earlier approach of not interfering in domestic disputes, many police departments now routinely arrest offending spouses. For these reasons, it is possible that spouses are less likely to *report* marital violence today than in the past, even though actual levels of violence remained the same. That is, the apparent decline in marital violence may reflect nothing more than an increased tendency to give socially desirable answers to survey questions on this topic.

If the decline in marital violence is due to response bias, then the decline should be stronger for husbands than for wives, given that the public views aggression as a more serious problem when it is initiated by men rather than women (Felson, 2002). Figure 2.4 shows the responses of husbands and wives to the two questions on marital violence. With respect to the marriage ever being violent, reports declined significantly for wives as well as husbands, and the extent of the decline did not differ by gender. With respect to marital violence within the previous three years, reports declined for wives as well as husbands, but the decline was significantly greater for husbands than for wives (as reflected in a significant decade-by-gender interaction). Reports of violence within the previous three years declined from 13% to 5% for husbands and from 11% to 7% for wives. These results suggest that re-

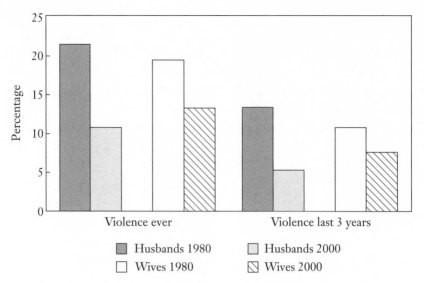

Figure 2.4   Percentage of husbands and wives reporting marital violence, 1980 and 2000

lying on husbands' reports may exaggerate the extent of the decline in marital violence, at least during the previous three years. Nevertheless, these results suggest that marital violence became less common, even when we rely exclusively on wives' reports.

Another way to assess the validity of this decline is to compare the associations between spouses' reports of marital violence and other aspects of marital quality in both decades. If the decline in reports of violence is due mainly to social desirability bias, then the correlation between violence and other dimensions of marital quality should have declined between surveys. This decline would occur because violence would be measured with greater error in 2000 than in 1980, and measurement error attenuates the magnitude of correlations. This is not what we found, however. For wives as well as husbands, the correlations between reports of violence and reports of marital happiness, marital problems, and divorce proneness did not change significantly between 1980 and 2000. Overall, our data do not suggest that reports of marital violence became less valid during this period.

The decline in reports of marital violence is consistent with crime data reported by the U.S. Department of Justice (Rennison, 2001). According to the National Crime Victimization Surveys, rates of intimate

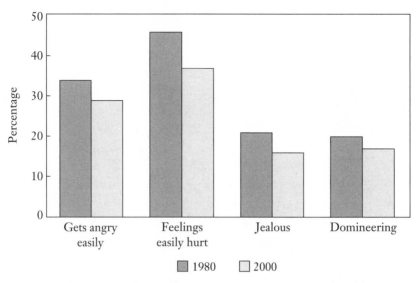

Figure 2.5 Percentage of respondents reporting particular marital problems, 1980 and 2000

partner violence declined by 41% between 1993 and 1999. This trend is consistent with general declines in most forms of violent crime during the 1990s. Our data indicate a comparable decline between 1980 and 2000: violence at any time in the marriage was down by 41%, and violence within the preceding three years was down by 47%. If we restrict the data to wives' reports, then violence at any time in the marriage was down by 32%, and violence during the preceding three years was down by 30%. Overall, these results suggest an important improvement in the quality of marital relationships during the last two decades of the twentieth century.

Marital problems. Although overall scores on the marital problems scale declined between 1980 and 2000, only four individual items changed significantly during this period. Figure 2.5 shows these four items: Getting angry easily, having feelings that are hurt easily, experiencing jealousy, and being domineering. All these items represented the interpersonal behavior factor that we described earlier. To cast additional light on this issue, we examined changes in the interpersonal behavior and antisocial behavior factor scores across surveys. The antisocial behavior factor changed little between decades, but the interpersonal behavior factor declined significantly. These results indicate that the decline in marital problems mainly involved interactional patterns between spouses. This finding makes intuitive sense, because behaviors that have an antisocial quality (getting in trouble with the police, drinking too much, using drugs, or having extramarital sex) probably reflect personality traits that are relatively resistant to change. Our data indicate that married couples were engaging in less problematic interpersonal behavior with their spouses in 2000 than in 1980.

Divorce proneness. Although the mean level of divorce proneness was stable between 1980 and 2000, responses to many of the individual items changed. Between surveys, married people were less likely to report thinking that they would enjoy living apart from their spouses (32% vs. 25%), thinking that their marriages ever had been in trouble (46% vs. 42%), thinking about divorce during the preceding three years (20% vs. 17%), discussing divorce with their spouses during the preceding three years (10% vs. 7%), or having a trial separation (11% vs. 8%). Given that all these changes represent declines in divorce proneness, why did the overall level of divorce proneness not decline as well?

The answer to this question involves the manner in which the divorce proneness scale was constructed. Recall that we scored this scale by weighting more recent indicators of marital instability more highly than earlier indicators. Consider the item on thinking that one's marriage is in trouble. The percentage of individuals who *ever* felt this was 46% in 1980 and 42% in 2000 (as we noted above). But among those individuals who answered "yes" to this question, those who had felt this way during the previous three years increased from 52% in 1980 to 60% in 2000. With respect to considering divorce within the previous three years, the percentages were 20% in 1980 and 17% in 2000, as we noted above. But among those who answered "yes" to the previous question, 12% were currently thinking about divorce in 1980, compared with 14% in 2000. So although the size of the group who reported few or no indicators of marital instability increased, so did the group of people who reported frequent and more extreme forms of instability. Because of this pattern, people in 2000, compared with people in 1980, were more likely to have either low or high levels of divorce proneness.

Figure 2.6 illustrates this pattern. To construct the figure, we divided people into three groups: those who reported no indicators of instabil-

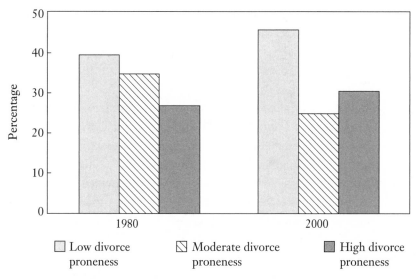

Figure 2.6 Percentage of respondents reporting low, medium, and high levels of divorce proneness, 1980 and 2000

ity, those who reported a small number of indicators (for example, occasionally thinking about living apart from one's spouse, thinking that one's marriage had been in trouble at some point during the marriage but not during the last three years, and discussing marital problems with the spouse within the last three years), and those who reported a large number of indicators, especially ones that were serious and recent (for example, thinking about divorce recently, talking with one's spouse recently about divorce, consulting an attorney, and having a trial separation within the previous three years). The figure reveals that the percentage of people with either a minimal level of divorce proneness or a high level of divorce proneness increased from 1980 to 2000. Correspondingly, the percentage of people with a moderate level of divorce proneness declined. This pattern is consistent with the finding, noted earlier, that the variance of the divorce proneness scale increased significantly across surveys.

The increased polarization of divorce proneness could represent two opposing trends. First, the same beneficial forces that decreased levels of marital conflict and marital problems during this period also may have decreased the level of divorce proneness, resulting in a larger proportion of stable marriages in the population. But at the same time, the increasing social acceptance of divorce may mean that once spouses begin to view their relationships as troubled, they move relatively quickly to more consequential thoughts and actions, such as thinking about divorce, talking with their spouses about divorce, consulting with an attorney, or having a trial separation.

Although it is not shown in the figure, an additional positive trend appeared in the data. Among people who thought that their marriages were in trouble, there was an increase in the proportion who discussed their marital problems with family members, friends, clergy, counselors, or social workers. The fact that people are increasingly likely to talk with others, including members of the helping professions, about their marital problems may be a healthy sign. Talking with relatives, friends, and professionals may lead to resolutions of problems or accommodations that curtail further steps toward dissolution.

Gender Differences

To supplement our presentation of changes in people's responses to specific questions, we examined the data separately for husbands and wives. This step was necessary because our findings would be misleading if husbands and wives exhibited substantially different patterns of change over time. Few gender differences were apparent, however.

Between 1980 and 2000 spouses of both genders became happier with the extent to which they agreed with their spouses, reported increased feelings of love, reported being less happy with their sexual relationships, and were less likely to believe that their marriages were better than most. Gender differences appeared for only two items. Between 1980 and 2000 wives—but not husbands—became happier with the amount of understanding received from their spouses. Wives also became happier with their husbands' work around the house, whereas husbands became less happy with their wives' work around the house. For both items, the interactions between year of survey and gender were significant, but the differences were small.

Husbands and wives reported similar declines in marital interaction. The proportion of spouses who reported "almost always" doing things together (including eating the main meal of the day, visiting friends, working on projects around the house, and going out for leisure activities) declined similarly for husbands and wives. For spouses of both genders, the largest drops occurred for visiting friends together and sharing leisure activities.

With respect to conflict, spouses of both genders reported declines in violence, but this change was greater for husbands than for wives, as we noted earlier. One additional item revealed an interaction between gender and decade: Wives, but not husbands, reported a small increase in arguments over the household division of labor. Husbands' and wives' reports of arguments over child care, however, were comparable between surveys.

Declines in reports of marital problems were nearly identical for husbands and wives. For both genders, reports of problems involving anger, jealousy, and having feelings that are easily hurt decreased between surveys.

As we reported earlier, some items on the divorce proneness scale tended to decrease over time, whereas other items increased, which led to greater variability in divorce proneness in 2000 than in 1980. This trend was similar for husbands and wives. For example, fewer spouses of both genders reported that they had *ever* thought that their marriages were in trouble. But among spouses who felt this way, husbands as well as wives were more likely to report that these feelings had continued into the present. Overall, the results for divorce proneness, like the results for our other four dimensions of marital quality, yielded surprisingly few differences between husbands and wives.

Within-Cohort and Cross-Cohort Change

One source of ambiguity in our study (and all studies like it) involves the impossibility of distinguishing between period, cohort, and age effects. Period effects refer to social events or processes associated with a particular historical era that have pervasive consequences for members of the population. For example, if the economy rallies in a particular period, then the financial well-being of most families will improve, irrespective of people's ages or the years in which they were born. Other forms of social change are due to cohort effects, which involve the unique experiences of a group of people born during adjacent years, such as the 1930s or the 1950s. Members of a birth cohort often carry with them, throughout their lives, traits that reflect the social milieus in which they were raised. For this reason, social change often occurs as members of older cohorts die and are replaced by members of younger cohorts. For example, if young people today hold relatively nontraditional attitudes toward gender roles in marriage, and if these attitudes are stable over the life course, then the population of married individuals gradually will become less traditional as older (and more traditional) couples die and are replaced with younger couples. Finally, age effects involve developmental processes that occur as people grow older. For example, the frequency of sexual activity in marriage tends to decrease with age, partly because of hormonal factors and growing health problems. (For discussion of period, cohort, and age effects, see Firebaugh, 1997, and Glenn, 1997).

A mathematical relationship exists among period, cohort, and age, in that any one of these factors can be determined precisely from the other two. For example, in the present study, if we know a person's year of birth and age, then we can calculate the year in which the survey was conducted (either 1980 or 2000) by adding the person's age to the person's year of birth (period = cohort + age). Similarly, we can calculate a person's year of birth by subtracting age at the time of the survey from the year of the survey (cohort = period − age). Finally, we can calculate a person's age by subtracting the person's year of birth from the year of the survey (age = period − cohort). Because of this mathematical relationship, survey researchers cannot use year of survey (period), year of birth (cohort), and age as predictors in a regression model simultaneously.

Although it is not possible to distinguish among age, period, and cohort effects, it is possible to decompose trends more generally into within-cohort and cross-cohort components. The within-cohort component refers to change that occurs among members of the same cohort over time, whereas the cross-cohort component refers to change due to the departure of older cohorts from the population and their replacement with younger cohorts. Following methods described by Firebaugh (1997), we decomposed the trend in each dimension of marital quality between 1980 and 2000 into within-cohort and between-cohort components. This analysis revealed no significant within-cohort or between-cohort trends for marital happiness. For the other four marital outcomes, however, both the within-cohort and the between-cohort components were significant. (Appendix 1 contains details on the calculations, and Tables 3 and 4 in Appendix 2 show the results of this procedure.)

The within-cohort components were *negative* for each marital outcome. In other words, within birth cohorts, all these dimensions of marital quality declined between 1980 and 2000. Keep in mind that within-cohort change can occur either because of period effects (which reflect people's exposure to historical events and processes) or aging effects (which reflect individual development). For example, the within-cohort decline in marital interaction between surveys could reflect greater employment demands since 1980 (a period effect) or a tendency for spouses to develop separate interests as they grow older (an aging effect).

Although unknown factors produced declines within cohorts in each of these marital dimensions between 1980 and 2000, cohort replacement slowed down the rate of change. In fact, cross-cohort change was *positive* for all marital outcomes. Cross-cohort change occurred because people left the married population, either through death, divorce, or (in the present study) by exceeding age 55. As married individuals from older birth cohorts left the married population, they were replaced by married individuals from more recent birth cohorts. And individuals from more recent birth cohorts, compared with ones from older birth cohorts, engaged in more interaction, experienced more conflict, reported more problems in their marriages, and were more divorce prone. The result for divorce proneness was particularly noteworthy, because overall change was almost perfectly offset by negative within-cohort and positive between-cohort effects.

Because these trends are difficult to understand, Figure 2.7 provides a concrete example. This figure shows the mean level of marital conflict by year of study and decade of birth. Birth cohorts (in ten-year intervals) are represented along the horizontal axis, and the two survey years are represented as separate lines. The rising lines for the 1980 and 2000 surveys show that marital conflict was higher among more recent birth cohorts than in earlier birth cohorts. The double-headed arrows identify birth cohorts that appeared in both surveys. Among individuals born in the 1940s the change across survey years amounted to $-.43$ of a standard deviation, and among individuals born in the 1950s the change across survey years amounted to $-.46$ of a standard deviation. Both these values are substantially greater than the overall value

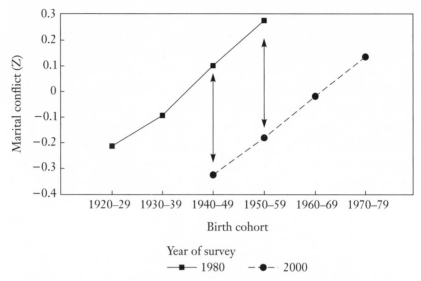

Figure 2.7   Change within and between cohorts: marital conflict, 1980 and 2000

of −.15 that we reported earlier (see Figure 2.1). If the 1980 to 2000 comparison were restricted to people born in the 1940s and 1950s, then the overall decline in marital conflict would have been greater than the value shown in Figure 2.1.

Note that individuals born in the 1920s and 1930s (with relatively low levels of marital conflict) appeared in the first survey but not in the second survey. Correspondingly, individuals born in the 1960s and 1970s (with relatively high levels of marital conflict) appeared in the second survey but were largely absent from the first survey. (The figure omits a small number of individuals who were born in the 1960s and appeared in the 1980 survey.) Cohort replacement resulted in older, low-conflict couples leaving the population and younger, high-conflict couples entering the population. Indeed, if we had compared the 1980 and 2000 surveys and omitted individuals from cohorts represented in both surveys, then marital conflict would have increased, rather than declined, between surveys. Cohort replacement did not happen fast enough, however, to balance the drop in marital conflict within cohorts (which may have been largely an aging effect), the result being a net decline in conflict in the married population.

In a parallel set of analyses, we replaced birth cohort (year of birth) with marriage cohort (year of marriage). These results (not shown) were nearly identical to the earlier results. That is, negative within-cohort differences were offset by positive between-cohort differences. Taken together, these results reveal the dynamic nature of marital quality at the end of the twentieth century. Young people from recent cohorts entered the married population with relatively high levels of interaction, conflict, problems, and divorce proneness. Some of these individuals exited the married population through divorce. But those who remained experienced gradual declines in interaction, conflict, problems, and divorce proneness. By the time these individuals reached their fifties, their marriages were relatively peaceful and stable. But by then, couples from more recent cohorts had joined the population, and these young couples raised the mean levels of conflict, problems, and divorce proneness in the population.

As we noted earlier, it is not mathematically possible to remove the effects of aging from the data to discover pure period and cohort effects. Nevertheless, the decomposition analysis suggests that a combination of period and cohort effects was present in the data. Therefore, our main analyses (reported in Chapters 3–6) focus on specific period and cohort factors (such as changes in labor-force participation, social integration, and attitudes toward marriage) that may be responsible for shifts in aggregate levels of marital quality in the U.S. population.

Selection Effects

Selection effects can reflect movement into marriage as well as movement out of marriage. Selection into marriage refers to the fact that the types of people who marry are different from the types of people who never marry. Selection out of marriage refers to the fact that the types of people who divorce are different from the types of people who remain married. Although selection into marriage is not an issue in the present context, selection out of marriage poses two potential challenges to our study.

First, our conclusions about changes in marital quality between 1980 and 2000 would be threatened if these results were driven primarily by an increase in the rate of divorce between surveys. Of course, as we pointed out in Chapter 1, divorce rates were relatively stable during this 20-year interval. But because divorce rates rose dramatically in the late 1960s and 1970s, there was more selection out of marriage in the

1980 sample than in the 2000 sample. The increase in selection out of marriage, however, was modest. Census data from 1980 and 2000 indicate that of all ever-married adults, 13% were divorced or separated in 1980, compared with 19% in 2000. (These percentages exclude widows and widowers.) With increased selection of people out of troubled marriages through divorce, one might expect remaining marriages to be of higher quality in 2000 than in 1980. If this is true, then the apparent stability in marital happiness and divorce proneness between surveys, for example, would represent a decline in the real level of these variables over time.

To see if this increase of 6 percentage points in the divorced population between surveys affected our results, we adopted two strategies. First, we restricted our decade comparisons to marriages of less than two years. Because these marriages are at risk for a short time, movement out of these marriages through separation and divorce is minimal (Bramlett and Mosher, 2002). Second, we estimated how marital quality would have changed if there had been no selection out of marriage through divorce in 1980 and 2000. To produce these estimates, we used "side" information on the quality of marriages before divorce from the longitudinal Marital Instability over the Life Course study. Both procedures indicated that the small increase in selection out of marriage between surveys did not distort our estimates of changes in marital quality. (See Appendix 1 for details.)

There is a second way in which selection out of marriage may have affected our results. As Norval Glenn (1990) pointed out, self-selection out of marriage is problematic in cross-sectional studies, because a single cross section of married people necessarily excludes a large group of unhappily married people who divorced before the time of data collection. For this reason, any cross-sectional study that attempts to understand the correlates and causes of marital quality omits some of the most important cases, that is, people with unhappy and short marriages. For example, marrying as a teenager is a well-known predictor of divorce (Bramlett and Mosher, 2002). But in a cross-sectional study of currently married individuals, the association between early marriage and marital quality will be underestimated because the most troubled young couples already have exited the married population. There is no way to avoid this problem, and all we can do is to caution readers that it exists. (We emphasize, however, that this is a limitation of all studies based on cross-sectional data—not just our own study.)

In summary, selection out of marriage did not appear to affect our estimates of overall changes in marital quality between 1980 and 2000. Selection out of marriage, however, means that many of the findings that we report in subsequent chapters about the links between specific demographic, social, and cultural variables and marital quality are likely to be underestimates of the true associations. In this sense, many of the findings reported in later chapters err on the conservative side.

Conclusions

Our goal in this chapter was to describe stability and change in five dimensions of marital quality between 1980 and 2000. Although some researchers restrict the term *marital quality* to marital happiness or satisfaction, we view marital quality as being multidimensional. We examined five conceptually and empirically distinct dimensions of marriage: happiness, interaction, conflict, problems, and divorce proneness. Because earlier research shows that these components of marital quality tend to correlate with external variables in distinct ways, we avoided the temptation to combine our measures into an overall marital quality score. Implicit in our approach is the assumption that dimensions of marital quality in the population may exhibit divergent (or even contrary) trends over time. In other words, "Have marriages improved or declined in quality in recent decades?" is too blunt a question. A more appropriate question is "How have various dimensions of marital quality changed over time?"

Our conceptualization and measurement of marital quality turned out to be a useful approach. The mean level of marital happiness did not change between surveys. Aggregate levels of marital interaction showed a clear downward trend: couples in 2000 were substantially less likely than couples in 1980 to eat together, visit friends together, go out for leisure activities together, or work on projects around the house together. In contrast, aggregate levels of marital conflict and marital problems declined during this period. Compared with spouses in 1980, spouses in 2000 reported fewer disagreements and substantially less relationship violence. Similarly, spouses in 2000 reported fewer interpersonal difficulties in their marriages, such as problems with anger and jealousy. Finally, although the mean level of divorce proneness did not change, marriages tended to be either higher or lower in divorce proneness in 2000 than in 1980.

Previous research indicates that wives tend to have less sanguine views of their marriages than do husbands (Lewis and Spanier, 1979). Wives also are more likely than husbands to initiate divorce (Amato and Previti, 2003; Kitson, 1992). Although our findings are consistent with earlier studies, it is important to point out that the gaps between husbands and wives were small in absolute terms. For example, the gender differences in happiness, conflict, and divorce proneness in 2000 were only about one-tenth of a standard deviation—differences that reflect relatively small effect size. (See our discussion of effect sizes in Appendix 1.) Even more notable is the finding that the gender gap in marital happiness closed significantly, from .30 of a standard deviation in 1980 to .12 of a standard deviation in 2000. If the feminist interpretation is correct (wives are less happy with their marriages because they benefit less from marriage than do husbands), then the relative benefits associated with marriage appear to have increased for wives since 1980. The gender gap in divorce proneness, however, did not close during this period, which indicates that wives continue to think more about ending their marriages than do husbands.

Overall, these results indicate a shift in the pattern of marital quality in the United States during the last two decades of the twentieth century. During this period marriages became more peaceful, with fewer disagreements, less aggression, and fewer interpersonal sources of tension between spouses. At the same time, the lives of husbands and wives became more separate, as spouses shared fewer activities. The trend for marital relationships to be less discordant and more individualistic appears to have had few implications for the overall level of satisfaction; spouses were as happy with their marriages in 2000 as they were two decades earlier. And with lower levels of conflict and perceived problems, stable marriages were more common in 2000 than in 1980. But somewhat paradoxically, unstable marriages also became more common. People who had *ever* thought that their marriages were in trouble were more likely to progress to advanced forms of instability, such as talking with their spouses about divorce. Presumably, tolerant public attitudes toward divorce and the legal ease of getting a divorce have made it easier for individuals with marital problems to think seriously about marital dissolution. Moreover, because marriages have become more individualistic since 1980, spouses may be less dependent emotionally on one another and hence less likely to invest time and resources in improving their marriages.

How do these findings relate to the debate about marital decline? As we noted in Chapter 1, two versions of the marital-decline perspective can be articulated. According to one version, because the rise in divorce has removed the least satisfying unions from the population, current marriages should be no worse in quality than were marriages in the past. A stronger version of the decline perspective, however, suggests that marriage is a more troubled arrangement now than in the past. Consequently, a recent snapshot of American marriages should reveal more tensions and sources of stress than would a snapshot from an earlier period.

Were married individuals in 2000 better or worse off than their counterparts in 1980? Our findings do not provide a simple answer to this question and do not lend consistent support to either a decline or a resilience perspective. The situation of contemporary married couples cannot be reduced to a simple "better or worse" conclusion. The results for divorce proneness, for example, were mixed, with an increase in the proportion of stable as well as unstable marriages in the population. Clearly, the declines in problems and conflict—especially the decrease in marital violence—are good news. But the decrease in marital interaction is a reason for concern. The benefits of reductions in discord and perceived problems are undermined if spouses have little time for shared activities or companionship. George Homans (1951) theorized that declines in interaction are followed by declines in positive sentiment, and two studies of married individuals provide empirical support for this proposition (White, 1983; Zuo, 1992). Another study (Hill, 1988) found that spouses who spend less time together are more likely to divorce than are spouses who spend more time together. Given these considerations, it is possible that the gradual decline in marital interaction between 1980 and 2000 will erode future marital happiness and increase subsequent levels of marital instability. In the remaining chapters we explore some of the probable causes of these shifts in marital quality.

~ 3

Rising Individualism and Demographic Change

$\mathcal{I}$N THE FIRST CHAPTER we discussed the historical shift from institutional to individualistic marriage. Marriage changed from a formal institution that meets the needs of the larger society to a companionate relationship that meets the needs of the couple and their children and then to a private pact that meets the psychological needs of individual spouses. This shift in the meaning of marriage was accompanied by a variety of demographic changes in the married population.

In this chapter we focus on five major demographic changes that reflect the continuing shift toward greater individualism and choice in American marriages: (1) the rise in premarital cohabitation, (2) the trend for young adults to delay marriage, (3) the increase in second and higher-order marriages, (4) the growing percentage of spouses who experienced parental divorce as children, and (5) the increase in marriages between spouses who differ in basic characteristics such as race and age. All these changes reflect the fact that individuals now have greater freedom to marry when they want, marry whom they want, and leave marriages that do not live up to their expectations. In analyzing these changes, we answer the following questions:

• How did these five characteristics of the married population change between 1980 and 2000?

- How were these characteristics related to dimensions of marital quality in 1980 and 2000?

- To what extent were changes in these characteristics between 1980 and 2000 associated with changes in mean levels of marital quality in the population?

Premarital Cohabitation

The Increase in Premarital Cohabitation

The relaxation of social rules about sexual behavior since the 1960s, combined with the rise of expressive individualism (with its focus on the importance of personal feelings, emotional gratification, and self-growth), made it easier and more attractive for couples to live together without marrying. In some European countries cohabitation has become an alternative to marriage for many couples (Kiernan, 2002). In the United States some unconventional couples also live together as an alternative to marriage. For most American couples, however, cohabitation can be viewed as an advanced form of dating, a prelude to marriage, or a stage in the marriage process (Casper and Bianchi, 2002; Heuveline and Timberlake, 2004). Although the specific reasons for living together vary, most cohabiting individuals see this as an opportunity to assess the suitability of their partners for longer-term relationships. Many women, for example, use this time to determine their partners' willingness to contribute equitably to household chores (Cherlin, 2000). In this sense, cohabitation reflects the increasing importance of finding the right person to meet one's needs—a spouse who will improve one's quality of life, facilitate one's personal growth, and be a true soul mate.

Our surveys reveal that the percentage of people who cohabited with their spouses before marriage more than doubled, rising from 16% in 1980 to 41% in 2000. Moreover, the increase in cohabitation occurred across a variety of social groups: younger and older individuals, high school graduates and college graduates, people in first and second marriages, people who attend religious services frequently and those who attend rarely or never, and people from a variety of racial and ethnic backgrounds. (Readers can find a full set of descriptive statistics for

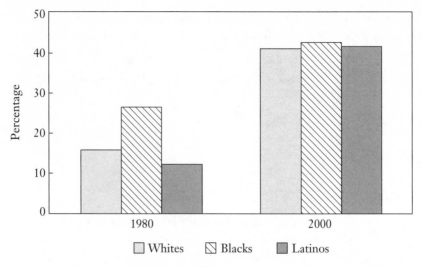

Figure 3.1   Percentage of couples cohabiting before marriage by race or ethnicity and decade

premarital cohabitation, along with other demographic characteristics of the two samples, in Table 5 in Appendix 2.)

Figure 3.1, for example, shows the percentage of white, black, and Latino couples who cohabited before marriage. In 1980 black couples were significantly more likely than white or Latino couples to have cohabited. By 2000, however, the three groups revealed nearly identical levels of premarital cohabitation. Previous studies have shown that blacks are more likely than whites to engage in nonmarital cohabitation (Raley, 2000). White couples, however, are more likely to translate these unions into marriages than are black couples (Manning and Smock, 1995). These trends produced a major demographic convergence: Among currently married couples, racial and ethnic differences in rates of cohabitation before marriage have largely disappeared (at least among these three groups).

We also examined the links between premarital cohabitation and the other demographic variables in our data. The factor that best predicted the increase in cohabitation between surveys was parental divorce. Studies indicate that adults with divorced parents are more likely to cohabit before marriage than are adults with continuously married parents, presumably because witnessing a parental divorce makes children more cautious about their own marital success (Amato and Booth,

1997). As we show in detail later, the percentage of married adults with divorced parents increased significantly between 1980 and 2000. So part of the increase in premarital cohabitation was due to the rise in divorce in the previous generation. Nevertheless, parental divorce accounted for only about one-seventh of the increase in cohabitation. Presumably, shifts in cultural values—individualism, sexual freedom, and the importance of trying out relationships before making long-term commitments—were the main reasons for the sharp increase in premarital cohabitation; a majority of Americans now view cohabitation as a normal, acceptable stage in the courtship process (Thornton and Young-DeMarco, 2001).

Premarital Cohabitation and Marital Quality

In this section we describe the connections between premarital cohabitation and the five dimensions of marital quality presented in Chapter 2. Our analyses involved three steps. First, we used ordinary least squares (OLS) regression to relate premarital cohabitation to dimensions of marital quality in 1980 and 2000. Second, we tested for the significance of the difference between regression coefficients in the two surveys. This procedure made it possible to determine if premarital cohabitation became a stronger or weaker predictor of marital quality between 1980 and 2000. Finally, we used decomposition methods to relate changes in premarital cohabitation between 1980 and 2000 to changes in mean levels of happiness, interaction, conflict, problems, and divorce proneness in the population. This analysis allowed us to determine if the increase in premarital cohabitation was associated with general improvements or declines in marital quality. (Readers can find a description of decomposition methods in Appendix 1 and the full decomposition results in Tables 9–13 in Appendix 2.)

Earlier research consistently shows that couples who cohabit before marriage are more likely to see their unions end in divorce than are couples who do not cohabit before marriage (Booth and Johnson, 1988; Bramlett and Mosher, 2002; Bumpass, Martin, and Sweet, 1991; Teachman and Polonko, 1990). Evidence on marital quality is less abundant, but existing studies suggest that premarital cohabitation is associated with more discord and less perceived stability within marriage (Amato and Booth, 1997; Dush, Cohan, and Amato, 2003). As we noted in Chapter 1, the experience of cohabitation may affect people in ways that undermine later marital quality and stability—for example, by making people less religious or eroding support for the norm of life-long marriage (Axinn and Thornton, 1992; Thornton, Axinn, and Hill, 1992). These findings also may reflect selection effects. That is, people who hold unconventional attitudes toward marriage, or who are poor marriage material, may be more likely to cohabit as well as to divorce (Bennett, Blanc, and Bloom, 1988; Booth and Johnson, 1988). The se-lection argument implies that the association between premarital co-habitation and poor marital quality will become weaker as the pro-portion of people who cohabit increases. With cohabitation before marriage being common these days, it should be less selective of people at risk of having troubled or unstable marriages. Recent studies, how-ever, indicate that the increased risk of divorce associated with premar-ital cohabitation has remained constant across recent decades (Dush, Cohan, and Amato, 2003; Teachman, 2002).

Premarital cohabitation was not related to marital happiness in ei-ther decade. Our data on marital interaction, however, provide some support for the selection perspective. Individuals who cohabited before marriage reported less interaction in 1980 but not in 2000—a finding that reflects a significant decade × remarriage interaction. Specifically, the gap in interaction between couples who did and did not cohabit be-fore marriage declined from one-fourth to one-twentieth of a standard deviation. The decline in the link between cohabitation and later mari-tal interaction is consistent with the notion that selection effects have become weaker as living together has become more common.

Other outcomes, in contrast, did not follow this pattern. Figure 3.2 indicates that individuals who cohabited with their spouses before mar-riage, compared with individuals who did not, reported more marital conflict, marital problems, and divorce proneness. (This figure shows means adjusted for all variables in the decomposition equation.) Al-though the differences in marital quality associated with cohabitation were somewhat smaller in 2000 than in 1980, these differences were not large enough to be significant. (That is, cohabitation did not inter-act with year of survey in predicting these dimensions of marital qual-ity.) For these three marital outcomes, the differences between those who cohabited before marriage and those who did not were modest, ranging from about one-tenth to one-fourth of a standard deviation. Nevertheless, our results indicate that cohabitation continued to be a

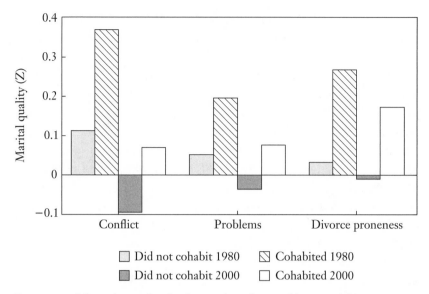

Figure 3.2 Adjusted mean levels of marital conflict, problems, and divorce proneness by premarital cohabitation and decade

risk factor for troubled marriages in 2000, despite the fact that more than 40% of all couples had lived together before marriage. This pattern of findings is consistent with the belief that something about the experience of cohabitation lowers subsequent marital quality.

Given that premarital cohabitation increased substantially between 1980 and 2000, and given that premarital cohabitation is associated with poorer marital quality, the rise in premarital cohabitation should correspond to declines in aggregate levels of marital quality in the population. Our decomposition analysis confirmed this expectation. The rise in cohabitation was associated with a decline in the mean level of marital interaction (.02 of a standard deviation), an increase in the mean level of marital conflict (.03 of a standard deviation), an increase in the mean number of marital problems (.03 of a standard deviation), and an increase in the mean level of divorce proneness (.05 of a standard deviation). Note that if the association between premarital cohabitation and marital interaction had not become weaker between surveys, the increase in cohabitation would have been accompanied by a larger decline in marital interaction in the population.

We cannot determine whether the links between cohabitation and dimensions of marital quality are causal or if they reflect a selection process. If the effect is causal, then the interpretation is clear: The increase in cohabitation before marriage during recent decades resulted in a decline in the general level of marital quality in the population. If the association is due to selection, however, then cohabitation can be viewed as an observed indicator of a set of unmeasured traits. These unmeasured traits would be attitudes or interpersonal orientations that both lead people to cohabit before marriage and interfere with the maintenance of harmonious, stable marital relationships. A selection perspective, therefore, implies that these unmeasured variables increased in the population between 1980 and 2000. Either way, the conclusion of our analysis is pessimistic. We suspect that some truth exists in both interpretations, although it is up to future research to determine more precisely the roles of causation versus selection in explaining the link between cohabitation and poor marital quality.

Age at Marriage

The Increase in Age at Marriage

The median age at first marriage for wives increased from 20 years in 1980 to 22 years in 2000, and the corresponding medians for husbands were 22 years and 23 years—findings that are consistent with other national data sets (Casper and Bianchi, 2002). Moreover, the increase in age at first marriage was comparable across all racial and ethnic groups. This trend reflects a substantial reduction in the percentage of wives who had married as teenagers—a figure that declined from 49% in 1980 to 31% in 2000. Correspondingly, the percentage of wives who married for the first time at 30 years of age or older increased from 1% to 9%.

Why did the average age at first marriage increase between 1980 and 2000? One explanation is that people are delaying marriage to complete their educations. And, in fact, respondents with 16 or more years of education married about two years later than did respondents with high school diplomas. Between the two surveys, however, age at first marriage increased significantly for people at *all* educational levels— even among people who did not graduate from high school. Another explanation refers to the growing popularity of cohabitation, which is likely to delay entry into marriage. Individuals who cohabited were about two years older by the time they married than were individuals who did not cohabit, which is consistent with this explanation. Nevertheless, even individuals who did not cohabit married at older ages in 2000 than in 1980. Further analysis reveals that the increases in education and cohabitation, taken together, accounted for only one-fourth of the rise in age at first marriage between 1980 and 2000, and with both these explanatory variables in the model, the increase in age at marriage still was significant.

In addition to increases in education and cohabitation, people may be marrying at later ages to give themselves more time to become secure economically (irrespective of educational level) or to enjoy a few additional years of being single. These explanations are consistent with Arnett's (2000) view that the period of adolescence has lengthened in recent decades: Most individuals now reach social adulthood in their mid-twenties or later. The social imperative to marry early has weakened, and single individuals have more sexual freedom now than in the past, so most young adults see little value in marrying as soon as possible. Moreover, postponing marriage provides more time for people to search for suitable spouses on the dating market. This interpretation is consistent with the notion that expectations for personal fulfillment from marriage have increased. All things being equal, the higher one's expectations for a spouse, the longer it will take to find the "right" person.

We also found an increase in age at second marriage for previously divorced individuals. In 1980 the median age at second marriage was 27 for wives and 31 for husbands. In 2000 these medians had increased to 30 and 32, respectively. A regression analysis revealed that the rise in age at second marriage was largely a reflection of the rise in age at first marriage. In other words, people who marry at older ages also tend to divorce and remarry at older ages.

Age at Marriage and Marital Quality

Marrying at a young age is one of the best predictors of divorce (Bumpass, Martin, and Sweet, 1991). Similarly, people who marry at young ages tend to report more problems in their marriages than do people who marry at older ages (Amato and Rogers, 1997; Booth and Edwards, 1985). Explanations for this phenomenon usually refer to the fact that young spouses, compared with older spouses, are less economically secure, are less mature and more naive about relationships, and have engaged in a shorter search process, all of which increases the chances of making a poor match. As was the case in the earlier research, age at marriage in our data was associated positively with marital interaction in 1980, negatively with marital problems in 1980, and negatively with divorce proneness in 1980 and 2000.

Most of the people in our data set, irrespective of the year of data collection, were in their first marriages. But what about individuals in second (or higher-order) marriages? Does age at marriage confer benefits on these individuals too? The answer appears to be yes. The links between age at marriage and marital quality did not vary with marriage order. Moreover, when we restricted the analysis to individuals in second or higher-order marriages, age at current marriage continued to be negatively associated with divorce proneness in 1980 and 2000. Marrying at older ages appears to promote marital stability, regardless of whether it is a first marriage or a higher-order marriage.

Research has shown that the link between early age at marriage and divorce occurs primarily among individuals who marry as teenagers. Once people enter their early to mid-twenties, the risk of divorce is attenuated (Bramlett and Mosher, 2002). Indeed, people who postpone marriage until their thirties face a dwindling supply of potential partners—a situation that may increase the likelihood of forming unions with partners who are not good marriage material (Glenn, 2004). In other words, marrying "too late" may increase the risk of having a troubled relationship. To check on this possibility, we examined marital quality among individuals who married in five age groups: 19 years or younger, 20 through 24, 25 through 29, 30 through 34, and 35 or higher. We restricted this analysis to people in first marriages. Figure 3.3 shows the mean levels of divorce proneness for these individuals in 1980 and 2000. Divorce proneness was highest among those who married as teenagers and lowest among those who married at age 35 or higher; increasing age at marriage corresponded to consistent declines in divorce proneness. The pattern was nearly identical in both decades. And although the figure refers to divorce proneness, similar results were apparent for marital interaction and problems. These results do not support the notion that waiting "too long" to marry is a risk factor for poor marital quality. Even if waiting to marry decreases the size of the pool of potential partners, this limitation may be offset by a longer search process that helps people to locate truly compatible partners.

Given that people who marry at older ages tend to have better marital quality, and given that age at marriage increased between 1980

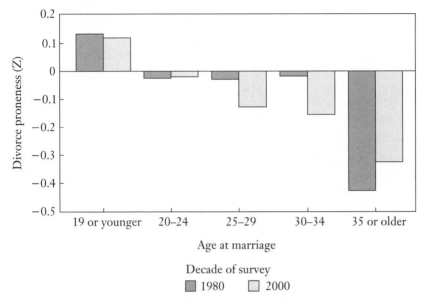

Figure 3.3   Adjusted mean levels of divorce proneness by age at marriage and decade

and 2000, these trends should have improved the mean level of marital quality in the population. Indeed, our decomposition analysis suggested that the rise in age at marriage had consistently positive implications for aggregate levels of marital quality. In particular, the change in age at marriage was associated with an increase in the mean level of marital interaction (.03 of a standard deviation), a decrease in the number of marital problems (.03 of a standard deviation), and a decline in the mean level of divorce proneness (.05 of a standard deviation). The trend for young adults to postpone marriage to complete their educations, become economically secure, find more suitable marriage partners, and ensure that they are psychologically ready appears to have benefited contemporary marital relationships.

Marriage Order

The Increase in Remarriage

The rise in divorce since the 1960s can be viewed as a direct result of the growth of individualism, along with changes in divorce laws that made it easier to leave unhappy unions and the relaxation of negative

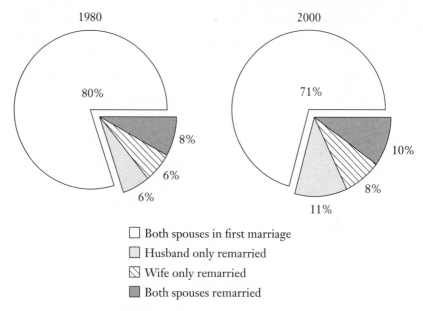

Figure 3.4   Percentage of remarried husbands and wives, 1980 and 2000

social attitudes toward divorce. In an earlier era, people stayed in less than satisfactory marriages because they felt a duty to remain married and were concerned that divorce might harm their children. The rise of expressive individualism, however, means that many people today place their own personal fulfillment above onerous social obligations, such as staying in an unhappy marriage. The increase in divorce has not meant, however, that people are rejecting marriage. Instead, this trend reflects a tendency for people to leave unsatisfactory relationships and seek out greater happiness with new partners. As a result, the proportion of second and higher-order marriages in the population has increased. Figure 3.4 shows the percentage of couples in which both spouses were in their first marriage, one spouse had been previously married, and both spouses had been previously married. Overall, the percentage of marriages that involved second or higher-order unions for one or both spouses increased from 20% in 1980 to 29% in 2000.

The picture looks slightly different when one takes race into account. The decrease in the percentage of couples in which both spouses were in first marriages was significant for whites (81% in 1980 to 69% in 2000) but not for blacks or Latinos. Although blacks are more likely than whites to see their marriages end in divorce, their rate of remarriage is lower (Cherlin, 1992). For this reason, higher divorce rates in recent decades do not seem to have increased the percentage of higher-order marriages among this group. The reason the percentage of higher-order marriages among Latinos did not increase is less clear, although it may reflect high rates of cohabitation, rather than remarriage, following divorce for this group (Casper and Bianchi, 2002).

Along with the increase in remarriage, we found an increase in the number of couples with resident stepchildren. In 1980 only 6% of married couples had a stepchild living in the household (that is, a child that either the husband or the wife brought to the marriage from a previous union). By 2000 the figure had increased to 11%. In both periods wives were more likely than husbands to have children from a previous union living with them. In other words, stepfather families were more common than stepmother families, irrespective of decade—a finding consistent with almost all other studies (ibid.).

Remarriage and Marital Quality

People in second or higher-order marriages are more likely to divorce than are people in first marriages (Bramlett and Mosher, 2002). This difference, however, may reflect a selection effect. That is, people who have dissolved a first marriage are likely to have traits (such as a low commitment to the norm of lifelong marriage or personality characteristics that interfere with relationship quality) that place their subsequent marriages at similar risk (Booth and Edwards, 1992). Alternatively, many remarriages involve the formation of stepfamilies, and the presence of stepchildren in the household may lead to complications and strains that ultimately undermine the marriage (White and Booth, 1985).

Our analysis suggested that marriage order (first marriages versus higher-order marriages) had few implications for marital quality. In 1980 (but not in 2000), being remarried was associated with *greater* marital happiness. In contrast, in 2000 (but not in 1980) being remarried was associated with higher divorce proneness. Aside from these contrary findings, we observed no other differences. The general lack of findings is consistent with earlier research showing relatively few differences in the quality of first marriages and subsequent marriages (Booth and Edwards, 1992; Vemer, Coleman, Ganong, and Cooper,

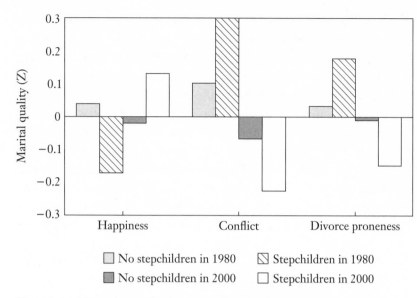

Figure 3.5 Adjusted mean levels of marital quality by presence of stepchildren in the household and decade

1989). We need to interpret this finding cautiously, however, because people in higher-order marriages tend to divorce more quickly than do people in first marriages. Consequently, cross-sectional studies may overrepresent longer-term remarriages that are relatively successful. Nevertheless, our decomposition analysis suggested that the increase in the percentage of second and higher-order marriages had no noteworthy consequences for overall levels of marital quality in the United States.

Our findings with respect to stepchildren are more interesting. In particular, the links between having stepchildren living in the household and marital quality changed between 1980 and 2000. Figure 3.5 shows the mean levels of marital happiness, marital conflict, and divorce proneness for respondents with and without stepchildren in the household. In 1980 the presence of stepchildren in the household was associated with less marital happiness, more conflict, and more divorce proneness. By 2000, however, the presence of stepchildren in the household was associated with more marital happiness, less marital conflict, and less divorce proneness. In other words, the presence of stepchildren appeared to lower marital quality in 1980 but to improve marital quality in 2000.

Earlier research indicated that stepchildren are often sources of tension between spouses (Hetherington and Jodl, 1994) and can increase the risk of divorce (White and Booth, 1985). In this context, Andrew Cherlin (1978) described stepfamilies as "incomplete institutions." By this he meant that the norms regulating relations between stepparents and stepchildren are ambiguous. For example, how much authority should stepparents exercise over their stepchildren? In a disagreement between a stepparent and a stepchild, to whom does the resident biological parent owe allegiance? Can stepchildren form close bonds with stepparents without putting their relationships with nonresident parents at risk? According to Cherlin, because there are few clear rules to provide guidance, families with stepchildren have a tendency to become disorganized and fragmented.

Although many stepfamilies may have suffered from these problems in 1980, our results suggest that stepfamily life was more harmonious and stable in 2000. This improvement may have occurred for several reasons. First, because stepfamilies have become more common, they may receive more support from their religious congregations, communities, and extended kin than in the past. Support groups and self-help books for stepfamilies are widely available these days, and more marriage therapists are trained to deal with stepfamily issues. In addition, an increasing number of married parents have grown up in stepfamilies—an experience that may provide insights into how these parents can make their own stepfamilies more successful.

Despite this positive trend, only a small percentage of married couples in either decade had stepchildren living in their households. For this reason, the decomposition analysis indicated that the increase in the proportion of marriages with stepchildren had no substantive consequences for aggregate levels of marital quality in the population.

Parental Divorce

The Increase in Parental Divorce

Given that the divorce rate increased dramatically between the mid-1960s and 1980, the percentage of adults in the population who, as children, experienced parental divorce should be higher in 2000 than in 1980. This expectation was confirmed in our data. Figure 3.6 shows

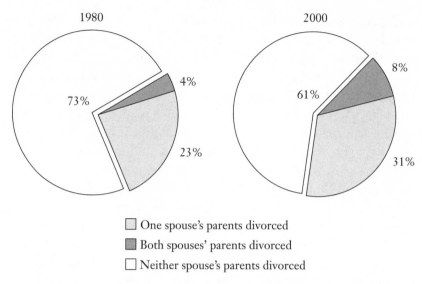

1980   2000

4%   8%

73%   61%

23%   31%

☐ One spouse's parents divorced
■ Both spouses' parents divorced
☐ Neither spouse's parents divorced

Figure 3.6   Percentage of respondents and spouses with divorced parents, 1980 and 2000

the percentage of marriages in which the husband, the wife, or both spouses experienced parental divorce while growing up. The percentage of cases in each of these groups increased significantly during this period, although the rise was most dramatic for marriages in which both spouses were adult children of divorce. The size of this particular group doubled, from 4% in 1980 to 8% in 2000. Overall, during this 20-year period, the percentage of marriages in which one or both spouses experienced a parental divorce increased from 27% to 39%. This increase was comparable for younger as well as older married individuals. Moreover, the percentage of adults with divorced parents increased similarly among whites and blacks, although the corresponding percentages among Latinos and Asians changed little across decades.

Parental Divorce and Marital Quality

A number of studies have indicated that parental divorce is a risk factor for seeing one's own marriage end in divorce (Amato, 1996; Bumpass, Martin, and Sweet, 1991; Feng, Giarrusso, Bengtson, and Frye, 1999; Glenn and Kramer, 1987; Wolfinger, 1999). Similarly, people who experience parental divorce while growing up report relatively less happiness and more problems in their own marriages (Amato and Booth, 1991; McLeod, 1991; Overall, Henry, and Woodward, 1974; Tallman, Gray, Kullberg, and Henderson, 1999). Our findings are consistent with these earlier studies. In both surveys, parental divorce was associated with higher levels of marital problems. In addition, in 2000 (but not in 1980) parental divorce was associated with a higher level of divorce proneness. The differences between spouses with divorced and continuously married parents were about one-fifth of a standard deviation, which reflects moderate effect sizes.

Adult children of divorce may be at risk for having troubled marriages for several reasons. First, parents who end their marriages in divorce may model poor communication, problem-solving, and conflict-resolution skills. As a result, some children from divorced families may reach adulthood with deficits in the kinds of interpersonal skills that facilitate rewarding and stable intimate relationships. Second, parents who divorce may demonstrate that marital dissolution is an acceptable solution to being in an unhappy marriage. Consequently, adult children of divorce, when experiencing serious marital problems, may prefer to obtain a divorce rather than invest time and energy in repairing their marriages. Finally, it is possible that a genetically inherited personality trait, such as a tendency toward antisocial behavior, may underlie the transmission of marital problems across generations (McGue and Lykken, 1992).

Additional insight into this issue is gained by dividing marriages into four groups: neither spouse experienced a parental divorce, the husband experienced a parental divorce, the wife experienced a parental divorce, and both spouses experienced a parental divorce. Figure 3.7 shows marital problems and divorce proneness scores for these groups in 2000. Marriages in which husbands (but not wives) had divorced parents had somewhat higher levels of problems and divorce proneness than did marriages in which neither spouse had divorced parents. Marital problems and divorce proneness were even higher when wives (but not husbands) had divorced parents. The most troubled marriages, however, were those in which both spouses had divorced parents.

Given that growing up with divorced parents is a risk factor for low marital quality, it is not surprising that marital problems are most common when both spouses come from divorced families. If one spouse reaches adulthood with weak relationships skills (having observed poor

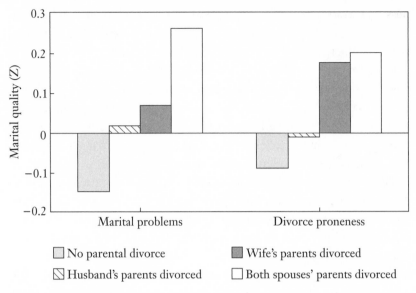

Figure 3.7 Adjusted mean levels of marital problems and divorce proneness by parental divorce, 2000

relationship models in the home), then the other spouse (who grew up with continuously married parents) may be able to compensate for this deficit. But if both spouses bring weak relationship skills to the marriage, then the likelihood of resolving difficulties amicably is substantially lower. With respect to divorce proneness, the implications for marriage appear to be stronger when wives rather than husbands were exposed to parental divorce. Adults with divorced parents tend to have reached adulthood with liberal attitudes toward divorce (Amato and Booth, 1991). Moreover, wives are more likely than husbands to initiate and file for divorce (Amato and Previti, 2003; Kitson, 1992). For these reasons, divorce proneness may be especially high in marriages in which wives, rather than husbands, see divorce as a reasonable solution to marital problems.

Nicholas Wolfinger (1999) argued that as parental divorce has become more common, the transmission of marital problems and instability across generations has become weaker. We did not find any evidence to support this hypothesis, however. The link between parental divorce and marital problems was similar in both surveys, and the association between parental divorce and divorce proneness was significant in 2000 but not in 1980 (although the interaction with year was not significant). Despite the fact that an increasing number of spouses grew up in divorced families, parental divorce continues to be a risk factor for poor marital outcomes.

In the decomposition analysis the increase in parental divorce between 1980 and 2000 was associated with increases in marital conflict (.01 of a standard deviation), marital problems (.02 of a standard deviation), and divorce proneness (.01 of a standard deviation) in the population. Overall, the rise in the number of married individuals who grew up with divorced parents appears to have had modest but negative implications for aggregate levels of marital quality in the United States.

Heterogamy

The Increase in Heterogamy

In both 2000 and 1980 homogamy (marrying someone with the same traits) was the rule, and heterogamy (marrying someone with different traits) was the exception. The majority of respondents in both surveys had spouses who were similar in terms of age, race, ethnicity, education, marriage order, and religion. With respect to age, for example, the correlation between husbands' and wives' ages was .89 in 1980 and .86 in 2000. Similarly, the correlation between husbands' and wives' years of education was .62 in 1980 and .56 in 2000.

Despite these trends, a decline in the social regulation of marriage, and a corresponding expansion of individual choice about marriage partners, has made it possible for individuals to seek out spouses who differ from themselves in basic social characteristics. Our study is consistent with this assumption in that it shows a substantial increase in marital heterogamy in the United States between 1980 and 2000. Figure 3.8 illustrates this change. Between surveys, the proportion of interracial or interethnic marriages more than doubled, from 4% in 1980 to 9% in 2000. A similar trend appeared for age. For this variable, we defined heterogamous unions as ones in which either husbands were more than ten years older than their wives, or wives were more than four years older than their husbands. By this definition, age heterogamy increased from 6% in 1980 to 10% in 2000.

Marriages also tend to be homogamous with respect to marriage order. Given that 17% of spouses in our sample were in second or higher-

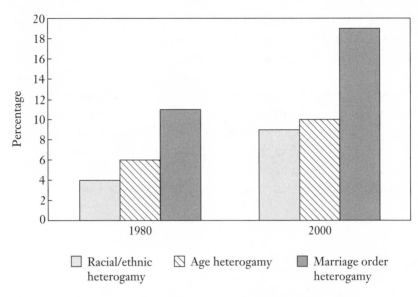

Figure 3.8   Three forms of marital heterogamy, 1980 and 2000

order marriages, we would expect only about 3% of all unions to represent a remarriage for both spouses if people did not use marriage order as a basis for mate selection (that is, .17 × .17). The percentage of couples in which both spouses were previously married, however, was 9—three times as many as one would expect by chance alone. Despite this tendency for previously married people to seek out spouses who also were previously married, the percentage of marriages in which one spouse was in a first marriage and the second spouse was in a second or higher-order marriage increased from 11% in 1980 to 19% in 2000.

In contrast to the trends just described, we found no evidence of a decline in the percentage of spouses with similar levels of education. Specifically, the percentage of marriages in which one spouse was better educated than the other (which we defined as a difference of four or more years of education) was 17% in 1980 and 18% in 2000. Similarly, the percentage of spouses who had different religious affiliations (21%) did not change during this time. Nevertheless, of the five characteristics that we investigated (race/ethnicity, age, marriage order, education, and religion), the percentage of couples that were heterogamous on at least one trait increased from 47% in 1980 to 59% in 2000. Although similarity remains a strong basis for attraction and marriage, married individuals have become less similar to their spouses, overall, in recent years—a finding consistent with a decline in the social control of marriage.

To simplify subsequent analyses, we created an index that reflected the sum of the five different forms of heterogamy. The resulting scores ranged from 0 (homogamous across all five variables) to 5 (heterogamous across all five variables). This index increased significantly between 1980 and 2000 by .30 of a standard deviation—a moderate effect size. Why did marital heterogamy increase during this period? We found that increases in five variables—parental divorce, remarriage, age at marriage, premarital cohabitation, and the size of the Latino population—accounted for nearly all of the rise in marital heterogamy. Although each of these variables is positively associated with heterogamy, parental divorce had the strongest influence. It is not clear why experiencing parental divorce leads people to choose spouses who differ from themselves in important respects. To our knowledge, this finding has not been reported previously. One possibility is that children from divorced families adopt less conventional views about marriage and family life in general and, hence, are more likely to choose spouses from outside their social groups.

Heterogamy and Marital Quality

Studies indicate that marital heterogamy is associated with lower marital quality and an elevated risk of divorce (Booth and Edwards, 1992; Curtis and Ellison, 2002; Heaton, 2002; Heaton and Pratt, 1990). Our heterogamy index was a consistent predictor of poor marital quality, which confirms earlier research. Across both surveys, marital heterogamy was associated with lower marital happiness, less interaction, more conflict, more problems, and greater divorce proneness. These associations were less likely to attain significance in 2000 than in 1980, which suggests some weakening of the links between heterogamy and marital quality. Nevertheless, even if American society has become more accepting of heterogamous marriages, differences between spouses in basic demographic characteristics continue to predispose couples to have more difficult marriages. Figure 3.9 illustrates this pattern with respect to marital happiness and problems in 2000. In general, marital happiness declined, and marital problems increased, as the number of forms of heterogamy increased.

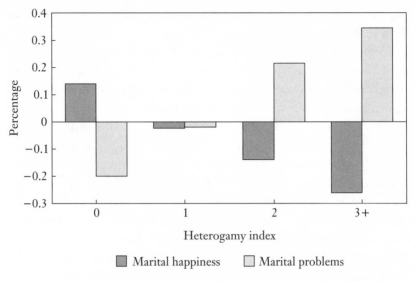

Figure 3.9   Adjusted mean levels of marital happiness and marital problems by heterogamy index, 2000

To gain further insight into these issues, we examined each component of the heterogamy index separately. The role of two forms of heterogamy grew weaker over time (as reflected in significant interactions involving decade). Age heterogamy was associated with greater marital conflict in 1980 but not in 2000. Declines in the implications of racial heterogamy were even more pronounced. Individuals in mixed-race marriages reported less marital interaction, more problems, and more divorce proneness than did individuals in same-race marriages in 1980 but not in 2000. These findings suggest that racial heterogamy and, to a lesser extent, age heterogamy became less problematic during this two-decade period.

The other heterogamy components had comparable links with marital quality across surveys. Individuals who differed from their spouses by four years or more of schooling reported less marital happiness, irrespective of decade. Religious heterogamy had especially wide-ranging implications. Compared with spouses who shared religious affiliations, spouses with different religions reported less marital happiness, less interaction, more conflict, more problems, and more divorce proneness, regardless of decade. Note, however, that neither educational heterogamy nor religious heterogamy increased between surveys (as we noted earlier), so these two forms of heterogamy cannot be responsible for shifts in aggregate levels of marital quality over time.

Heterogamy with respect to marriage order (that is, unions in which one spouse was in a first marriage and the other spouse was in a second or higher-order marriage) also was a consistent predictor of marital quality in both surveys. Individuals in these "mixed" marriages reported less marital happiness, less marital interaction, more conflict, more problems, and more divorce proneness. Further analysis with this variable confirmed that marital quality tended to be more positive either when both spouses were in a first marriage or when both spouses were previously married. Correspondingly, marital quality tended to be less positive when either the husband or the wife (but not both) had been previously married. Although most marriage researchers have not considered heterogamy with respect to marriage order, our study suggests that this factor makes a substantial contribution to marital quality. When both spouses have been previously divorced, spouses may have a better understanding of one another's past experiences and may be more flexible when dealing with children from former marriages or ex-spouses. Given the increase in remarriage during the last 20 years, greater attention to this factor seems warranted.

The decomposition analysis indicated that the increase in marital heterogamy between 1980 and 2000 (mostly with respect to age, race, and marriage order) was associated with modest shifts in aggregate levels of marital quality, including a decrease in marital happiness (.02 of a standard deviation), a decrease in marital interaction (.02 of a standard deviation), an increase in marital conflict (.02 of a standard deviation), an increase in marital problems (.02 of a standard deviation), and an increase in divorce proneness (.02 of a standard deviation).

Summary of Other Demographic Changes

So far, we have focused on several major demographic shifts that reflect the continuing deinstitutionalization of marriage. But the demographic composition of the married population changed in other ways between 1980 and 2000, and some of these changes appear to have had implications for marital quality. We briefly review these changes here.

Race and Ethnicity

Between 1980 and 2000 the racial and ethnic composition of the married population became more diverse. Whites were the majority group in both years, but their representation declined from 85% in 1980 to 76% in 2000. The size of the black group remained relatively constant at about 7% in both years. The largest gain occurred among Latinos, who increased from 6% of the married population in 1980 to 11% in 2000. Modest increases also occurred in the percentages of Asians and Native Americans, although these groups remained small in absolute numbers.

In both surveys blacks tended to report lower levels of marital quality than did whites. This finding is consistent with earlier studies showing that blacks are more likely than whites to report being unhappy with their marriages (Broman, 1993) and to divorce (Cherlin, 1992; Kreider and Fields, 2002). Despite these differences, however, the proportion of blacks in the married population did not change between 1980 and 2000. The proportion of Latinos increased substantially between surveys, but Latinos did not differ from the majority group (whites) in mean levels of marital quality. Consequently, although the racial and ethnic composition of the married population became more diverse between 1980 and 2000, this change had few implications for aggregate levels of marital quality.

Education

Between surveys, husbands' mean years of education increased from 13.2 to 13.9, and wives' mean years of education increased from 12.7 to 13.9. Note that the gender gap in education closed during this period. These figures reflect notable shifts in the percentage of people who achieved specific educational qualifications. In 1980, 17% of spouses had not graduated from high school, compared with only 9% in 2000. Correspondingly, the percentage of married individuals with bachelor's degrees increased from 21% in 1980 to 32% in 2000. Increases in education occurred in every racial and ethnic group.

Earlier studies suggest that education is positively associated with marital quality and stability (Kreider and Fields, 2002; Lehrer, 2003; Lewis and Spanier, 1979). Educational attainment, however, was not linked with better marital quality in our study. Indeed, education was associated with less marital interaction in 1980 and more marital conflict in 2000. Given the general absence of findings, it is not surprising that our decomposition analysis found that the increase in educational attainment between 1980 and 2000 had no implications for mean levels of marital quality in the population.

Age

Husbands as well as wives were older in 2000 than in 1980. During this time, the mean age of husbands increased from 37 to 40, and the mean age of wives increased from 35 to 38. This increase in the age of the married population is a direct result of the postponement of marriage among young adults, as we noted earlier. In fact, the increase in age at first marriage accounted for about one-half of the increase in the current age of married individuals. We also considered duration of current marriage, but this variable did not change between 1980 and 2000. In both decades, the average duration of marriage was about 13 years. Therefore, spouses in 2000, compared with spouses in 1980, were older and had married at later ages, but they did not differ in the duration of their marriages.

Our decomposition analysis revealed that the rise in age was associated with declines in four dimensions of marital quality: marital happiness (.02 of a standard deviation), interaction (.04 of a standard deviation), conflict (.03 of a standard deviation), and problems (.01 of a standard deviation). As individuals grow older, they may develop interests and friendship networks that diverge from those of their spouses. At the same time, older spouses may have resolved sources of tension that existed earlier in their marriages. More generally, the decline in positive as well as negative dimensions of marital quality is consistent with research showing that as individuals age, they tend to report fewer positive as well as negative emotions and experiences—a trend that reflects a flattening of affect (Steverink, Westerhof, Bode, and Dittmann-Kohli, 2001).

Children

A small but significant decline occurred in the percentage of married couples with children. In 1980, 71% of married couples had one or more children 18 years of age or younger living in the household, compared with 67% in 2000. Among couples with children, however, the number of children living in the household did not change. Well-educated couples were more likely to be childless than were poorly educated couples, and the increase in education between 1980 and 2000 completely explained the small decline in family size during this period.

In 1980, as well as in 2000, the number of children in the household was negatively associated with marital happiness and marital interaction. In general, childless couples in our surveys had the highest level of marital quality. These findings are consistent with studies showing that having a child is followed by a decline in marital quality (Cowan and Cowan, 1992; Glenn and McLanahan, 1982). Cowan and Cowan (1992) argued that parenthood is harder these days because couples are more isolated from supportive networks of kin, mothers are more likely to be employed during the preschool years, and husbands and wives must negotiate a new division of child-care responsibilities that previous generations took for granted. Our analysis, however, did not indicate that having children was associated with marital quality more strongly in 2000 than in 1980. The small decline in the mean number of children between surveys, overall, resulted in only a minor increase in aggregate levels of marital interaction (.01 of a standard deviation).

Conclusions

Our surveys demonstrate that substantial changes in the institution of marriage occurred during the last two decades of the twentieth century. Many of these changes can be interpreted as recent manifestations of the long-term deinstitutionalization of marriage. Marriage today is based on the ability of spouses to promote one another's self-expression and personal growth. For this reason, finding the "right" partner is critical to marital happiness and stability. Mate selection is more successful if young people have a variety of experiences before marriage that increase their understanding of close relationships and provide them with useful interpersonal skills. For this reason, a prolonged period of dating increases the chances of having a successful marriage. As is consistent with this reasoning, our analysis suggests that the continuing rise in age at first marriage had positive implications for marital quality. Couples who are older at the time of marriage have had more time to become economically secure, are more mature psychologically, and have had more experience with members of the opposite sex—factors that are likely to improve the quality and stability of resulting unions.

Other reflections of growing individualism, however, appear to have had negative consequences for marital quality. People are more likely to cohabit these days—a step that allows couples to get to know one another more deeply before marriage. Although living together before making a firm commitment seems like a sensible strategy in an era of high divorce rates, our analysis suggests that the spread of cohabitation between 1980 and 2000 eroded multiple aspects of marital quality.

The increase in marital heterogamy in recent decades also is consistent with the shift toward more individual choice in marriage. As schools and communities become more diverse, and as parents, extended kin, and community members exercise less influence on youth, it becomes easier for young adults to chose partners from different races, age groups, and marriage orders. But heterogamous marriages are prone to a variety of problems, and the increase in "mixed marriages" appears to have had largely negative consequences for marital quality.

When people hold high expectations for personal fulfillment from marriage, a relatively high level of marital instability is to be expected, and the increase in divorce during the 1960s and 1970s allowed many unhappily married individuals to seek greater happiness with new partners. At the same time, however, the increase in divorce produced a generation of youth who did not have the advantage of growing up with two continuously married parents. Because parental divorce appears to elevate the risk of marital discord among offspring, the freedom to divorce in one generation exerts downward pressure on marital quality in the next generation.

Overall, our decomposition analysis indicated that shifts in basic demographic characteristics between 1980 and 2000 were associated with only modest shifts in marital quality. The variables described in this chapter, collectively, were associated with a decline in marital happiness (.03 of a standard deviation), a decline in marital interaction (.03 of a standard deviation), an increase in marital conflict (.02 of a standard deviation), an increase in marital problems (.02 of a standard deviation), and an increase in divorce proneness (.03 of a standard deviation).

These modest overall shifts, however, partly reflect the fact that the estimated effects of some demographic characteristics offset one an-other. Consider the case of marital interaction. Changes in several vari-ables (increases in age, premarital cohabitation, and marital heterog-amy) were associated collectively with a decline in the level of marital interaction in the population equivalent to .08 of a standard deviation. Other changes, especially the rise in age at marriage, were associated with an increase in the level of interaction in the population—an in-crease that reduced the net decline in interaction by more than half. In other words, if age at marriage had not changed, the level of interaction in the married population would have declined even more substantially.

Offsetting trends can be illustrated with reference to other marital outcomes as well. For example, increases in premarital cohabitation, heterogamy, and parental divorce were associated collectively with an elevation of marital conflict in the population equivalent to .05 of a standard deviation. At the same time, the rise in age was associated with a decline in marital conflict in the population equivalent to .03 of a standard deviation. Similarly, increases in premarital cohabitation, pa-rental divorce, and heterogamy were associated with an elevation of marital problems in the population equivalent to .07 of a standard devi-ation. Changes in age and age at marriage, however, offset this trend by .04 of a standard deviation. Finally, increases in premarital cohabita-tion, parental divorce, and heterogamy were associated with an in-crease in divorce proneness of about .08 of a standard deviation, but age at marriage offset this effect by .05 of a standard deviation. In gen-eral, it appears that the beneficial effects of an older age at marriage partly ameliorated many of the negative consequences of other changes that occurred during this time. These results are consistent with our assumption (stated in Chapter 1) that the mean level of marital quality in the population at a given time can be thought of as a balancing point between multiple opposing forces.

Overall, however, the continuing deinstitutionalization of marriage appears to have had more detrimental than beneficial consequences for marital quality in the United States. This conclusion would be prema-ture, however, because we considered only demographic factors in this chapter. In subsequent chapters, we focus on changes in employment, financial well-being, gender equity, and other aspects of marriage. Af-ter reviewing this evidence, we should be in a better position to under-stand how marital quality has changed in recent decades and, to a cer-tain extent, how marital quality may continue to change in the future.

ॐ 4

Who Benefited from the Rise of Dual-Earner Marriage— and Who Did Not?

*A*LTHOUGH SCHOLARS have written a great deal about wives' economic role in the family during the last few decades, marriage *always* has been an economic arrangement between men and women. Before the mid-nineteenth century, when most families in the United States lived on farms, husbands and wives worked together to produce food, shelter, furniture, clothing, and other necessities of life. It was not until the industrial revolution, and the movement of jobs from rural settings to urban areas, that husbands and wives adopted what we think of as a "traditional" marital division of labor. As men took jobs in factories and became primary breadwinners, women became domestic specialists, with their primary responsibilities involving housework and child care. Of course, in many working-class and poor families, wives worked outside the home or engaged in other tasks (such as taking in washing) that brought money into the household. Other wives looked after boarders and lodgers in their homes, which was common before the twentieth century (Mintz and Kellogg, 1988). Nevertheless, the breadwinner-homemaker family became the ideal to which most couples aspired. Indeed, sociologists in the 1950s, such as Talcott Parsons (Parsons and Bales, 1955), believed that this domestic arrangement was ideally suited for the smooth functioning of an urban, industrial society.

The breadwinner-homemaker arrangement was the dominant form

of marriage in the United States from around 1900 until the early 1970s (Hernandez, 1993). This form of marriage turned out to be surprisingly short-lived, however, and by the mid-1970s dual-earner families had replaced breadwinner-homemaker families as the statistical norm for married couples (Spain and Bianchi, 1996). But even during the relatively short era when most husbands were breadwinners and most wives were homemakers, we should not underestimate the extent to which women's domestic labor contributed to the economic well-being of their families. The fact that wives performed housework and child care made it possible for husbands to devote time and energy to their jobs and careers—an arrangement that allowed men to become more effective providers. As feminist authors have noted, because wives are not paid for their household labor, their economic contributions are largely invisible (Ferree, 1990). Seen in this light, marriage always has been a financial partnership between men and women, irrespective of historical period or family form.

The shift from breadwinner-homemaker families to dual-earner families can be viewed as part of the long-term transition from institutional to individualistic marriage. Ernest Burgess and his colleagues (Burgess and Wallin, 1954; Burgess, Locke, and Thomes, 1963) argued that institutional marriage was fundamentally patriarchal: the husband's authority was based on his control of the family's economic resources. During the twentieth century, however, women's growing labor-force participation weakened the economic dependence of wives on husbands—an important step toward a more egalitarian, companionate form of marriage. Although Burgess recognized that economic independence also made it easier for wives to leave troubled marriages, he believed that wives' employment, in the long run, would strengthen the bond between spouses.

Like Burgess, many current scholars have stressed the benefits of gender equality and role sharing for marriage (Blumstein and Schwartz, 1983; Coltrane, 1996; Deutsch, 1999; Risman and Johnson-Sumerford, 1998; Scanzoni, 1978). According to these authors, equal relationships (unlike hierarchical relationships) promote feelings of warmth, closeness, and friendship between spouses. Moreover, dual-earner couples have more in common than do breadwinner-homemaker couples, and this similarity promotes mutual understanding and communication. The employment of wives also strengthens marriage indirectly by enhancing financial security and stability—factors that are especially important in an era of stagnating male wages (Oppenheimer, 1997; Spain and Bianchi, 1996; White and Rogers, 2000).

In contrast, other scholars have emphasized the potentially desta-bilizing effects of wives' employment on marriage (Becker, 1981; Nock, 1998; Parsons and Bales, 1955). According to this view, special-ization within marriage—the division of paid labor and family work by gender—creates interdependence between spouses. Specialization not only is an efficient arrangement for ensuring that tasks are performed successfully, but also maximizes feelings of solidarity. Abandoning the traditional, complementary roles of husband and wife, therefore, weak-ens mutual dependence and erodes marital cohesion. The employment of wives also can lead to "status competition" with husbands, which in-creases the potential for marital disagreements and conflict.

These views can be traced to the work of the French sociologist Emile Durkheim, who wrote around the turn of the twentieth century. Durkheim claimed that all social systems develop specialized divisions of labor over time, with interdependence between individuals produc-ing greater "organic solidarity" and stability. In applying this general principle to families, Durkheim argued that marital harmony is facili-tated when wives serve as domestic specialists and husbands serve as primary income earners. Moreover, Durkheim warned that strict gen-der equality and female autonomy (as advocated by feminist writers of the time) would undermine women's privileged status within the fam-ily, weaken the conjugal bond, and lower women's emotional well-be-ing. (See Lamanna, 2002, for a discussion of Durkheim's views on mar-riage.) Although these views seem out of step with the present era, they continue to influence the work of some contemporary scholars.

Other research literature has focused on the potential for wives' la-bor-force participation to create work-family conflict. Many individu-als in dual-earner marriages are frustrated by the lack of free time avail-able to spend either with their families or in solitary leisure pursuits (Hochschild, 1997; Nomaguchi, Milkie, and Bianchi, 2005). These feelings can exacerbate tension between spouses over issues such as housework and child care and lead tired spouses to withdraw from fam-ily interaction (Booth, Johnson, White, and Edwards, 1984; Glass and Fujimoto, 1994; Perry-Jenkins, Repetti, and Crouter, 2000; Repetti, 1989, 1994). Some research also suggests that job strain between husbands and wives increases the risk of marital violence (Fox, Benson, DeMaris, and Van Wyk, 2002).

Given these contrary perspectives, it is difficult to determine how recent shifts in the employment of wives may have affected aggregate levels of marital quality in the United States. Wives' labor-force participation increases family income (which lowers economic stress) but also requires balancing the competing demands of two full-time jobs and family life, especially among couples with children. In other words, the large-scale shift toward dual-earner marriage is likely to have involved costs as well as benefits for married couples. Moreover, we suspect that these costs and benefits were not distributed equally within the population; some couples benefited more than others. Our goal in this chapter is to cast more light on these issues by describing changes in spouses' employment patterns between 1980 and 2000, as well as changes in married couples' financial well-being. We also describe the links between these economic factors and the five measures of marital quality described in chapter 2: happiness, interaction, conflict, problems, and divorce proneness. Finally, we assess the extent to which changes in these economic factors were associated with changes in marital quality between 1980 and 2000.

Changes in Employment

In this section we first focus on *objective* conditions of employment, including whether husbands and wives were in the labor force, the number of hours that husbands and wives worked, and the number of demands that spouses' jobs involved (such as working on weekends or in the evenings). We then focus on *subjective* aspects of employment, such as people's perceptions that their jobs (or their spouses' jobs) interfered with family life, husbands' feelings about their wives' jobs, wives' employment preferences, wives' reasons for being employed, and both spouses' job satisfaction. (Details on the variables described in this chapter are available in Table 6 in Appendix 2.)

Changes in Objective Aspects of Employment

Changes in labor-force participation. In both surveys we asked about the number of hours that husbands and wives spent in the paid labor force

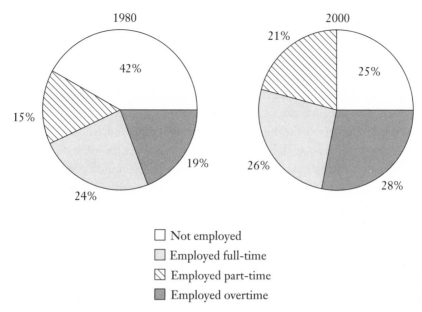

Figure 4.1 Wives' employment status, 1980 and 2000

during a typical week, including time spent driving to and from work. (Respondents provided information on their spouses' jobs as well as their own jobs.) Like other national data, our surveys indicate that wives' labor-force participation increased substantially between 1980 and 2000, rising from 58% in 1980 to 75% in 2000. Figure 4.1 shows this change in greater detail. In this figure, *part-time* refers to being in the labor force up to 34 hours per week, *full-time* refers to being in the labor force between 35 and 44 hours per week, and *overtime* refers to being in the labor force 45 or more hours per week. Note that the largest increase was in the overtime category; only 19% of wives worked 45 hours or more per week in 1980, compared with 28% of wives in 2000. Despite the large increase in the percentage of employed wives, the mean number of hours that wives spent at work (counting employed wives only) increased only slightly, from 38 to 40. This minor increase in hours is consistent with other national data collected during this period (Jacobs and Gerson, 2004). In other words, the major change during this period involved the movement of full-time homemakers into the labor force, rather than an increase in the number of hours that employed wives spent at work.

In both surveys wives' labor-force participation was most common among blacks and least common among Latinas. Despite these differences, however, significant increases in wives' employment occurred among all racial and ethnic groups. Wives' participation in the labor force increased from 57% to 76% among whites, from 75% to 85% among blacks, and from 51% to 68% among Latinas. Significant increases in employment also occurred among older wives as well as younger wives, and among mothers as well as women without children. The increase in wives' labor-force participation was impressive, both in terms of its magnitude and its pervasiveness in the population.

We assumed that the movement of wives into paid employment between 1980 and 2000 was related to several of the demographic shifts described in Chapter 3. As some observers have noted, well-educated wives experience more opportunity costs than do poorly educated wives by remaining out of the paid labor force (Jacobs and Gerson, 2004; Spain and Bianchi, 1996). That is, wives with a high potential for earning income give up more by avoiding employment than do other wives. Moreover, education is positively associated with job commitment and job satisfaction—two factors that should increase wives' labor-force attachment. Also, because mothers traditionally have assumed the major responsibility for child care, the decline in family size in recent decades made it easier for wives to be employed (Casper and Bianchi, 2002; Jacobs and Gerson, 2004). Finally, research shows that remarried wives are more likely to be in the paid labor force than are wives in first marriages (Booth and Edwards, 1992). Presumably, wives who saw their first marriages end in divorce wish to maintain a degree of financial independence to protect themselves in the event of a second divorce.

We found support for all these explanations in our data. Wives' employment (measured in hours) was positively associated with wives' education, negatively associated with the number of children in the household, and positively associated with being in a second or higher-order marriage. Taken together, changes in these three factors between 1980 and 2000 explained over one-third (35%) of the increase in wives' hours of employment. Nevertheless, even after taking education, children, and remarriage into account, the difference between decades was significant, which indicates that other factors (in addition to the three that we considered) played a role in increasing wives' labor-force participation. Large-scale structural and cultural shifts, such as rising employment opportunities for women in the service sector, improvements in women's real wages during the last two decades, and the growing social acceptance of maternal employment, probably contributed to this change.

The employment trend for husbands moved in an opposite direction. In 1980, 95% of the husbands in our sample were employed, but by 2000 this figure had declined to 92%. A small part of the decline in men's employment reflected an increase in the percentage of househusbands in the population. Only one husband in the 1980 survey was a full-time homemaker, compared with 20 husbands (1% of the sample) in 2000. The decline in men's employment also was due to a small increase in the percentage of husbands who had retired by age 55 (from less than 1% in 1980 to 2% in 2000). These two trends largely accounted for the decline in the percentage of employed husbands between surveys. Despite the modest drop in men's labor-force participation, the mean length of the workweek (including commute time) among employed husbands rose only slightly, from 51 to 52 hours—a result that is consistent with other national data (Jacobs and Gerson, 2004).

Some couples may deal with potential work-family conflicts by taking their spouses' hours of employment into account when making decisions about their own level of job involvement. For example, when wives increase their hours of employment, some husbands may decrease their hours of employment to compensate, which results in little net change in spouses' total work hours. Although this may happen in some cases, there is no correlation between husbands' and wives' hours of employment in our data, which indicates that husbands' and wives' hours of employment are largely independent of one another.

Labor-force participation and marital quality. What were the implications of changes in husbands' and wives' employment patterns for marital quality? Husbands' labor-force participation was not associated, in general, with marital quality. The one exception involved marital interaction, which was negatively associated with husbands' weekly hours of employment in 1980 and 2000. Not surprisingly, husbands who work long hours have less time available to engage in shared activities with their spouses.

Existing research on the impact of wives' labor-force participation on marital quality is equivocal; some studies suggest negative effects

(Booth, Johnson, White, and Edwards, 1984) and other studies suggest positive effects (Rogers and DeBoer, 2001). Our analysis provides modest support for the notion that wives' jobs are a source of marital stress, although these trends were more apparent in 2000 than in 1980. In particular, the number of hours that wives were employed every week was associated with less marital happiness and interaction in 2000, and this trend did not vary with the gender of the respondent. These results applied mainly to wives who worked relatively long hours; that is, wives' employment was not linked with poorer marital quality unless they worked 45 or more hours per week. Of course, it is possible that wives who are unhappy with their marriages spend more time at work (Rogers, 1999). We cannot sort out the causal order of these variables with our data, although it is likely that one interpretation is true in some cases and the other interpretation is valid in others.

The pattern differed for marital problems. In 2000 the mean level of problems was significantly *lower* when wives were employed part-time than when wives were not employed. This finding—which held for husbands as well as wives—is consistent with the notion that, for many couples, part-time employment is a less stressful and more satisfying arrangement than either full-time employment or full-time homemaking. Apparently, for many wives, part-time employment is an optimal way to balance work and family commitments (Spain and Bianchi, 1996).

The decomposition analysis revealed that changes in husbands' and wives' employment between 1980 and 2000 were not associated with changes in aggregate levels of marital quality, in general. The one exception involved marital happiness. For this outcome, the increase in wives' hours of employment was associated with a decrease in marital happiness in the population equivalent to .03 of a standard deviation. Overall, however, the substantial changes in wives' labor-force participation during the last two decades of the twentieth century had few implications for marital quality—a surprising conclusion, given the large research literature devoted to the effects of wives' employment on marriage and family life.

Changes in job demands. Although working a relatively large number of hours every week can lead to work-family strain, other job demands also may affect marital quality. Presser (2003) argued that the growth in women's employment, combined with recent changes in technology, gave rise to a growing demand for late-shift and weekend employment. Nonstandard work schedules, however, make it difficult for spouses to spend high-quality time with their families. To assess how common these work demands were, we asked respondents whether their own or their spouses' jobs involved irregular hours, nonstandard shifts, evening meetings, or overnight trips away from home.

The percentage of employed husbands who reported irregular hours, shift work, or evening work did not change between 1980 and 2000. The percentage of husbands with jobs that involved overnight trips, however, increased significantly, from 33% to 37%. We also combined these four questions into a summary index of job demands, with scores ranging from 0 to 4. Husbands' scores on this index did not differ between 1980 and 2000.

With respect to employed wives, increases between surveys occurred for evening meetings (23% versus 27%) and overnight trips (8% versus 19%), although the percentage of wives who worked irregular hours or nonstandard shifts did not change (about 33% and 17% in both years, respectively). Correspondingly, the summary index of job demands increased from 0.79 to 0.92. The fact that the mean of the scale was less than zero in both surveys indicates that the majority of wives did not experience any of these demands. Nevertheless, some wives held very demanding jobs. For example, among employed wives in 2000, 18% reported two demands and 10% reported three or four demands. (The corresponding values in 1980 were 15% and 7%, respectively.) Therefore, wives were more likely not only to be employed in 2000 than in 1980, but also to hold demanding jobs with the potential to interfere with home life.

Presser (ibid.) argued that the growth in nonstandard work arrangements occurred primarily among low-income couples. Our measure of wives' work demands, however, was positively correlated with wives' education, income, and occupational status. (Similarly, our measure of husbands' work demands was positively correlated with husbands' education, income, and occupational status.) Disaggregating our measure of work demands helps to explain this apparent discrepancy. Among husbands as well as wives, education was negatively associated with doing shift work—a finding consistent with Presser's claim that poorly educated men and women are especially likely to have nonstandard work arrangements. Among husbands as well as wives, however, educa-

tion and occupational status were positively associated with working irregular hours, attending evening meetings, and taking overnight trips.
Overall, our findings suggest that the increase in wives' work demands
between 1980 and 2000, and the corresponding burdens these demands may have posed for family life, fell on the shoulders of middle-
class as well as working-class wives.

Job demands and marital quality. Previous research has shown that the
stress associated with excessive work demands can spill over and affect
family life. For example, some studies have suggested that doing shift
work increases the risk of divorce (Presser, 2000; White and Keith,
1990). We found that, contrary to these studies, husbands' work demands were not related to marital quality. Wives' scores on the work
demands index, in contrast, were positively associated with marital
problems and divorce proneness in 2000. But despite these associations, the decomposition analysis suggested that the increase in wives'
work demands did not have any implications for changes in mean levels
of marital quality in the population.

Changes in Subjective Aspects of Employment

Perceived job interference in family life. As we noted earlier, the percentage of employed wives increased between 1980 and 2000, irrespective of age, race, or number of children. In addition, a larger proportion of wives reported working 45 or more hours per week, working in
the evenings, and making overnight job-related trips. One result of
these changes may be an increase in conflict between the demands of
work and family roles, which, in turn, may influence the quality of marital relationships. One recent study (Winslow, 2005) found that married people's reports of work-family conflict increased between 1977
and 1997, especially for parents. Interestingly, this study also found
that husbands reported as much work-family conflict as did wives. To
assess perceptions of work-family conflict in our study, we asked the
following questions: "How much does your job interfere with your
family life?" and "How much does your spouse's job interfere with your
family life?" For both questions, response options were (1) not at all,
(2) a little bit, (3) somewhat, or (4) a lot. Figure 4.2 shows the percentage of husbands and wives who reported "somewhat" or "a lot" by the
year of the survey.

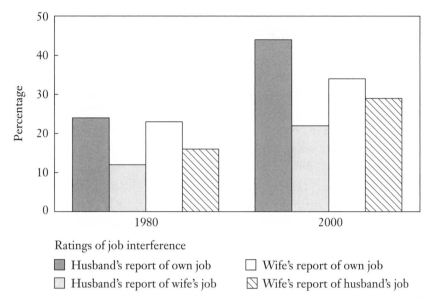

Figure 4.2 Percentage of spouses reporting that jobs interfered with family life, 1980 and 2000

Overall, most respondents reported that husbands' and wives' jobs interfered relatively little with family life, with the most common responses being "not at all" or "a little bit" in both surveys. Nevertheless, the figure reveals several noteworthy trends. For example, the percentage of spouses who reported that husbands' jobs interfered with family life was higher in 2000 than in 1980, and this was true irrespective of whether husbands or wives served as respondents.

The increase in perceptions that the husband's job intruded on family life is surprising, given the modest rise in husbands' hours of employment and work demands (described above). Nevertheless, this finding is consistent with some earlier research (ibid.). Additional analysis indicated that men's hours of employment, number of work demands, and having children in the household (especially preschool children) were positively associated with perceptions of job-family interference. That is, spouses of both genders were more likely to see the husband's job as being intrusive when men worked long hours, had especially demanding jobs, or were fathers of young children. Spouses also were more likely to believe that husbands' jobs interfered with family life when husbands had a high level of education, although this association was mediated entirely by the greater work demands of well-educated husbands. We also found that perceptions that the husband's job interfered with family life were not related to whether his wife was employed. Overall, the modest increases in men's hours of employment and work demands explained less than one-fifth (19%) of the increase in reports of job-family interference between 1980 and 2000. Presumably, the increase in perceptions of problems had less to do with changes in men's objective conditions of employment than with changes in people's expectations. If husbands are expected to be more involved in family life today than they were a generation ago (whether or not their wives are employed), then the same level of job involvement that was normative in the past may be seen as problematic in the present.

Figure 4.2 also reveals a rise in husbands' and wives' reports that the wife's job interfered with family life. Women's hours of employment and work demands were positively associated with perceptions of interference. In 2000, for example, when wives worked part-time, only 15% of husbands felt that their wives' jobs intruded on family life. But when wives worked full-time, 25% of husbands felt this way. This effect was even stronger for wives. Only 16% of wives who worked part-time felt that their jobs intruded on family life, compared with 35% of wives who worked full-time. Spouses also were more likely to report that the wife's job interfered with family life when children lived in the household than when the household was childless. Spouses also perceived wives' jobs to be more disruptive when wives were well-educated or held professional positions, primarily because well-educated wives tended to have more demanding jobs. Overall, changes in wives' hours of employment and work demands accounted for about one-fourth (26%) of the increase in the perception that the wife's job was intrusive. In other words, spouses were more likely to see the wife's job as causing problems in 2000 than in 1980 partly because wives were working longer hours and experiencing more work demands (especially evening work and overnight trips). After taking these two variables into account, however, the increase in perceptions of job interference between surveys continued to be significant. Once again, people's perceptions of work-family conflict may have as much to do with changing expectations as with changes in the objective circumstances of employment.

Figure 4.2 reveals one more significant trend of interest. In both decades, husbands viewed their own jobs as being more disruptive to family life than their wives' jobs. Given that husbands worked longer hours and experienced more work demands than did wives, this finding is not surprising. Nevertheless, these results suggest that husbands place most of the "blame" for work-family conflict on their own jobs. Although most of the research literature on work-family conflict has focused on wives' employment, our findings suggest that greater attention should be focused on husbands' jobs as a source of family tension.

Perceived job interference in family life and marital quality. People who reported job-family interference also tended to report relatively low levels of marital quality. This finding held for husbands' as well as for wives' jobs and did not depend on whether husbands or wives served as respondents. Moreover, this pattern was apparent in both time periods and held across all five dimensions of marital quality. These findings suggest that perceptions of job interference in family life have pervasive, detrimental consequences for marital quality. The effect sizes were modest in magnitude, however, ranging from .08 to .23. The intrusiveness of the husband's job turned out to be a consistently better predictor of marital quality than was the intrusiveness of the wife's job. This difference may reflect the fact that men, compared with women, tend to work longer hours and experience more work demands. For these reasons, husbands' jobs appear to have more potential than wives' jobs to conflict with family routines and responsibilities and, hence, to create tension in the marital relationship. These results support our contention, noted above, that research should focus more attention on men's jobs as sources of marital distress.

Changes in husbands' feelings about their wives' jobs. Another indicator of work-family conflict involves husbands' feelings about their wives' employment. In both surveys we asked husbands how they felt; the response options were (1) strongly disapprove, (2) disapprove, (3) neither approve nor disapprove, (4) approve, and (5) strongly approve. We also asked employed wives how much approval they received from their husbands, with the same response options. Irrespective of whether husbands described their own views or wives reported on their husbands' views, the large majority of husbands supported their wives' employment in both decades. This support became even stronger between surveys. In 1980, 9% of husbands disapproved or strongly disapproved of their wives' jobs, compared with only 1% of husbands in 2000.

These findings are consistent with the notion that the labor-force participation of wives had become almost universally accepted in American society by the end of the twentieth century.

To gain a more detailed understanding of how husbands felt about their wives' employment, we asked a series of questions about job-related concerns. Specifically, we asked, "Are any of the following aspects of your wife's job a cause of concern for you?"

- She comes home crabby or irritable?
- Not having time to do all the things she should?
- Having time to take care of the house?
- Meeting too many men?
- Not having time to do things together?
- Taking proper care of the children?

For each item, response options were (1) not a concern, (2) a concern but not a serious one, and (3) a serious concern. The majority of husbands had few concerns about their wives' jobs, irrespective of decade. Across both surveys, the percentage of husbands with serious concerns was 9% for coming home crabby and irritable, 6% for not having time to do all the things she should, 6% for having time to take care of the house, 1% for meeting too many men, 11% for not having time to do things together, and 6% for taking proper care of the children (among couples with children). Of course, it is possible that when husbands have serious concerns, their wives are more likely to quit their jobs.

Even among husbands who held serious concerns, most supported their wives' employment. Specifically, among husbands who had at least one serious concern, 75% approved of their wives' employment, either strongly or very strongly, and another 13% had neutral feelings. Only 11% of husbands in this group expressed disapproval. (The pattern was nearly identical when wives reported on their husbands' feelings.) Presumably, even husbands who held serious concerns appreciated the higher standard of living provided by their wives' jobs and were willing to accept a degree of inconvenience as part of a package deal.

Husbands' support for wives' jobs and marital quality. Although the great majority of husbands approved of their wives' employment, marital happiness was lower and marital conflict and marital problems were higher in both surveys when husbands disapproved. These trends held whether husbands reported on their own disapproval or wives reported on their husbands' disapproval. These findings indicate that lack of support from husbands is a source of marital discord—but only in a small number of dual-earner couples. Similarly, we found that when husbands held serious concerns about their wives' jobs, marital quality tended to be lower, irrespective of the year of the survey or whether husbands or wives served as respondents. Moreover, the effect sizes were moderate in magnitude and ranged from .22 to .37. Nevertheless, it is important to keep in mind that only a minority of husbands were concerned about problems arising from their wives' employment.

Changes in wives' employment preferences. Despite the large increase in wives' labor-force participation, not all employed wives are necessarily happy with these arrangements. Indeed, studies have shown that a substantial percentage of employed women as well as men would prefer to work fewer hours (Christensen, 2005; Jacobs and Gerson, 2004). To gain insight into wives' employment preferences, we asked, "If you had a choice, would you prefer to have a part-time job, a full-time job, or no job at all?" Given the large-scale movement of wives and mothers into the labor force during the second half of the twentieth century, we assumed that the percentage of wives who preferred employment to nonemployment had increased between 1980 and 2000. The results, however, were contrary to our expectations. Between the two surveys, the percentage of *all* wives who preferred "no job at all" *increased* from 25 to 34. Correspondingly, the percentage of all wives who preferred a full-time job *decreased* from 27 to 19. The percentage of wives who preferred a part-time job was essentially the same, at 48 and 47. These figures indicate that, irrespective of decade, the modal choice of married women was for a part-time job. When we looked only at wives who were in the labor force at the time of the surveys, the results revealed a similar trend. For example, among employed wives, the percentage who preferred not to have a job doubled from 14 to 28. These results demonstrate that although wives were less likely to be employed in 1980 than in 2000, women's preferences shifted slightly in the direction of being full-time homemakers. Indeed, one-third of all wives in 2000 preferred to be full-time homemakers.

To understand this trend better, we examined wives' work preferences in relation to their current employment status. Among wives who were not employed at the time of the survey, 59% wished for either a part-time or full-time job in 1980, compared with only 48% in 2000. This decline suggests that by the end of the 1990s, it had become easier for wives who wanted to be employed to obtain jobs. Nevertheless, even in the more recent survey, nearly half of all wives without jobs preferred to be employed, suggesting that many wives continued to face obstacles to entering the labor force.

The picture for employed wives was quite different. Among wives employed part-time, 16% preferred to be homemakers in 1980, compared with 30% in 2000. And among wives employed full-time, 18% preferred to be homemakers in 1980 compared with 25% in 2000. Overall, the percentage of employed wives who preferred to be working either fewer hours or not at all increased from 48% in 1980 to 59% in 2000. Although wives' labor-force involvement increased substantially during the last two decades of the twentieth century, many wives were not enthusiastic about their new economic role.

One explanation for these contradictory trends (increases in wives' hours of employment coupled with increases in wives' preferences to work fewer hours) is that many wives were employed not because they wished to have a career, but because their paychecks were necessary to meet their families' financial needs. This situation is likely to arise when husbands earn relatively little income. In fact, husbands' income was negatively associated with wives' preferences to leave the labor force. If husbands earned relatively little money, then employed wives were especially likely to want to be full-time homemakers—a finding consistent with the notion that many wives were working because of economic necessity rather than personal interest. In addition, employed wives were more likely to express a preference to leave the labor force when their husbands did not approve of their jobs. That is, wives were most likely to wish to leave the labor force when husbands earned relatively little income *and* disapproved of their employment—a situation that placed wives in a difficult position.

Wives also were more likely to want to quit their jobs when there were children in the household, especially preschool-age children. This finding is not surprising for several reasons: employed mothers often find it difficult to find affordable child care, trying to balance work and parenting can lead to feelings of exhaustion and role overload, and most fathers continue to do less than half of child care, especially when children are young (see Chapter 5). Some employed mothers prefer to spend more time at home, either because they feel that it would be better for their children's development or because they enjoy spending time with their children (Robinson, 1993). Presumably, these mothers held jobs either because their families needed the additional income or because they did not want to sacrifice future earning potential by dropping out of the labor force.

We did not ask whether husbands would prefer to work fewer hours in 1980, but we included this question in the 2000 survey. Although the great majority of husbands were working full-time in that year, only 55% preferred to be working full-time, 20% preferred to be working part-time, and 25% preferred not to be working. These results indicate that many husbands, like wives, would prefer to spend less time at their jobs. Our findings are consistent with another national study showing that one-third of men, compared with 40% of women, prefer to work fewer hours (Reynolds, 2003). So a desire to spend less time in the labor force appears to hold for many husbands as well as wives.

Before we leave this topic, one more aspect of these findings merits attention. Our data indicate a substantial mismatch between wives' employment preferences and their labor-force participation. In 2000 about half of all nonemployed wives preferred to be employed, whereas the majority of employed wives preferred to work fewer hours or not at all. If we think in terms of three categories (nonemployment, part-time employment, and full-time employment), then there are nine combinations of work preferences and work statuses (3 preferences × 3 statuses = 9 combinations). Three of these combinations reflect good matches (for example, preferring full-time employment and being employed full-time) and six of these combinations reflect mismatches (for example, preferring part-time employment and not being employed). Based on these nine categories, only 26% of wives had employment statuses that were consistent with their preferences in 1980, compared with 32% of wives in 2000. These results indicate that wives were better able to match their behavior with their preferences in more recent years. Nevertheless, two-thirds of wives in the 2000 survey were in employment statuses that did not match their preferences.

Wives' employment preferences and marital quality. Given that most wives do not experience a good fit between their work status and their

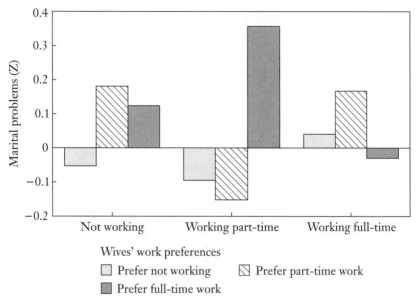

Figure 4.3   Adjusted mean level of marital problems by wives' employment status and wives' employment preferences, 2000

work preferences, does a poor fit have implications for marital quality? According to our data, the answer is yes. In both surveys wives who reported a good fit between their employment preferences and their actual behavior, compared with wives who reported a poor fit, were happier with their marriages and experienced less conflict, fewer problems, and lower divorce proneness. Most of these differences were about one-fifth of a standard deviation—modest but nontrivial effect sizes.

Figure 4.3 shows wives' reports of marital problems, based on data from the 2000 survey. Wives who preferred not to be in the labor force reported relatively few marital problems when they were not employed and more marital problems when they were employed in part-time or full-time jobs. When wives preferred part-time employment, they reported the fewest marital problems when they held part-time jobs and the most marital problems when they worked full-time. And wives who wanted full-time employment reported fewer problems when they held full-time jobs and more problems when they were not employed at all or held part-time jobs. In general, wives see their marriages as being less troubled when their work preferences are consistent with their labor-force status. These findings suggest that wives' unhappiness with their work hours (whether they want to work more or fewer hours) can spill over and affect their marital quality.

Some of these differences may reflect the effect of marital unhappiness on wives' work preferences (Rogers, 1999). For example, full-time homemakers in troubled marriages might prefer employment to get away from their husbands, find an alternative source of emotional fulfillment, or accumulate financial assets in case their marriages end in divorce. In other cases, full-time homemakers who wish to be employed may experience the disapproval of their husbands, which results in frustration on the part of wives and tension in the marriage. In yet other cases, wives who are employed full-time but prefer to be working fewer hours may experience job-related stress that spills over into the marriage. In general, the links between wives' marital quality and wives' employment are complex, and no single explanation is likely to be applicable to all cases.

Changes in wives' reasons for employment. Earlier we assumed that many wives entered the labor force during the last few decades not because they wanted to but because their families needed the additional income. To explore wives' motivations for being in the labor force, we asked employed wives in both surveys to rate the importance of eight reasons for employment. Specifically, we said, "I want to read you some reasons why people work. Please tell me how important each is as a reason why you have worked during the time of your marriage."

- Your earnings are necessary to make ends meet.
- To have enough money to get some of the better things.
- You want a career.
- For a feeling of accomplishment.
- To get away from the family or children.
- You don't like staying at home.
- You like contact with people.
- To make you more financially independent.

To rate these reasons, respondents used the following options: (1) not important at all, (2) not very important, (3) pretty important, (4) and very important.

Wives' ratings in both surveys are summarized in Figure 4.4. In 1980

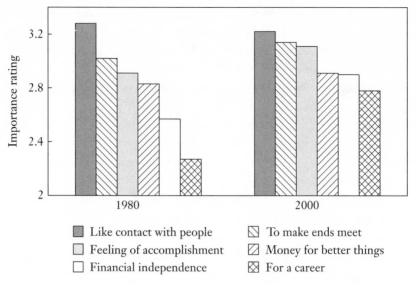

Figure 4.4   Wives' reasons for working: ratings of importance, 1980 and 2000

wives rated contact with people as the most important reason for working. The second most important reason was to make ends meet, followed by feeling of accomplishment, money for some of the better things, financial independence, and wanting a career. Although they are not shown in the figure, don't like staying at home and to get away from the family or children were rated as the least important reasons.

The ranking of reasons was the same in 2000. Nevertheless, wives rated several reasons as being more important in 2000 than in 1980. Working to make ends meet, feeling of accomplishment, money for some of the better things, financial independence, and wanting a career all received higher ratings in 2000 than in 1980. The largest jumps occurred for wanting a career and financial independence. These results indicate that motivations related to career and financial independence became more important, relative to the other motives, between 1980 and 2000. This increased focus on career and financial independence reflects the rise in women's education and the improved possibilities for upward occupational mobility among women during the last few decades.

To explore these trends further, we subjected these motives to a factor analysis. This procedure revealed three general factors that reflected a strong career orientation (wanting a career, feeling of accomplishment, financial independence, and contact with people), economic need (to make ends meet, money for some of the better things, and financial independence), and escape from the home (to get away from the family or children and don't like staying at home). (Note that financial independence loaded on two factors.) As the results reported earlier led us to expect, scores on the career and economic-need factors increased over time, whereas scores on the escape from home factor decreased over time.

We then correlated wives' scores on these factors with several variables of interest. Wives with high scores on the career factor tended to work long hours and reported a relatively large number of work demands. These wives were well educated; 61% had two years of college or more. Many (49%) worked in professional and managerial positions, and both they and their husbands had high earnings. These wives also tended to have few children, reported strong approval for their jobs from their husbands, preferred to be in the labor force, and had no wish to be full-time homemakers. Finally, and importantly, wives' scores on the career factor were stronger in 2000 than in 1980.

Wives who scored high on the economic factor also tended to work long hours and have moderately high earnings. In contrast to wives with career motives, however, these wives had jobs that involved relatively few additional demands. Most of these wives were not well educated (62% had no post–high school education), relatively few worked in professional or managerial positions (28%), and their incomes reflected their long work hours rather than the status of their jobs. These wives appeared to be in the labor force largely because their husbands had relatively low earnings. In addition, wives who worked because they needed the income tended to feel that their jobs interfered with family life, and most preferred not to be employed. Although the majority claimed that their husbands approved of their jobs, many also reported that their husbands had concerns about the negative effects of their jobs on family life—a combination that suggests ambivalent feelings on the part of husbands. Like the career motive, this motive for employment was stronger in 2000 than in 1980.

Finally, wives who viewed employment as an escape from the home tended to work few hours (primarily part-time rather than full-time). They also reported a moderate level of work demands, especially nonstandard hours (that is, working on evenings or weekends, while their husbands and children were at home). Their jobs did not generate much in the way of earnings. Although their husbands expressed some concerns, these wives preferred to be employed and had no wish to be full-time homemakers. In contrast to women's endorsement of career and financial-need motives, women expressed this motive less often in 2000 than in 1980.

To understand how common these motives were in the population, we categorized wives into three groups, depending on which of the three factors they endorsed most strongly. Using this method, we found that 24% of wives in 1980 worked primarily for career reasons, 36% worked primarily to meet economic needs, and 40% worked primarily to get away from the home. By 2000, 33% of wives worked primarily for career reasons, 40% worked primarily to meet economic needs, and 27% worked primarily to get away from the home. Thus, between 1980 and 2000 the percentage of wives who worked for careers or to make ends meet increased, and the percentage of wives who viewed employment as an escape from a less-than-satisfying home life declined.

In general, these results indicate that two very different motives for wives' employment became more common after 1980. Some wives entered the labor force because they were well educated and committed to their careers. Other wives were not well educated and preferred not to be in the labor force, but they needed to compensate for their husbands' low earnings. The movement of wives into the labor force during the last two decades of the twentieth century appears to have originated in two distinct social contexts, one reflecting the conditions of middle-class families and the other reflecting the conditions of working-class families. As we noted in Chapter 1, the earnings of men without college degrees have been stagnant in recent decades, so increases in wives' hours of employment represent the only route to upward economic mobility for most working-class couples.

Wives' reasons for employment and marital quality. Wives' reasons for being employed were associated with aspects of marital quality in similar ways in both time periods. Not surprisingly, wives who worked because they did not like spending time at home with their families reported relatively low levels of marital happiness and relatively high levels of marital conflict, marital problems, and divorce proneness. These effect sizes were modest, however, and ranged from .10 to .22. We also found that many wives in this group had preschool children in the home. For these wives, employment appeared to serve as an escape not only from a somewhat stressful marriage, but also from the demands of rearing young children.

Earlier in this chapter, we pointed out that wives who worked to make ends meet tended to be married to men with relatively low earnings. Moreover, many of these wives felt that their jobs interfered with family life and preferred not to be employed. For these reasons, we expected that wives who worked primarily because of economic need would be at risk for having troubled marriages. These expectations were confirmed. Wives who worked because their families needed the extra income tended to report relatively low levels of marital happiness and relatively high levels of conflict, problems, and divorce proneness. Apparently, employment under these circumstances has the potential to generate turmoil within these unions. Nevertheless, the effect sizes, which ranged from .09 to .23, reflected modest rather than strong associations.

In contrast, wives' scores on the career and accomplishment factor were not associated with dimensions of wives' marital quality in either time period. Although career-oriented wives tended to work long hours and reported a relatively large number of work demands, these wives also had high levels of education, substantial earnings, few children, and strong support from their husbands. Moreover, most of these wives were in the labor force because they wanted to have jobs and not because their families needed the additional income. Overall, the negative aspects of these jobs (long hours and other work demands) may have balanced the positive aspects, the result being no overall links with marital quality.

Changes in job satisfaction. The extent to which people are satisfied with their jobs is also relevant to understanding the interface between employment and marital quality. As we noted earlier, a large number of scholars have pointed out that stress at work can spill over and affect the quality of family life. For this reason, we asked husbands and wives to describe whether they were very satisfied, somewhat satisfied, a little dissatisfied, or very dissatisfied with their jobs.

In both decades the majority of husbands and wives reported being satisfied with their jobs. For example, 88% of husbands were either very or moderately satisfied with their jobs, and this percentage did not vary across surveys. Similarly, 89% of wives were either very or moderately satisfied with their jobs across both surveys. For the great majority of employed spouses, a high level of job satisfaction was the norm. Nevertheless, job satisfaction was especially high among men and women who worked longer hours, had higher occupational status, and earned more income. We also found that wives were less satisfied when they were employed primarily to make ends meet and more satisfied when they were employed primarily for career reasons or to get away from the home. As we expected, wives who preferred to be full-time homemakers were less satisfied with their jobs than were other employed wives. Interestingly, having children (including preschool children) was not related to the job satisfaction of husbands or wives, which suggests that the additional stress of balancing employment and parenting did not detract from parents' satisfaction with their work.

Job satisfaction and marital quality. One avenue through which work experiences can influence the quality of family life is through the spillover of positive and negative psychological states from one role to the other. Experiences in the workplace that leave people feeling frustrated, depressed, or ineffective may contribute to withdrawal or hostility in family interaction, general feelings of dissatisfaction with family life, or lowered performance as a spouse and parent. Similarly, experiences at work that generate feelings of competence, enjoyment, and stimulation may contribute to warmth and involvement in interaction, general satisfaction with family life, and improved role performance (Crouter, Perry-Jenkins, Huston, and Crawford, 1989; Hughes, Galinsky, and Morris, 1992; Roberts and Levenson, 2001; Voydanoff, 1988). Moreover, several studies indicate that husbands and wives have similar experiences of spillover between work and family domains (Duxbury, Higgins, and Lee, 1994; Rogers and May, 2003).

We found that job satisfaction was consistently associated with marital quality in both decades, which is in keeping with this research literature. In 1980 and 2000 wives' job satisfaction was positively associated with marital happiness and interaction and negatively associated with marital conflict, marital problems, and divorce proneness. Correspondingly, in both surveys, husbands' job satisfaction was associated in the expected direction with each dimension of marital quality. Although most of these effect sizes were modest or moderate in magnitude, it appears that how people feel about their jobs has pervasive implications for the quality of their marriages.

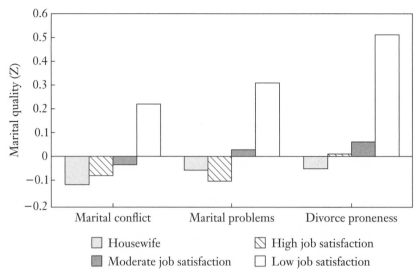

Figure 4.5 Wives' adjusted mean levels of marital quality by wives' job satisfaction, 2000

To understand this trend more fully, we compared marital quality among four groups of wives in 2000: those who were very satisfied with their jobs, those who were moderately satisfied, those who were dissatisfied (either a little or a great deal), and those who were not employed. As Figure 4.5 indicates, few differences were apparent in the marital quality of wives who were very satisfied with their jobs, wives who were moderately satisfied with their jobs, and wives who were not employed. Wives who were dissatisfied with their jobs, in contrast, reported more marital conflict, more problems, and greater divorce proneness than did wives in the other three groups. And although it is not shown in the figure, wives who were dissatisfied with their jobs also reported lower marital happiness and interaction. These results suggest that positive feelings about one's job do not improve marital quality. That is, wives who were very satisfied with their jobs did not differ from full-time homemakers in their levels of marital quality. In contrast, wives' negative feelings about their jobs appear to spill over and affect their marriages negatively. Of course, it is likely that negative marital experiences are transmitted to the workplace, just as negative workplace experiences are transmitted to the home. (It is also possible that a personality trait, such as a general tendency to be satisfied or dissatisfied, is partly responsible for this association.) Regardless of the interpretation, our study indicates that the connections between well-being in these two domains—the workplace and the marriage—are strong and consistent across decades.

Summary of Changes in Employment and Marital Quality

Between 1980 and 2000 substantial changes occurred in the labor-force participation and experiences of married couples. The percentage of wives in the labor force rose, while the percentage of husbands in the labor force fell slightly. An increasing number of wives held full-time jobs rather than part-time jobs, and wives' jobs involved more evening work and overnight trips—employment demands that previously were associated with husbands' jobs. We also found an increase in the percentage of employed mothers with preschool-age children, which indicates a tendency for mothers to return to the labor force relatively quickly after the birth of a child. These trends illustrate the continuing convergence in the work roles of husbands and wives (Spain and Bianchi, 1996; White and Rogers, 2000). The specialized breadwinner-homemaker arrangement, common in the 1950s, was rare among married couples at the beginning of the new millennium.

Numerous authors have pointed out that changes in employment have exacerbated the potential for work-family conflict. Our surveys likewise revealed an increase in the number of people who felt that their jobs (or their spouses' jobs) interfered with family life, and this change was similar for husbands and wives. Moreover, people who reported that their jobs or their spouses' jobs intruded on family life tended to report lower marital quality. The increase in people's perceptions that their jobs (or their spouses') intruded on family life was only partly explained by increases in work hours and job demands. We suspect that this finding reflects an increase in the perceived demands of family life during the last two decades of the twentieth century. Studies—as well as anecdotal evidence—indicate that parents are spending an increasing amount of time managing and "cultivating" their children's experiences (Hochschild, 1997; Jacobs and Gerson, 2004; Lareau, 2003). Middle-class parents, in particular, fill their children's lives with organized sports, music lessons, and other cultural and artistic activities that may enhance children's cognitive development and school success. To the extent that child rearing has become a more time-consuming task, the increase in the perceived "interference" of jobs on family life may have more to do with rising expectations for high-quality child rearing than with changes in parents' objective work conditions. This interpretation is consistent with the finding, noted earlier, that perceived job-family interference was especially pronounced among couples with children.

Some authors have suggested that many men feel challenged by their wives' jobs because they lose the privileges associated with being the sole breadwinner (Goode, 1980). Our study shows, however, that the great majority of husbands approved of their wives' jobs, and few husbands reported problems caused by their wives' employment. The main exception occurred when wives worked 45 or more hours per week—a situation that exacerbated some men's concerns about the effects of their wives' jobs on the family. More generally, in 1980 as well as in 2000, husbands were more likely to believe that their own jobs (rather than their wives' jobs) were the primary source of interference in family life.

A different view emerged when we looked at wives' work preferences and reasons for employment. Somewhat paradoxically, as the percentage of wives in the labor force increased, so did the number of employed wives who wanted to work fewer hours or be full-time homemakers. This apparent paradox is due to the fact that two very different groups of wives increased their labor force participation between 1980 and 2000. On the one hand, an increasing percentage of wives entered the labor force because they wanted to have careers and enjoyed the associated feelings of accomplishment. These women were generally well educated and worked in high-paying jobs, as did their husbands. On the other hand, an increasing percentage of wives entered the labor force because their families needed the additional income. This shift was due largely to stagnation in wages for men without college degrees combined with a rise in women's wages (in constant dollars). As a result, many wives married to working-class men were drawn into the labor force, or increased their hours of employment, to help make ends meet and give their families a higher standard of living. This increase in employment, however, came with a cost: many of these wives experienced low job satisfaction, felt that their jobs interfered with family life, and preferred to work fewer hours (or be full-time homemakers). Presumably, many of these couples were not able to afford services, such as high-quality child care, take-out meals, and home cleaning, that help to ease the family burdens associated with dual employment. Moreover, wives who worked primarily for financial reasons and who preferred to be working fewer hours tended to have relatively troubled marriages. The bottom line is that economic trends since 1980 appear to have benefited many middle-class couples but made life more difficult for many working-class couples.

Changes in Economic Well-Being

Changes in Income

Earned income is one of the best indicators of economic well-being. Figure 4.6 shows the mean annual earned income (in constant 2000 dollars) for husbands and wives in 1980 and 2000. The mean income of husbands increased slightly during this period, from $45,400 to $48,800, which represents an increase of about 7%. Wives' income rose more dramatically, from $17,200 in 1980 to $28,200 in 2000—an increase of 64%. Combining the earnings of husbands and wives across all households, mean family income increased from about $55,600 to about $70,000 in 2000, an increase of 26%. Alternatively, the median family income increased from $47,000 to $65,000, an increase of 38% in constant dollars. (We excluded husbands and wives who were not in the labor force from these calculations. This is why husbands' and wives' incomes do not add up to total family income.) As these figures demonstrate, married couples were earning substantially more income in 2000 than in 1980, and most of this increase was due to wives' economic contributions.

The rise in wives' income was due to an increase in the hours that wives worked, along with an increase in their hourly earnings. To create a rough indicator of the latter variable, we divided the wife's annual income by the estimated number of hours she worked in a year. This measure was approximate, because our measure of weekly hours of employment included time spent driving to and from work—time for which workers usually are not paid. Nevertheless, our calculations indicate that wives' hourly earnings increased from a median of just under $8 an hour in 1980 to $12 an hour in 2000 (in constant 2000 dollars). In comparison, husbands' earnings increased from a median of $15.80 an

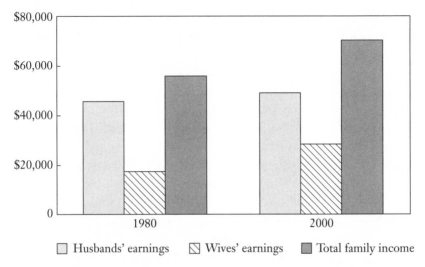

Figure 4.6 Married couples' mean earned income (in constant 2000 dollars), 1980 and 2000

hour in 1980 to only $16.80 an hour in 2000. These values represent approximately a 50% increase in hourly earnings for wives, compared with only a 6% increase in hourly earnings for husbands.

These two trends—a significant rise in wives' incomes and a small increase in husbands' incomes—substantially narrowed the earnings gap between spouses. If we restrict our calculations to dual-earner couples, then the earnings gap between husbands and wives was about $24,000 in 1980 and $18,000 in 2000. The earnings gap was even smaller in 2000 (about $14,000) in households in which both spouses were employed full-time (that is, 35 or more hours per week). Moreover, when we eliminated older wives from these calculations (that is, wives who were 40 years of age or older), then the earnings gap was only about $11,000 in 2000. (We eliminated older wives from these calculations because younger wives are better educated and tend to have higher earnings.) These findings indicate that although husbands continue to earn more than their wives, the gender difference in earned income narrowed considerably during the last two decades of the twentieth century.

Another way of looking at changes in income is to consider the income-to-needs ratio. This figure represents the ratio of total family income to the poverty threshold for families of various sizes, as established by the U.S. government. The income-to-needs ratio is superior to earnings as an indicator of overall standard of living, because it takes into account the number of people who depend on these earnings to live. This ratio increased substantially between decades, from 3.64 in 1980 to 4.70 in 2000. In other words, the typical married couple lived at 364% of the poverty threshold in 1980 and at 470% of the poverty threshold in 2000. Although the number of couples living below the poverty threshold was small in both surveys, this group declined from 4% to 3%. (These small values reflect the fact that poverty among married-couple families is rare in the United States.) If we include couples who were "near poor" (that is, couples who earned 150% or less of the poverty threshold), then the decline was more pronounced, from 11% to 7%. On the other side of the spectrum, the share of relatively affluent couples who earned 600% or more of the poverty threshold doubled, from 12% to 25%. Overall, these results reveal a substantial decline in economic hardship, as well as a substantial increase in family affluence, between decades.

Changes in the Value of Assets

Another major change is reflected in the accumulated assets of husbands and wives. We asked respondents to estimate the value of their homes, along with the value of other joint marital property, such as vacation homes, stocks, or bonds. The total mean value of these assets (in constant 2000 dollars) increased from $125,500 in 1980 to $228,300 in 2000, an increase of 82% in the net worth of married couples. Other objective indicators of economic well-being showed similar improvements between 1980 and 2000. The percentage of married couples who owned or were purchasing their homes increased slightly (but significantly) from 76% to 79%. Correspondingly, the percentage of married couples who had relied on some form of government assistance during the previous three years (such as food stamps or Medicaid) declined from 11% to 7%. Of course, the year 2000 represented the end of an unprecedented decade of economic growth in the United States. During this time married couples with assets saw the value of their homes and their retirement portfolios appreciate considerably. Many of these couples were not as well off a year or two later, as the economy dipped into recession.

Changes in Perceptions of Economic Hardship

To capture people's perceptions of economic well-being, we asked respondents how satisfied they were with their financial situation (1 = not very satisfied, 2 = pretty satisfied, 3 = very satisfied). Unlike our results for income and assets, people's responses to this question did not shift between 1980 and 2000. We also asked, "During the last few years, has your financial situation been getting better, getting worse, or has it stayed about the same?" Between surveys, the percentage of people who reported that their financial situations were getting worse declined from 14% to 7%. Correspondingly, the percentage of people who reported that their financial situations were getting better increased slightly, from 60% to 63%. We combined these two questions to create a measure of perceived economic hardship. If people reported that they were dissatisfied with their current financial situation, or if they reported that their financial situation had grown worse during the previous three years, they received a score of 1, and all other respondents received a score of 0. Based on this variable, the percentage of people who reported economic hardship declined from 22 in 1980 to 17 in 2000.

In general, people's responses to these questions were consistent with other data showing improvements in the economic well-being of married couples during the 1990s. People's subjective perceptions of well-being, however, did not change as dramatically as did the objective indicators. Although median family income increased by 38% and the value of assets increased by 82%, people's mean ratings of financial satisfaction were nearly identical in the two surveys. One explanation for this apparent contradiction is that people's expectations for a higher standard of living increased at the same pace as their incomes. To check this idea, we used regression analysis to predict people's financial satisfaction in 2000 from their total family income. We then used the regression equation to predict what people's level of satisfaction would have been in 2000 if the mean level of earnings had not increased over time. This procedure revealed that if family income had remained the same between surveys, then financial satisfaction would have declined significantly by about one-fifth of a standard deviation. These results are consistent with the notion that married people's financial expectations rose even faster than their incomes during the last two decades of the twentieth century.

Variations in Economic Well-Being

With respect to race, differences between groups were predictable; white couples had the highest level of economic well-being, followed by couples in the "other" category (mostly Asian), black couples, and Latino couples. People in all four groups experienced similar improvements in economic well-being between surveys, however. For this reason, the same ranking of groups existed at both points in time. Black couples did especially well with respect to reliance on public assistance during the three years preceding each survey, which declined from 20% in 1980 to only 7% in 2000. (This trend was reflected in a significant interaction between being black, the year of the survey, and using public assistance.)

These improvements were not shared equally by all married couples, however. Dual-earner couples experienced greater gains in economic security than did traditional breadwinner-homemaker families. For example, mean family income increased by 29% during this period among dual-earner families but by only 14% among breadwinner-homemaker families. Similarly, the increase in home ownership and the decline in the use of public assistance were apparent only for dual-earner families and not for breadwinner-homemaker families. This pattern is consistent with other reports indicating that single-earner families have lost ground relative to dual-earner families during the last couple of decades (Casper and Bianchi, 2002, chap. 9).

To illustrate these results more clearly, Figure 4.7 shows the mean income-to-needs ratio for three types of marriages: marriages in which husbands were the sole breadwinner, marriages in which wives worked part-time, and marriages in which wives worked full-time. (Husbands were employed at least part-time in all three groups.) The figure also displays these trends separately for families in which husbands had or did not have a college degree (defined as an associate degree or more). Among husbands with a college degree (on the right side of the figure), the income-to-needs ratio increased for all three groups. Nevertheless, the change was most pronounced among couples with two earners (wives with either full-time or part-time jobs), who experienced a 26% improvement in standard of living. Breadwinner-homemaker families, in contrast, experienced only a 13% improvement in standard of living. This divergence in economic well-being was even more pronounced

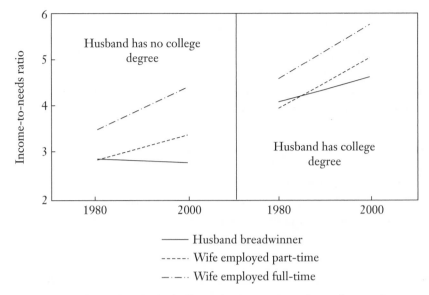

Figure 4.7 Changes in standard of living between 1980 and 2000 by wives' employment status and husbands' education

for husbands without any post–high school education (on the left side of the figure). Among these couples, breadwinner-homemaker families experienced a 3% decline in standard of living during this period, compared with a 26% improvement when both spouses worked full-time. Note that inequality between families was greater in 2000 than in 1980, especially for those in which husbands did not attend college. Note also that by 2000 couples without a college-educated husband but with a wife in the labor force full-time had surpassed the standard of living of couples in 1980 with a college-educated husband but without a wife in the labor force full-time. These dramatic differences illustrate the strong economic incentives that exist for wives married to men without college degrees to enter the paid labor force.

Family Income and Marital Quality

How were changes in family income related to marital quality? Our analysis revealed only one noteworthy result for family income: a positive association with marital happiness in 1980. The general absence of significant results seems surprising, given that earlier studies have found links between earnings and marital quality and stability (Bramlett and Mosher, 2002; Conger and Elder, 1994; Fox and Chancey, 1998). Some observers have noted, however, that income is an inconsistent predictor of marital quality (White and Rogers, 2000). Moreover, family income was associated negatively with perceived economic hardship, and perceived economic hardship, in turn, was consistently associated with marital quality. The direct effect of income is weak, therefore, because most of its effect operates through perceptions of economic hardship. Indeed, with perceived economic hardship omitted from the regression equation, family income was related to most dimensions of marital quality in the expected direction in both surveys. Readers should not assume, therefore, that income has no consequences for marital quality. Moreover, the decomposition analysis revealed that the increase in family income between 1980 and 2000 was associated with an increase of .02 of a standard deviation in the aggregate level of marital happiness in the population—an increase that was independent of the role of perceived economic distress.

Use of Public Assistance and Marital Quality

Spouses who used public assistance during the three years preceding the surveys had more troubled marriages than did spouses who had not used public assistance. Specifically, public assistance was associated with less marital interaction in 2000, more marital conflict in 1980, more marital problems in 2000, and greater divorce proneness in 1980 and 2000. These associations were moderate in magnitude, ranging from about one-fifth to one-fourth of a standard deviation.

Couples who use public assistance not only experience financial strain, but also must deal with the stigma of being on welfare. Husbands, in particular, are likely to find that not being able to support their wives and children is a demoralizing experience. Not surprisingly, these sources of tension can lead to discord in the marriage. As we noted earlier, the economic prosperity of the 1990s resulted in a decline in the use of public assistance between our two surveys: from 11% in 1980 to 7% in 2000. Because the decline was modest, however, our decomposition analysis found that the consequences of this change for marital quality in the population also were modest—a decline of about .01 of a standard deviation in marital problems and divorce proneness.

Perceived Economic Hardship and Marital Quality

Of all the economic variables that we consider in this chapter, perceived economic hardship had the most consistent associations with marital quality. In fact, economic distress was associated with all five dimensions of marital quality in at least one survey. This finding is consistent with the work of Rand Conger and his associates, who have shown that declines in family income exacerbate perceptions of economic distress, which, in turn, are related to increases in marital conflict and declines in marital happiness in Iowa farm families (Conger et al., 1990; Conger and Elder, 1994). Similar findings have been observed in African American families (McLoyd, Cauce, Takeuchi, and Wilson, 2000).

We also found that the estimated effects of economic distress on marital quality became stronger between surveys. With the exception of marital conflict, the associations between economic distress and the various dimensions of marital quality were significantly larger in 2000 than in 1980. These trends are revealed in Figure 4.8, which includes data for divorce proneness. Economic distress was associated with a small increase in divorce proneness in 1980 and a large increase in 2000. The results for marital happiness, interaction, and problems were of comparable magnitude. Why did these associations become stronger over time? As we noted earlier in this chapter, it is likely that during the economic boom of the 1990s, people's expectations for a "reasonable" standard of living increased. Consequently, as the average level of family prosperity increased, those couples who were left behind felt increasingly stressed. Research on relative deprivation indicates that it not so much one's absolute level of deprivation that counts, but the extent to which one feels disadvantaged relative to others.

Although the apparent effects of economic distress on marital quality became stronger between surveys, the percentage of people who reported economic hardship fell from 22% in 1980 to 17% in 2000. Our decomposition analysis indicated that the decline in economic distress was associated with increases in the mean levels of marital happiness and interaction, and with declines in the mean levels of marital conflict, marital problems, and divorce proneness in the population. Despite the broad, positive implications of lower economic distress, these associa-

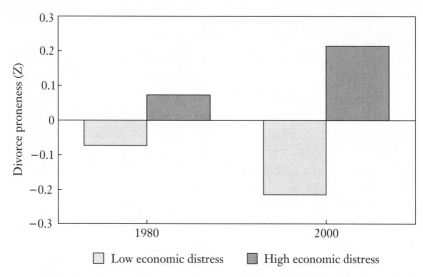

Figure 4.8   Adjusted mean levels of divorce proneness by perceived economic distress, 1980 and 2000

tions were relatively weak; most represented about .01 of a standard deviation.

Direct versus Indirect Effects

One of the limitations of a decomposition analysis is that it estimates the direct effects of variables and ignores the indirect effects. This limitation reflects the fact that a decomposition analysis is not the same as a causal analysis. In the previous section, for example, we noted that most of the estimated effects of family income on marital quality appeared to operate through perceptions of economic hardship. One might reach a similar conclusion about wives' hours of employment. As we noted earlier, we found few direct links between wives' hours of employment and marital quality. Wives who work longer hours, however, also earn more income, all things being equal. Consequently, it is possible that wives' hours of employment had indirect implications for marital quality that operated through family income and perceptions of economic hardship.

We tested these ideas using path analytic methods. Figure 4.9 shows the results of an analysis in which we assumed that (1) wives' hours of employment affect family income, (2) family income affects percep-

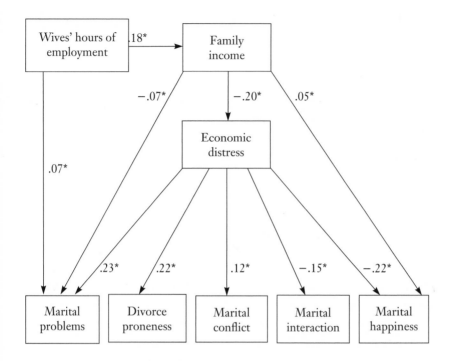

Significant indirect effects:

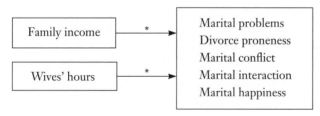

Figure 4.9   Path model showing direct and indirect associations among wives' hours of employment, family income, and dimensions of marital quality (*p < .05)

tions of hardship, and (3) perceptions of hardship affect marital quality. Although the model is based on the 2000 survey data, similar trends appeared in 1980. (To simplify the presentation, the figure excludes control variables and nonsignificant paths.) The figure reveals that wives' labor-force participation was positively related to family income as well as to marital problems. Family income was related to fewer marital problems, greater marital happiness, and less economic distress. Economic distress, in turn, was linked with all five marital outcomes.

More important, the figure demonstrates that the direct effects of wives' employment and family income were not as consistent as their indirect effects. The bottom part of the figure summarizes the significant indirect effects of these two variables on the five dimensions of marital quality. Family income (through lowering perceptions of economic distress) was related to increased happiness and interaction and lower conflict, problems, and divorce proneness. Similarly, wives' hours of employment (by increasing family income) appeared to have indirect effects on all five marital outcomes—raising happiness and interaction and lowering conflict, problems, and divorce proneness. Note that wives' income had a direct *positive* effect on marital problems and an indirect *negative* effect on marital problems. These results reveal the complexity of understanding the effect of wives' labor-force participation on marital quality. On the one hand, wives' full-time employment has the potential to improve marital quality by increasing income and lowering perceptions of economic distress. On the other hand, wives' long hours of employment can exacerbate work-family conflict and create other problems within the marriage. For example, with family income held constant, an increase in wives' hours of employment can result in a *lower* standard of living, given that wives' jobs often create extra expenses, such as greater child-care costs. The decomposition analysis described in Appendix 1 focuses on direct effects, so the indirect effects of distal variables (such as wives' hours of employment and family income) are largely captured by more proximal variables (such as perceptions of economic hardship).

Summary of Changes in Economic Well-Being

Married couples were substantially better off in 2000 than they were in 1980. Total family income increased, the value of accumulated assets rose, home ownership went up, and the use of public assistance went down. Clearly, many families benefited from the large-scale expansion of the U.S. economy during the 1990s. Most of these benefits accrued to dual-earner families, however, rather than to single-earner families. For this reason, dual-earner couples cashed in on the economic good times of the 1990s, whereas many traditional single-earner families, especially those with poorly educated husbands, fell further behind. Somewhat paradoxically, we also found that people's perceptions of economic well-being increased only slightly during this period of strong economic growth. Apparently, people's expectations about what constitutes an acceptable standard of living rose along with their incomes.

We assumed that improvements in economic well-being during this time had positive implications for marriage. Our results for three economic variables—family income, public assistance, and perceived economic distress—were noteworthy. Taken together, changes in these variables between 1980 and 2000 were associated with an increase of .04 of a standard deviation in the mean level of marital happiness in the population and an increase of .03 of a standard deviation in the mean level of marital interaction in the population. Corresponding to these changes were reductions in marital conflict (.02), marital problems (.02), and divorce proneness (.02). Interestingly, perceived economic distress became a more powerful predictor of marital quality between 1980 and 2000. Presumably, as the average level of family prosperity increased, spouses who felt left behind became increasingly stressed. Nevertheless, general improvements in the economic well-being of married couples during the last two decades of the twentieth century had widespread, positive consequences for marital quality.

But good times do not last forever. After dramatic growth during the 1990s, the U.S. economy slowed during the early years of the twenty-first century, the value of the stock market plunged, and the unemployment rate increased. These changes are likely to have eroded many of the benefits experienced by married couples during the previous decade. Presumably, dual-earner couples fared better than did single-earner couples. As others have pointed out (Oppenheimer, 1997; Spain and Bianchi, 1996; White and Rogers, 2000), the employment of a second spouse helps to buffer the family against declines in income or the loss of a job on the part of the primary earner. Economic recessions, therefore, represent a greater threat to the economic well-being of single-earner couples than to that of dual-earner couples.

Conclusions

Our surveys are consistent with the research of others in revealing a continuing convergence in the economic roles of wives and husbands (Casper and Bianchi, 2002; White and Rogers, 2000). More spouses are in dual-earner marriages, and the demands of overtime work, travel, and evening meeting—demands that once were associated primarily with husbands' jobs—have become common in wives' jobs. At the beginning of this chapter, we suggested that the shift toward dual-earner marriage involved costs as well as benefits for couples. On the one hand, the increases in economic resources improved people's standard of living and lowered their perceptions of financial distress. A higher standard of living made it possible for couples to purchase more consumer goods, move into larger homes, enjoy a wider range of leisure interests, provide resources for the educational enrichment of their children, and save more for retirement or future medical needs. Wives with college degrees, in particular, were able to find jobs and careers that provided a high level of personal satisfaction. On the other hand, however, husbands and wives were more likely to report that their jobs interfered with family life in 2000 than in 1980. Dual-earner couples are likely to experience time constraints as they try to get home in time for dinner with their families, supervise their children's homework, get their children to bed on time, and reconnect emotionally with their spouses in the evening.

As husbands' and wives' economic roles continue to converge, both spouses may experience the emotional and physiological stress that sometimes accompanies the demands of paid employment. These demands, if excessive, can deplete the psychological resources of husbands and wives and limit their ability to maintain warm, supportive, and relaxed family environments for themselves and their children. Although men remain the primary breadwinners in most families, norms that once allowed tired husbands to withdraw from family life after dinner are eroding. Many men with demanding jobs like to relax in the evenings by reading or watching television (Repetti, 1989), but this option is less likely as an increasing number of employed wives depend on their husbands to help with food preparation, household chores, and child care after work.

Despite the vast literature on work-family stress, however, we found surprisingly little evidence that the increase in wives' hours of employment and work demands had generally negative consequences for marital quality. Of course, having a demanding job does not necessarily result in experiences of emotional distress or problems in family relationships. People can define job demands as stimulating challenges or onerous burdens, depending on a variety of individual and family characteristics. For example, the extent to which wives' work preferences are consistent with their employment status appears to be a factor that determines whether work is experienced as stressful and has negative consequences for family relationships. Our study indicates that wives' full-time employment is problematic mainly when wives are working to make ends meet and would prefer to work fewer hours or not at all— circumstances that became more common between 1980 and 2000. These wives tend to report general dissatisfaction with their jobs as well as an elevated number of difficulties in their marriages.

Another relevant factor is the extent to which husbands are supportive of their wives' participation in the labor force. We find that the great majority of husbands approve of their wives' jobs, and only a minority of husbands are concerned that their wives' jobs have a negative impact on family life. Nevertheless, when husbands do not approve of their wives' employment, or when husbands have concerns about the effects of their wives' jobs on family life, wives are less satisfied with their jobs as well as their marriages. Of course, the extent to which husbands provide practical support in the form of household chores and child care, rather than verbal approval and emotional support, is also likely to affect the level of stress experienced by employed wives—a topic we explore in Chapter 5.

Although wives' employment can have detrimental consequences for marital quality under certain conditions, it is important to note that the majority of spouses in dual-earner marriages (husbands as well as wives) felt that the husband's jobs interfered more with family life than did the wife's job. Moreover, interference from the husband's job was a stronger and more consistent predictor of poor marital quality than was interference from the wife's job. The research literature on work-family stress has focused primarily on wives' employment, presumably because the dramatic increase in wives' labor-force participation during the last several decades captured most of the attention. In contrast, our study suggests that researchers should give greater attention to the ways in which men's jobs pose challenges for marriage and family life.

Perhaps the most striking finding to emerge in this chapter is that the increase in wives' employment between 1980 and 2000 occurred in two groups of families that occupy distinct positions in the American class structure. In middle-class families, employed wives are well-educated, work disproportionately in managerial and professional positions, and earn relatively high incomes. Similarly, their husbands are well-educated, are employed mainly in managerial and professional positions, and earn above-average levels of income. These husbands and wives are career-oriented and expect to spend long hours at the office, work in the evenings occasionally, or take work-related trips out of town. Moreover, these couples are generally satisfied with their jobs, which suggests that they perceive their employment demands as challenges rather than burdens. Moreover, the sharing of career orientations appears to buffer these couples from job-related stress, and their combined income provides a substantial degree of economic security that minimizes the potentially harmful effects of economic problems. Our data suggest that the movement of these wives into full-time employment had generally beneficial consequences for marriages.

A different picture emerges, however, when we consider the increased labor-force participation of working-class wives. These wives do not have college degrees, earn a moderate level of income, are not typically employed in professional or managerial jobs, and have few work demands (or challenges, depending on one's point of view). Most of these wives are employed primarily to make ends meet, prefer to work fewer hours or not at all, and are either moderately satisfied or dissatisfied with their jobs. Moreover, their husbands do not have college degrees and earn relatively low incomes. These wives are employed not because they want to have careers, but because their husbands' earnings are insufficient to provide a desirable standard of living and a reasonable degree of economic security. Furthermore, these husbands and wives appear to be vulnerable to work-family strains that translate into lower marital quality. The increase in the percentage of these couples in the married population, therefore, has placed additional stress on many marriages.

These findings reveal that dual-earner arrangements do not have universally positive or negative consequences for marital quality—a conclusion that contradicts the two perspectives outlined at the beginning of this chapter. As we noted earlier, Ernest Burgess believed that the increase in wives' employment would facilitate the transition to companionate, mutually satisfying marriages. Many contemporary observers also have stressed the benefits of dual-earner marriage for marital quality (Blumstein and Schwartz, 1983; Coltrane, 1996; Deutsch,

1999; Risman and Johnson-Sumerford, 1998; Scanzoni, 1978). In contrast, other observers have stressed the potentially destabilizing effects of wives' employment (Becker, 1981; Parsons and Bales, 1955) and the potential for work-family conflict when both spouses hold full-time jobs (Booth, Johnson, White, and Edwards, 1984; Glass and Fujimoto, 1994; Repetti, 1989, 1994). Our analysis suggests that these perspective do not capture the full complexity of current work and family experiences, primarily because they do not take into account the differential effect of wives' employment in working-class and middle-class families. In general, dual-earner arrangements are linked with positive marital quality among middle-class couples and with negative marital quality among working-class couples. Although the additional income provided by working-class wives helps to improve the standard of living of their families, these financial benefits come with a steep price in the form of greater marital tension, low job satisfaction, and a desire on the part of many wives to decrease their hours of employment or return to full-time homemaking.

The rise of dual-earner marriages between 1980 and 2000 appears to have had costs as well as benefits for marital quality. Although these costs and benefits appear to have offset one another at the aggregate level, they are not distributed evenly throughout the married population. The shift from the specialized division of labor that characterized families in the 1950s to the dual-earner arrangements that characterized families at the end of the twentieth century produced losers as well as winners.

❧ 5

Changing Gender Relations in Marriage

$\mathcal{T}$HE REALIGNMENT OF GENDER relations within marriage represents one of the most important changes in family life during the last half century. In the 1950s breadwinner-homemaker marriages—in which husbands were responsible for earning income and wives were responsible for housework and child care—represented the dominant pattern. This form of marriage was not universal, of course, and many wives, especially those married to men with low earnings, spent much of their married lives in the labor force. Nevertheless, the breadwinner-homemaker model was the cultural ideal to which most couples aspired (Mintz and Kellogg, 1988).

During the second half of the twentieth century, the large-scale movement of wives and mothers into the labor force altered marriage in fundamental ways. As we pointed out in Chapter 3, about three-fourths of wives under age 55 are currently in the labor force. Furthermore, women are increasingly demonstrating a pattern of consistent attachment to their jobs, with most remaining in the labor force throughout the prime years of childbearing (Spain and Bianchi, 1996). The American public now views women's economic contributions to family life as being not only acceptable, but also desirable. Correspondingly, a majority of men and women now expect husbands to perform a greater share of household chores and child care than they did in the past (Thornton and Young-DeMarco, 2001).

Did the growing labor-force participation of wives precipitate a shift toward more egalitarian—and perhaps more emotionally satisfying—marriages? Are these new marriages happier and more stable than traditional marriages? As we reported in Chapter 4, the links between wives' employment and marital quality are complex. On the one hand, the increase in wives' hours of employment, especially among wives who worked 45 or more hours per week, was associated with a small decline in marital happiness in the population. On the other hand, increases in wives' earnings between 1980 and 2000 improved the economic well-being of most families, and this development appears to have had broadly positive consequences for marital quality. The trade-off between potential work-family conflict and a higher standard of living, however, appears to have worked more smoothly for middle-class couples than for working-class couples. Unlike middle-class wives who enjoy the status and challenges of professional careers, many working-class wives are employed primarily to offset their husbands' low earnings, are not satisfied with their jobs, and would prefer to be working fewer hours or not at all. Moreover, less affluent, working-class couples are less able to purchase services that offset the demands of two careers, such as high-quality child care, restaurant or take-out meals, and home cleaning. This constellation of factors appears to have made dual-earner arrangements less satisfying and more problematic for working-class couples than for middle-class couples. To understand these contrary effects better, it is necessary to delve more deeply into how wives' growing economic responsibilities are linked with gender arrangements within marriage.

In this chapter we explore changes in gender relations and the implications of these changes for marital quality. Specifically, we present data on wives' percentage of family earnings, spouses' attitudes toward the gender division of labor in marriage, husbands' share of housework and child care, perceptions of unfairness in the household division of labor, and the extent of decision-making equality between spouses. As in previous chapters, our presentation involves three steps. First, we describe how these factors changed between 1980 and 2000. Second, we show how gender arrangements are related to marital quality. And third, we use decomposition methods to understand how changes in gender relations between 1980 and 2000 were related to shifts in marital quality in the U.S. population during this period.

Changes in Gender Relations

Wives' Percentage of Family Income

In the previous chapter we described the substantial increase in wives' hours of employment between 1980 and 2000. This increase, combined with the rise in women's wages, led to a rise in wives' share of earned family income. Wives earned 21% of family income in 1980, on average, compared with 32% in 2000. (Family income is based on the total earned income of husbands and wives.) Figure 5.1 shows this trend in greater deal. In 1980 more than one-third of wives (37%) earned 0% of family income, compared with only 16% of wives in 2000. Correspondingly, there was a substantial increase in the percentage of wives earning between one-third and one-half of family income. The percentage of wives who earned more than their husbands was small in both surveys. Nevertheless, the percentage of wives earning 51% or more of family income rose from 4% in 1980 to 12% in 2000— a threefold increase. By this definition, at the beginning of the new millennium about one of every eight wives was the primary breadwinner. (Details on the variables described in this chapter are available in Table 7 in Appendix 2.)

Significant increases in wives' percentage of family income occurred for whites, blacks, and Latinas. The greatest degree of change occurred among whites, who increased their average share of family income from 19% to 31%. Corresponding increases were from 32% to 42% among blacks and from 23% to 30% among Latinas. Despite the general increase in wives' economic contributions to their families, black wives earned the largest percentage of family income in both survey years. This finding is consistent with the historical trend for black wives to have especially high rates of labor-force participation and for black men to be overrepresented in low-wage jobs or among the unemployed (Spain and Bianchi, 1996).

We considered the extent to which the increase in wives' percentage of family income between 1980 and 2000 was due to several factors, in-

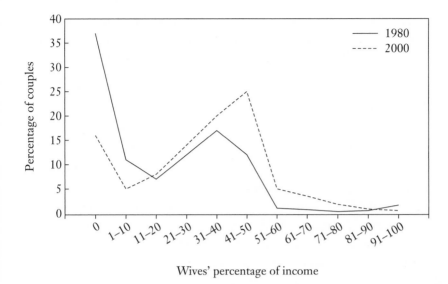

Figure 5.1 Frequency distribution of wives' percentage of family income, 1980 and 2000

cluding the increase in wives' education (noted in Chapter 3), the small decline in husbands' labor-force participation, the increase in wives' hours of employment, and the increase in wives' hourly earnings (all described in Chapter 4). Our analysis revealed that increases in wives' hours of employment and hourly earnings accounted for about three-fourths of the rise in wives' percentage of family income. In other words, wives contributed a greater share of family income in 2000, not only because they were working longer hours, but also because they were getting paid more for the hours they worked. Another 10% of the increase in wives' share of household income was due to the small increase in the proportion of husbands who were not in the labor force.

Wives' education was not a significant predictor of wives' percentage of family income. As we noted in Chapter 4, however, wives' education was positively associated with hourly earnings and hours of employment. Not surprisingly, well-educated women obtain better-paying jobs than do poorly educated women. Education also appears to increase the number of hours that wives spend in employment, presumably because the opportunity costs of not working are greater when wives have a high potential to earn income. The increase in wives' edu-

cation between 1980 and 2000 accounted for 17% of the increase in
wives' hourly earnings and 16% of the increase in wives' hours of employment during this period. In other words, improvements in wives'
education helped to raise wives' contributions to family income indirectly by increasing wives' hourly wages and hours of employment.

Attitudes toward Gender Arrangements in Marriage

By 2000 the majority of wives shared the breadwinner role with their
husbands. Did people's attitudes change in ways that acknowledged this
new reality? To assess spouses' attitudes, we asked people to respond to
a series of seven statements dealing with gender arrangements in marriage. Because women's roles changed more than men's roles in recent
decades, these statements focused mainly on wives' employment and
motherhood. The seven statements were:

1. A woman's most important task in life should be taking care of
   her children.
2. A husband should earn a larger salary than his wife.
3. If jobs are scarce, a woman whose husband can support her
   ought not to have a job.
4. Even though a wife works outside the home, the husband
   should be the main breadwinner and the wife should have the
   responsibility for the home and the children.
5. If his wife works full-time, a husband should share equally in
   household tasks, such as cooking, cleaning, and washing.
6. It should not bother the husband if a wife's job sometimes
   requires her to be away from home overnight.
7. A working mother can establish just as good a relationship with
   her children as a mother who does not work.

After hearing each statement, people indicated whether they disagreed
strongly, disagreed, agreed, or agreed strongly. People who agreed
with the first four statements and disagreed with the last three statements held relatively conservative views about gender roles; that is,
they supported the view that husbands should be breadwinners and
wives should be homemakers. In contrast, people who disagreed with
the first four statements and agreed with the last three statements held
relatively liberal views about gender roles.

Husbands became consistently less traditional between 1980 and

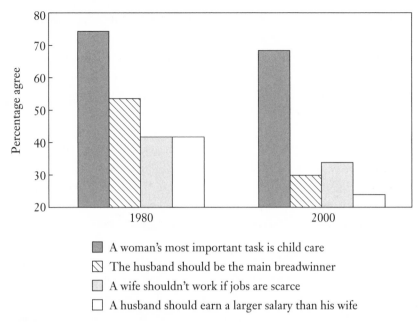

Figure 5.2 Husbands' traditional views of gender roles in marriage, 1980 and 2000

2000. Figure 5.2 shows the percentage of husbands who either agreed or strongly agreed with the first four statements about gender. Agreement with the statement that a woman's most important task in life should be taking care of her children declined from 75% in 1980 to 69% in 2000. Similarly, support for the belief that the husband should be the main breadwinner dropped from 54% to 30%. Agreement with the statement that a wife should not take a job if her husband can support her declined from 42% to 34%, and support for the belief that a husband should earn a larger salary than his wife dropped from 42% to 24%. Although they are not shown in the figure, corresponding changes occurred in husbands' responses to the three liberal statements. Between 1980 and 2000 support for the belief that a husband should share housework equally if his wife is employed increased from 91% to 95%. Similarly, agreement with the statement that it is okay for a wife's job to involve occasional overnight trips increased from 54% to 68%, and agreement with the statement that employed and non-employed wives can establish equally positive relationships with their children increased from 53% to 59%. Although not all these shifts in percentages were large, they reflected consistently growing support for wives' employment and the sharing of breadwinning and family responsibilities between spouses.

Even in 1980 relatively few husbands held consistently traditional attitudes toward gender roles in marriage. For example, only 11% of husbands gave conservative responses to at least six of the seven statements in that year. By 2000, however, only 4% of husbands gave conservative responses to at least six statements. Correspondingly, the percentage of husbands who gave liberal responses to six or seven items increased from 22% in 1980 to 36% in 2000. Although husbands became less traditional in their attitudes during the 1980s and 1990s, it is important to note that the majority of men held a mix of liberal and conservative views in both years, which suggests some ambivalence in men's attitudes.

In general, wives tended to be less traditional than husbands in their responses to these statements in both surveys. For example, wives were more likely than husbands to support the statement that it is okay for a wife's job to involve occasional overnight trips (80% of wives versus 68% of husbands in 2000) and the statement that employed wives can be just as close to their children as are nonemployed wives (74% of wives versus 59% of husbands in 2000). Nevertheless, wives' responses to these statements, like husbands' responses, revealed a general shift toward less traditional views about marital roles between 1980 and 2000.

To illustrate this trend, we combined the seven items into a single scale, with high scores indicating more traditional attitudes (alpha reliability = .61). To facilitate interpretation of this scale, we standardized the distribution of scores to have a mean of zero and a standard deviation of one. Figure 5.3 shows the mean scores of husbands and wives on this scale. Between 1980 and 2000 the mean score for husbands declined by .41 of a standard deviation, which represents a moderately large change. During this same period the mean score for wives declined by .31 of a standard deviation. Although the decline was somewhat larger for men than for women, the difference in the rate of change was not statistically significant. These results reveal that although husbands continue to be more traditional than wives in their attitudes toward marital roles, spouses of both genders adopted less traditional attitudes during this period.

It is informative to note that the mean score for husbands in 2000

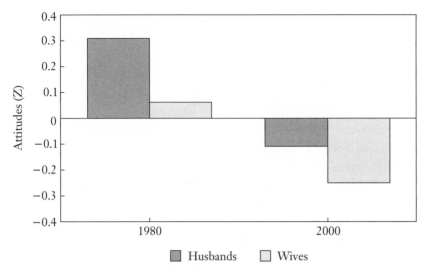

Figure 5.3   Husbands' and wives' mean scores on a scale of conservative gender attitudes, 1980 and 2000

was *lower* than the mean score for wives in 1980. That is, husbands in 2000, as a group, were less traditional in their views about gender than wives had been 20 years earlier. By the end of the 1990s, the majority of husbands believed that spouses should share breadwinning, that it is acceptable for a wife to earn more income than her husband, that a wife's employment does not interfere with her role as a mother, and that husbands should take on a greater share of the housework when their wives are employed. These attitudes represent a significant departure from the model of the breadwinner-homemaker family that dominated the 1950s.

Across both surveys, respondents held less traditional attitudes toward gender roles if they were younger rather than older. Our analysis indicated that this difference largely reflected a cohort effect (rather than an aging effect), with older respondents having been raised in an era when most people held traditional views about gender and marriage. Attitudes also were less traditional among well-educated than among poorly educated respondents. The association with education probably reflects the fact that well-educated individuals, because of their exposure to new perspectives in college, tend to hold less traditional views about a range of issues, including gender. Not surprisingly, spouses held less traditional attitudes when wives were employed full-time, although it is not clear if wives' employment is a cause or a consequence of these attitudes. People with children in the household—especially preschool children—tended to have more conservative views about gender roles. Once again, the causal direction between these two variables is unclear. Having traditional views about gender may lead couples to have children, or couples with young children may become more conventional in their views about gender. This latter possibility may occur because many married couples—even those with nontraditional views—adopt a more traditional division of labor following the birth of their first child (Coltrane, 2000; Cowan and Cowan, 1992). Finally, blacks held more traditional views than whites—a difference that held for husbands as well as wives. This finding was unexpected, because black couples are more likely than white couples to share breadwinning, as we noted in Chapter 4. The relatively high labor-force participation of black wives, however, may have more to do with financial need than with beliefs about the optimal division of labor between spouses. Finally, Latinos were no more or less traditional than whites. This finding appears to contradict the assumption, noted by some observers, that Latino men are relatively traditional in their views on gender (Oropesa and Gorman, 2000; Zinn and Wells, 2000).

Husbands' Share of Housework and Child Care

Some studies indicate that husbands have adopted a greater share of household labor in recent decades, although the amount of change has been modest rather than large (Coltrane, 2000; Robinson and Godbey, 1997). How large was this shift between 1980 and 2000? To answer this question, we asked respondents the following question: "In every family there are a lot of routine tasks that have to be done, such as cleaning the house, doing laundry, cooking meals, and cleaning up after meals. How much of this type of work is usually done by you?" (Note that the examples we provided all referred to traditionally female household tasks.) We coded people's responses to reflect the husband's approximate proportion of household labor: 0 = none, .25 = less than half, .50 = about half, .75 = more than half, and 1.00 = all of it. When respondents had children living in the household, we asked a second question about child care: "How much of the looking after children is done by you?" As we had with the question on housework, we coded people's responses to reflect the husband's approximate share of child care.

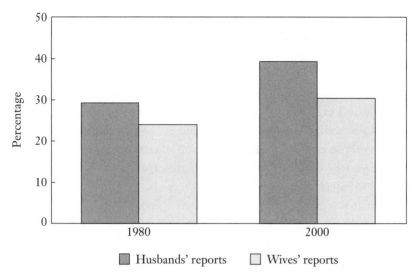

Figure 5.4 Percentage of housework performed by husbands: reports of husbands and wives, 1980 and 2000

Earlier in this chapter we reported that husbands as well as wives held less traditional attitudes toward gender in 2000 than in 1980. Men's reports of their share of housework increased during this period, which is consistent with this change in attitudes. Figure 5.4 shows the proportion of housework done by husbands in both surveys, as reported by husbands and wives. Husbands' reports of their share of housework increased from 29% in 1980 to 39% in 2000. Correspondingly, wives' reports of their husbands' share of housework increased from 24% to 30%. These figures are consistent with other national estimates, which suggest that husbands do about one-fourth to one-third of the housework these days (Lee, 2005; Presser, 1994; Robinson and Godbey, 1997; Shelton, 2000).

In both survey years, husbands reported doing a greater proportion of household chores than wives reported their husbands doing. Although husbands and wives in our surveys were not married to one another, this finding is comparable to results obtained from studies that have interviewed both spouses (Casper and Bianchi, 2002, chap. 5; Lee, 2005). The tendency for husbands to report doing more family work than wives acknowledge may reflect a self-serving bias, as husbands wish to present themselves in a positive light while being interviewed. In fairness to husbands, this difference also may reflect a respondent's point of view: respondents (husbands as well as wives) are aware of work that they have performed around the house that their spouses may not have observed.

Although the percentage of housework performed by husbands increased irrespective of which spouse was interviewed, the increase was significantly larger when reported by husbands than when reported by wives (as reflected in a significant interaction between the gender of the respondent and the decade of the survey). Nevertheless, the fact that wives also reported a significant increase indicates that this trend cannot be accounted for entirely by a desire on the part of husbands to present themselves in a positive light. Of course, it is likely that some of the increase reported by husbands was due to a decline in the number of chores performed by wives, rather than an increase in the number of chores performed by husbands. Compared with full-time homemakers, wives with full-time jobs may delegate more chores to older children, utilize housecleaning and laundry services more often, purchase food from restaurants more frequently, and simply get used to having the house less clean. The overall increase in men's *proportion* of housework, therefore, may reflect an increase in husbands' absolute hours of household work combined with a decrease in wives' absolute hours of household work—a trend documented in several studies (Berardo, Shehan, and Leslie, 1987; Coltrane, 2000).

We relied on wives' reports (which we assumed were less likely than husbands' reports to be affected by self-serving bias) to explore the shift in husbands' housework in greater detail. In 1980, 29% of wives reported that their husbands did not do any housework. By 2000, however, this figure had declined to 16%. Correspondingly, 22% of wives reported that their husbands did 50% or more of the housework in 1980—a figure that increased to 32% in 2000. In other words, by the end of the century, about one-third of wives reported an equal division of household chores with their husbands. Although the majority of married couples remain unequal in this respect, the percentage of husbands who share housework equally appears to be larger than many observers suggest (e.g., Deutsch, 1999; Hochschild, 1989; Shelton and John, 1996).

When we look only at couples with children in the household, fathers did slightly more child care in 2000 than in 1980. The increase in child care, however, was not as large as the increase in housework. Between surveys, the increase was 38% to 42% (based on fathers' reports) and 31% to 32% (based on mothers' reports). Although this increase was significant for fathers' reports, it was not for mothers'. The fact that mothers' and fathers' reports did not agree casts doubt on whether real change occurred during this time. Nevertheless, 34% of mothers claimed that their husbands did 50% of more of the child care in 2000. As was the case for housework, about one-third of couples these days appear to have an egalitarian division of child care.

The modest increase in fathers' share of child care clashes with the results of several other investigations (Pleck and Masciadrelli, 2004). For example, in a study based on time diaries, Sandberg and Hofferth (2001) found that paternal engagement with children doubled between 1981 and 1997. Comparing directly across studies is difficult, however, because researchers rely on different conceptual and operational definitions of father involvement. In our study the absence of an increase in men's share of child care may be due to several factors. Many couples continue to believe that child care is primarily the responsibility of mothers, and many fathers still feel uncomfortable in this role, especially with infants and children of preschool age (Cowan and Cowan, 1992). Moreover, the greater earnings of husbands, compared with wives, motivates some to invest more time in breadwinning than in caring for children. Until these circumstances change, it is unlikely that most fathers will provide the same level of child care that mothers do.

Other researchers have put forward three major explanations to account for variation between families in the amount of housework done by husbands. First, a time-availability perspective assumes that husbands' involvement in housework is negatively related to their hours of paid employment and positively related to their wives' hours of paid employment. In other words, the amount of household labor performed by husbands depends on the amount of time that husbands and wives have left over after returning from their jobs. Second, a resources (or power) perspective assumes that spouses who earn high incomes (and hence contribute disproportionately to their family's standard of living) are able to negotiate a smaller share of housework. And third, a social psychological perspective assumes that husbands who hold nontraditional, egalitarian attitudes about gender perform a larger share of housework then do husbands who hold traditional views. (For discussions of these three perspectives, see Casper and Bianchi, 2002; Coltrane, 1996, 2000; Shelton and John, 1996.)

With respect to housework, we found support for all three of these explanations, irrespective of whether husbands or wives served as respondents. Husbands performed a larger proportion of housework when they were employed fewer hours and when their wives were employed longer hours which is consistent with the time-availability perspective. Husbands performed less housework when they earned the largest share of income, when husbands' and wives' hours of employment were held constant, a finding that conforms to the power perspective. And finally, husbands performed a greater share of housework when they (or their wives) held nontraditional attitudes about gender. All three of these factors made independent contributions to the proportion of housework done by husbands. In addition, husbands' and wives' years of education were positively associated with the husband's share of housework, independent of spouses' hours of employment, wives' percentage of family income, and gender attitudes.

These variables accounted for 42% of the two-decade increase in husbands' reports of housework, and nearly one-half (48%) of the increase in wives' reports of husbands' housework. In other words, husbands appear to have increased their share of housework between 1980 and 2000 because wives worked longer hours, wives earned a larger share of household income, spouses became more egalitarian in their gender attitudes, and spouses' years of education increased. Even with these variables taken into account, however, the increase in husbands' share of housework continued to be significant, which suggests that other factors not considered here also contributed to this process. The same variables that predicted men's share of housework also predicted their share of child care. Among couples with children, the proportion of child care done by husbands was negatively related to husbands' hours of employment, positively related to wives' hours of employment, positively related to wives' share of income, positively related to husbands' (and wives') nontraditional attitudes toward gender, and positively related to husbands' and wives' years of education. Moreover, these results did not depend on whether husbands or wives served as respondents. Once again, these results suggest that men's share of family work is related to time availability, power, and attitudes about gender.

We also considered racial and ethnic variations in housework. Black and Latino husbands both performed more housework than did white husbands. The result for black men is consistent with our report in Chapter 4 that black wives had the highest rate of labor-force participation of any racial or ethnic group. With respect to Hispanics, our results clash with the commonly held imagine of traditionally masculine Latino men (Oropesa and Gorman, 2000)—a finding consistent with our results for gender attitudes, as noted earlier. The macho image associated with Latino husbands may be more of a stereotype than a reality.

Perceived Unfairness in the Household Division of Labor

Some observers have argued that marital disagreements these days are especially likely to revolve around issues of fairness and justice, with the household division of labor being a key source of contention between spouses (Sabatelli and Ripoll, 2004). To address this issue, we asked respondents if they felt that the division of housework between spouses was "about right," "unfair to you," or "unfair to your spouse." For respondents with children in the household, we asked a similar question about the division of child care between spouses. Because few people reported that the household division of labor was unfair to their spouses, we have omitted this response from the present discussion.

Figure 5.5 shows the percentage of husbands and wives who felt that the division of housework or child care was unfair to them. With respect to housework, wives were considerably more likely than husbands to report unfairness. In 1980 only 3% of husbands felt that they were doing more than their fair share of housework, compared with one-fourth of wives. Similarly, mothers were substantially more likely than fathers to feel that they were doing more than their fair share of child care. In 1980 only 1% of fathers reported that the division of child care was unfair to them, compared with 18% of mothers. These findings are consistent with earlier research showing that wives are more likely than husbands to view housework and child care as sources of marital friction (Hochschild, 1989; Thompson, 1991). These findings also are consistent with recent time diary studies showing that wives have less daily leisure time than do husbands, which is likely to be a source of frustration for wives (Mattingly and Bianchi, 2003).

Between 1980 and 2000 the percentage of husbands who reported doing more than their fair share of housework increased slightly but

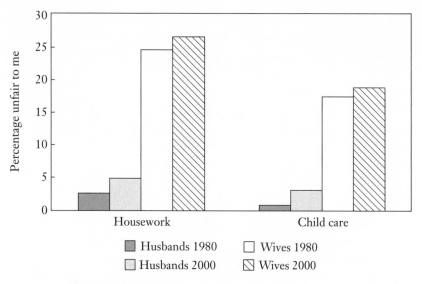

Figure 5.5 Division of household labor is unfair to me: views of husbands and wives, 1980 and 2000

significantly to 5%. Although the percentage of wives who reported doing more than their fair share of housework increased to 27%, this change was not significant. Similarly, the percentage of fathers who felt that the division of child care was unfair to them increased slightly but significantly to 3%. Mothers, in contrast, were no more likely to report that the division of child care was unfair in 2000 than in 1980. Given that men's share of housework increased between surveys, one might have expected wives' perceptions of unfairness to have declined. Of course, wives' labor-force participation also increased during this period, which probably raised their expectations for sharing family work with their husbands. Nevertheless, it is useful to note that the majority of wives (as well as the majority of husbands) in both time periods did *not* view the division of family labor as problematic—a finding that is consistent with earlier research (Coltrane, 2000; Shelton and John, 1996).

Figure 5.5 also reveals that wives were more likely to feel that the division of housework is unfair than they were to feel that the division of child care is unfair. Of course, the data for housework in this figure are based on all respondents, whereas the data on child care are based only on respondents with children, so the two sets of results are not strictly comparable. Nevertheless, the same pattern emerged when we restricted the analysis to couples with children in the household. In 2000, 29% of mothers felt that the division of housework was unfair, whereas only 19% of mothers felt that the division of child care was unfair. This finding is of interest, given that men were doing similar proportions of housework and child care: about one-third in each case. Apparently, some mothers feel that they are doing more than their fair share of housework but not more than their fair share of child care, despite the fact that their husbands are doing about the same proportion of work in each domain. This discrepancy may occur because some mothers believe that they are better suited than their husbands to care for children and, hence, do not mind doing most of the child care. Moreover, caring for children is probably more enjoyable than doing mundane household chores, such as washing dishes, ironing, and vacuuming. Consequently, even though some mothers are comfortable being their children's primary caregivers, they may resent the fact that their husbands are reluctant to take on a greater share of everyday housework (see Deutsch, 1999, for a discussion of this issue).

We also looked at the factors that lead wives to feel that the division of household labor is unfair. Not surprisingly, the percentage of housework performed by husbands was the best predictor of wives' perceptions of unfairness. For example, when wives reported that their husbands performed no housework at all, 59% felt that the division of housework was unfair. In contrast, only 5% of wives felt that the division of housework was unfair when their husbands performed half or more of the housework. This finding is consistent with common sense, as well as a number of earlier investigations (Blair and Johnson, 1992; Sanchez, 1994).

Another factor that was closely associated with wives' perceptions of unfairness was the number of hours that wives spent in the labor force. The more hours that wives spent in employment, the more likely they were to feel that the division of housework was unfair. In addition, wives were more likely to report unfairness if they earned a relatively high income, had children living in the household, were well educated, and held nontraditional gender attitudes. As the power perspective suggests, wives who earn a substantial share of family income may feel that their economic contributions entitle them to do less housework, and they are likely to be unhappy if their husbands do not share the labor equitably. Obviously, children require a great deal of care and supervision. In addition to direct care, having children in the household means that more food must be prepared, more dishes need to be washed, more clothes have to be laundered, rooms must be cleaned more often, and more shopping has to be done. Because children create substantially more housework, it is not surprising that their presence increases wives' perceptions that they are unfairly overworked. With respect to education, well-educated wives may have more egalitarian expectations for the household division of labor—expectations that many husbands (even well-educated husbands) may fail to meet. And, of course, wives who hold nontraditional views about the household division of labor are likely to be especially disappointed when their husbands do not share housework equitably.

We also looked at the factors that predict mothers' feelings of unfairness with the division of child care. As was true of our findings for housework, the best predictor of a woman's feelings of unfairness was the husband's share of child care. For example, 58% of mothers felt that the division of child care was unfair when fathers did no child care at all, whereas only 3% of mothers felt this way when fathers did half of the child care. In addition, mothers with children of preschool age (0–4) reported more unfairness than did mothers with children of primary school age (5–12) or adolescents (13–18). Given that young children demand a great deal of parents' time, this finding is not surprising. Moreover, fathers tend to become increasingly involved as their children grow older (Amato, 1989; Deutsch, 1999). Other than these trends, however, we were unable to locate factors associated with mothers' feelings of unfairness in the division of child care. As we noted earlier, norms about mothers' special responsibilities for children probably reduce mothers' perceptions of unfairness about child care in comparison to their perceptions of unfairness over housework.

As we noted earlier, wives are not only increasing their participation in the labor force, but also earning a growing share of total family income. Yet many employed wives come home from their paid jobs every day to cook dinner, wash dishes, and clean the house—a phenomenon that Arlie Hochschild (1989) referred to as the "second shift." According to Hochschild, doing the second shift is a major source of feelings of unfairness and distress among wives and a common source of tension and disagreement between spouses.

These considerations lead to two interesting questions: What percentage of wives are burdened with a second shift? And has this percentage changed over time? To answer these questions, we focused only on wives with full-time jobs, that is, wives who spent 35 or more hours per week in paid employment. Presumably, wives with part-time jobs are less likely than wives with full-time jobs to feel that doing most of the housework is unfair. We also required that the difference between husbands' and wives' work hours be no greater than five. For example, if a wife is employed 40 hours per week and her husband is employed 50 hours per week, then it would not be unreasonable for the husband to do somewhat less than half of the housework. But if a wife is employed 40 hours per week and her husband is employed 43 hours per week, then she might reasonably expect her husband to do about half of the housework. Finally, for couples without children, we assumed that wives did a second shift when their husbands did less than 50% of the housework. For couples with children, however, wives did a second shift when their husbands did less than 50% of housework *and* less than 50% of child care.

Figure 5.6 shows the result of this examination. The left-hand side of the figure shows that 41% of all wives in full-time employment in 1980 reported doing a second shift, compared with 32% in 2000. In contrast, 35% of all husbands reported that their wives did a second shift in 1980, compared with 20% in 2000. Although wives were more likely than husbands to report doing a second shift, the decline across decades was significant for spouses of both genders. Apparently, the increase in men's share of housework more than offset the increase in the number of hours that wives were employed, leading to an overall decline in the percentage of wives burdened with a second shift. Irrespective of decade, however, wives doing a second shift were considerably more likely than other wives to view the household division of labor as unfair (47% versus 25%). Perhaps more interesting is the fact that slightly more than half of wives performing a second shift did *not* see this arrangement as unfair.

Given the different perceptions of husbands and wives, it is not possible to give a definitive estimate of the percentage of wives who performed a second shift. The estimate also depends on which women are included in the denominator. As we noted earlier, if we use wives' reports and count only wives who are in full-time employment, then

Figure 5.6 Percentage of dual-earner couples in which wives did a second shift or had an egalitarian division of labor, 1980 and 2000

about one-third (32%) were doing a second shift in 2000. If we count *all employed wives,* including those working less than full-time, then the percentage of wives doing a second shift declines to 25%. And if we count *all wives,* irrespective of employment status, then the figure declines to 20%. No matter how the calculations are made, however, it is clear that the large majority of married women do not experience a second shift.

These considerations lead to an additional question of interest: What percentage of husbands are doing a second shift? To address this question, we used a procedure similar to the one described earlier for wives. Husbands doing a second shift worked full-time, about the same number of hours as their wives (or more), did 50% or more of the housework, and, if they had children, did 50% or more of the child care. Based on husbands' reports, 2% of men were doing a second shift in 1980, compared with 4% in 2000—a small but significant increase. In contrast, 2% of wives in both surveys reported that their husbands were doing a second shift. Clearly, the percentage of husbands burdened with a second shift is small, regardless of the source of data or decade. Nevertheless, husbands who did a second shift were considerably more likely than other husbands to feel that the household division of labor was unfair to them. Specifically, 20% of husbands doing a second shift reported unfairness, compared with only 4% of other husbands. But like wives, the majority of husbands doing a second shift did not feel that the division of labor was unfair. Apparently, feelings of fairness—for husbands as well as wives—are based on more than objective circumstances.

The right-hand side of the figure shows a different trend: the percentage of couples who reported an egalitarian division of labor. These couples spent about the same amount of time in the paid labor force (within five hours), shared housework equally, and shared child care equally if they had children. Based on husbands' reports, the percentage of egalitarian couples increased from 15% to 23% between surveys. The corresponding figures for wives were 13% and 17%. Although fewer wives than husbands reported an egalitarian division of labor, the percentages increased no matter which spouses served as the respondent. Taken together, our results demonstrate a decline in second-shift arrangements and an increase in egalitarian arrangements between 1980 and 2000. (The remaining couples, not represented in the figure, had a division of labor that was somewhere between the exploitive, second-shift pattern and the equalitarian pattern.)

Decision Making

In the middle of the twentieth century, most people believed that the husband should be the head of the household and, hence, should have more power than wives to make key decisions. Since then, wives have increased their share of family income, as we pointed out earlier in this chapter. Economic resources are a basis of marital power, and wives often expect (and get) more decision-making power when they make financial contributions to the marriage (Blumberg and Coleman, 1989). Moreover, the feminist movement fundamentally challenged the notion that the husband is the head of the household. Most people these days believe that egalitarian marriages, in which decision-making power is shared equally between spouses, are preferable to traditional patriarchal arrangements (Thornton and Young-DeMarco, 2001).

Deciding whether the husband or the wife has more power in a marriage is a difficult task. Although researchers disagree about how marital power should be measured, "final word" measures continue to be the most commonly used method for assessing this construct (Mizan,

1994). Following this tradition, we relied on three questions to assess marital power. We began by asking: "Now I would like you to take a minute and think about the way decisions are made at your house. Are there any kind of decisions made in your house in which your decision is the final word? What about your spouse? Are there kinds of decisions in which his/her decision is the final word?" We followed these questions with a final item: "Overall, considering all the types of decisions you two make, does your spouse more often have the final word or do you?"

The responses to these questions revealed an unmistakable trend away from patriarchal marriages. With respect to the question about one spouse having the final word for certain types of decisions, respondents of both genders were less likely to report that husbands had the final word in 2000 than in 1980. For example, in the earlier survey, 70% of husbands reported that they sometimes had the final word, compared with 61% of husbands in the later survey. Husbands' reports that their wives sometimes had the final word also declined across surveys, from 37% to 30%. In contrast, wives' reports that they sometimes had the final word increased across surveys, from 63% to 70%. (This difference represents a significant interaction between the gender of the respondent and decade.) These findings indicate that husbands moved toward greater equality by reporting less decision making on the part of either spouse, whereas wives moved toward greater equality by reporting less decision making on their husbands' part and more decision making on their own part.

Irrespective of decade, most husbands and wives reported that they had the final word with respect to some decisions and that their spouses had the final word with respect to other decisions. In 2000, for example, 61% of husbands and 74% of wives reported that husbands sometimes had the final word, and 65% of husbands and 70% of wives reported that wives sometimes had the final word. These results are consistent with other studies of family decision making, which suggest that many husbands and wives have different spheres of interest and influence. In an early and influential study, Blood and Wolfe (1965) noted that wives typically made decisions about household matters (such as choice of meals), husbands typically made decisions about large purchases (such as a new car), and spouses jointly made decisions about other matters (such as where to go on a vacation). Although the pattern

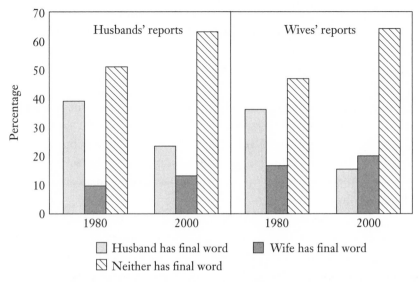

Figure 5.7   Percentage of husbands and wives reporting on who has the final word, 1980 and 2000

of decision making may be less stereotypical now than in the past, it appears that most husbands and wives continue to have particular areas of expertise in which their word is final.

The shift toward more egalitarian decision making is especially clear when we turn to people's responses to the question on who has the final word most often. Figure 5.7 shows the percentage of spouses in both surveys who reported that husbands usually have the final word, that wives usually have the final word, or that decision making is equal. The trends over time for husbands and wives were similar. Between 1980 and 2000 the percentage of spouses who reported that husbands usually have the final word declined, whereas the percentage of people who reported that neither spouse had the final word increased. The small increase in the percentage of spouses reporting that wives had more power was significant but relatively small. Overall, husbands' reports of equal decision making increased from 51% to 63%, and wives' reports increased from 47% to 64%.

In both decades people's gender attitudes (described earlier in this chapter) were associated with greater equality in decision making. Husbands as well as wives who held conservative views about gender arrangements were less likely to report egalitarian decision making and more likely to report that husbands generally had the final word. The amount of housework done by husbands also was associated with equal decision making in both surveys: The more housework husbands did, the more likely spouses were to report equal decision making. Apparently, couples who shared decision making tended to share housework as well. The percentage of income earned by wives was not related to decision-making equality—a finding that contradicts the assumption that wives' marital power is based on their economic contributions. Instead, wives' decision-making power appeared to be based more on spouses' attitudes toward gender roles in marriage than on spouses' share of household earnings.

Other variables associated with decision-making equality varied with the year of the survey. In 2000 couples were more likely to report equality if they were childless than if they had children, were Latino rather than white, and had a high rather than a low level of family income. Earlier studies have shown that the transition to parenthood is associated with a more traditional division of family labor, even among couples who begin their marriages with relatively egalitarian attitudes (Coltrane, 2000; Cowan and Cowan, 1992). Our data suggest that having children is associated with more traditional power arrangements in the family as well. Our results for ethnicity contradict the notion that Latino men are relatively domineering and traditional in their gender orientations—a view that may be more of a stereotype than a reality, as we noted earlier in this chapter. Finally, our results for income suggest that economic security facilitates power sharing between spouses. Perhaps decision making is easier when economic resources are plentiful. After all, deciding whether to take a family vacation in the Caribbean or the South Pacific seems less urgent than deciding whether to spend extra money at the end of the month on repairing the family car or fixing a hole in the roof. Moreover, couples with abundant economic resources can outsource some household chores (such as cleaning, laundry, and yard work), thereby reducing disagreements about which spouse should do this labor.

We also asked individuals how satisfied they were with the amount of influence they had in family decision making. The differences across decades were small, but the trends differed for husbands and wives. Between 1980 and 2000 the percentage of husbands who felt dissatisfied with decision making *increased* from 2% to 4%, whereas the percentage of wives who felt dissatisfied *decreased* from 8% to 4%. (Both differences were statistically significant, as was the interaction between gender of respondent and decade.) These trends in dissatisfaction mirror the decline in men's decision-making power and the increase in women's decision-making power, noted earlier. Nevertheless, it is important to keep in mind that the great majority of husbands and wives were satisfied with how decisions are made in their households. Dissatisfaction over decision making does not appear to be a salient issue for the great majority of American couples.

Summary of Changes in Gender Relations

Between 1980 and 2000 gender relations within marriage continued to shift away from the patriarchal breadwinner-homemaker model and toward a new model involving joint breadwinning, shared family work, and equal decision making. Women's contributions to family income increased during this period, and by the end of the twentieth century one of eight wives earned more income than her husband. Correspondingly, men's share of housework increased, and by 2000 one of three husbands performed one-half (or more) of the household chores and child care. Furthermore, equal decision making (rather than husbands having the final word) became the norm in the majority of marriages. Bolstering these changes in behaviors were changes in attitudes; men as well as women became less conservative in their beliefs about wives' employment, wives' earnings, and men's share of housework. Taken together, these findings provide strong evidence that American marriages became substantially less patriarchal during the last two decades of the twentieth century.

Gender Relations and Marital Quality

As we pointed out earlier in this book, many observers have argued that gender equality is a prerequisite for the development of closeness and intimacy in marriage. If this perspective is accurate, then the shift away from the patriarchal breadwinner-homemaker model of marriage should have brought about general improvements in the quality of marital relationships. This view stands in contrast to that of an earlier generation of scholars, who believed that the specialization of roles within marriage, and the identification of the husband as the head of the household, is critical for maintaining a high level of marital quality and stability. If this earlier perspective is valid, then the shift away from the patriarchal breadwinner-homemaker model of marriage should have brought about general declines in the quality of marital relationships. We compare these contrasting predictions in the remainder of this chapter.

Wives' Percentage of Family Income and Marital Quality

Some studies have shown that wives' proportion of family income is positively associated with divorce, whereas other studies suggest that the relationship is negative or curvilinear. (See Rogers, 2004, for a review.) The complex nature of findings in this research literature makes it difficult to predict how wives' proportion of income might be related to marital quality. We found in this study that wives' proportion of income was not related to any dimension of marital quality, including divorce proneness, in 1980 or 2000. We also considered the possibility that these associations differed for husbands and wives, but the interaction between the respondent's gender and wives' income was not significant for any marital outcome. Corresponding to these null findings, the indication of our decomposition analysis was that the increase in wives' proportion of family income was not associated with shifts in marital quality during this period. Overall, our study suggests that the increase in the proportion of family income generated by wives had few implications for marital quality.

Husbands' Share of Housework and Marital Quality

Some research suggests that marriages tend to be happier and more stable when husbands do a substantial share of housework (Coltrane, 2000; Kalmijn, 1999; Pleck and Masciadrelli, 2004). Our finding, which is consistent with this prior work, is that the husband's share of housework was related to greater marital interaction in 1980 as well as in 2000. This association may occur because men who do substantial amounts of housework also value sharing leisure time with their spouses. Correspondingly, wives may appreciate their husbands' company more when their husbands perform a greater share of housework.

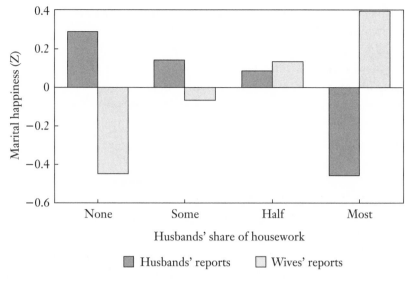

Figure 5.8   Adjusted mean level of marital happiness by gender and husbands' share of housework, 2000

Other links between housework and marital quality were obscured, however, when we combined wives and husbands in the same analysis. In 2000, among wives, the husband's share of housework was associated with greater marital happiness, fewer marital problems, and less divorce proneness. In contrast, among husbands, the husband's share of housework was associated with lower marital happiness, more marital problems, and higher divorce proneness. (These findings reflect significant interactions between the gender of the respondent and the husband's share of housework.) The same trends—although not as pronounced—were present in 1980. In general, when husbands did a substantial amount of housework, wives tended to experience better marital quality and husbands tended to experience worse marital quality.

Figure 5.8 illustrates this pattern with respect to marital happiness. Wives who reported that their husbands did "none" of the housework were generally unhappy with their marriages, which is reflected in a mean Z score of −.45. Wives who reported that their husbands did "some" or "about half" of the housework were moderately happy with their marriages. And wives who reported that their husbands did "most" of the housework were very happy, with a mean Z score of +.4. The difference between wives with husbands who did no housework and wives with husbands who did most of the housework was six-sevenths of a standard deviation—a very large effect size. In contrast, husbands who did no housework were relatively happy with their marriages, whereas husbands who did most of the housework were relatively unhappy. The difference between these two groups of husbands represented three-fourths of a standard deviation—also a very large effect size. The patterns for marital problems and divorce proneness were nearly identical in direction and magnitude.

In general, these results suggest that no one likes to do housework, and that when one spouse does substantially more than the other, bad feelings spill over and affect the quality of the marriage. Correspondingly, when the burden of housework is shared, each spouse is likely to appreciate the other spouse's contribution, and there may be more leisure time for shared activities. Interestingly, Figure 5.8 indicates that it was only when husbands and wives shared housework equally that husbands as well as wives had above-average levels of marital happiness (that is, scores higher than 0). In other words, this was the situation that produced the maximum *joint* benefit for spouses.

Although the increase in men's share of housework appeared to have different implications for husbands and wives, the positive associations with marital interaction were consistent irrespective of gender. For this reason, the decomposition analysis revealed that the increase in husbands' share of housework between 1980 and 2000 was associated with an increase in marital interaction in the population equivalent to .04 of a standard deviation.

Results for the husband's share of child care were similar to the results for the husband's share of housework. In general, as fathers did more child care, mothers became happier with their marriages and fathers became less happy—a pattern that appeared in 1980 as well as in 2000. Although caring for children may be more rewarding than doing ironing and washing dishes, it still involves a great deal of hard work, and most mothers appreciate sharing this labor with their husbands. Moreover, when fathers do little or no child care, mothers may interpret this behavior as a lack of concern for the children. Most people value fathers' involvement, not only because it is fair to mothers, but also because it promotes children's development. To the extent that fathers are disengaged from their children, mothers are likely to feel that their husbands are poor fathers. The implications of paternal non-involvement are strong. In 2000, for example, mothers who reported that their husbands did little or no child care scored more than two-thirds of a standard deviation below the mean in marital happiness and two-thirds of a standard deviation above the mean in divorce proneness. These findings represent very strong estimated effects.

Attitudes toward Gender and Marital Quality

Earlier studies suggest that the links between gender attitudes and marital quality differ for men and women. For example, a longitudinal study by Amato and Booth (1995) found that husbands became happier with their marriages if they adopted more liberal views toward gender. In contrast, wives who adopted more liberal views toward gender became less happy with their marriages.

Our data revealed that people with conservative views about gender tended to have poorer-quality marriages in 1980 as well as in 2000. In particular, holding conservative attitudes was associated with less marital happiness, less marital interaction, and more marital problems. Contrary to studies cited earlier, these trends were similar for husbands and wives. These findings suggest that traditional beliefs about the roles of men and women no longer fit well with the realities of contemporary married life. As we noted in Chapter 4, between 1980 and 2000 the percentage of wives in the labor force increased, as did wives' earnings. During this time economic opportunities for men—especially young men without college degrees—declined, so fewer husbands were able to be the sole breadwinner for their families. With three-fourths of wives being employed in 2000 (mostly in full-time jobs), spouses who value the breadwinner-homemaker model of marriage are likely to experience a clash between their expectations and their ability to enact these traditional roles. In fact, it was primarily when spouses held conservative views about gender and wives were employed full-time that marital happiness was low and marital problems were elevated, and this was true in both time periods.

Figure 5.9 shows how marital happiness varied with wives' attitudes toward gender roles in marriage and wives' employment status in 2000. In some respects, the links between marital happiness and employment were similar for wives with traditional and nontraditional attitudes. For both groups, marital happiness was highest when wives worked part-

Figure 5.9   Wives' adjusted mean level of marital happiness by wives'
employment and gender attitudes, 2000

time. Marital happiness was especially low, however, among wives who
held traditional views and were employed full-time. Part-time employment among wives is not contrary to a traditional model of marriage,
because it still allows husbands be the primary breadwinner and wives
to be the primary homemaker. Full-time employment among wives, in
contrast, is inconsistent with a specialized marital division of labor. As
we noted earlier, the pattern in Figure 5.9 was similar for husbands and
wives. Presumably, wives' full-time employment threatens traditional
men's claims to be breadwinners (with all of the responsibilities and
privileges this implies), just as it threatens traditional women's desires
to be full-time homemakers and mothers with their own responsibilities and privileges.

   Because traditional attitudes toward gender were associated with
lower marital quality, and because attitudes became less traditional during these decades, the overall estimated consequences for marital quality were positive. Our decomposition analysis indicated that attitude
change was associated with an increase in marital happiness (.03 of a
standard deviation), an increase in interaction (.02 of a standard deviation), and a decrease in marital problems (.02 of a standard deviation)
in the population.

Perceived Unfairness and Marital Quality

Like other research (Coltrane, 2000; Perry-Jenkins and Folk, 1994), our surveys revealed that spouses who felt that the household division of labor was unfair to them reported consistently poorer marital quality than did spouses who felt otherwise. Irrespective of the year of the survey, people who felt that current arrangements were unfair were less happy with their marriages, engaged in less interaction with their spouses, experienced more conflict with their spouses, perceived more problems in their marriages, and had higher levels of divorce proneness. These effect sizes were large; the differences between people who did and did not feel that the household division of labor was unfair ranged between one-half and three-fourths of a standard deviation. These associations were equally strong in both decades and were as pronounced for husbands as they were for wives. That is, husbands who felt that the household division of labor was unfair to them reported levels of marital quality that were comparable to those of wives who felt unfairly treated. Moreover, the source of these reports was relatively unimportant. That is, whether the husband or the wife was interviewed, if the respondent reported that either spouse felt that the division of labor was unfair, marital quality tended to be lower.

Of course, as we noted earlier in this chapter, wives were more likely than husbands to feel that the division of labor was unfair, so perceived unfairness was more likely to affect the marital quality of wives than of husbands. The percentage of wives who reported unfairness, however, did not increase between decades, whereas the percentage of husbands who reported unfairness increased modestly but significantly. For this reason, the decomposition analysis indicated that the change in men's experiences of unfairness was associated with a small decline in marital happiness (.01 of a standard deviation), and small increases in conflict, problems, and divorce proneness (.01 of a standard deviation in each case).

Perceptions of unfairness with child care yielded similar results. Individuals who felt that the division of child care was unfair to them (compared with individuals who felt that the division of child care was fair) reported less happiness, less interaction, more conflict, more problems, and more divorce proneness. In fact, unfairness with child care was associated more strongly with marital quality than was unfairness with housework. For example, in 2000 individuals who felt that child-care arrangements were unfair scored a full standard deviation lower in marital happiness. Once again, these findings held for husbands as well as wives, although wives were more likely than husbands to report unfairness.

Regardless of gender, perceptions of unfairness in family labor appear to seriously erode marital quality. These findings are consistent with several other studies (Greenstein, 1996; Hochschild, 1989; Perry-Jenkins and Folk, 1994; Pina and Bengtson, 1993) and support feminist scholars who argue that housework and child care are major sources of contention in contemporary marriages (Thompson and Walker, 1991). As we noted earlier, men who do more housework tend to be less happy with their marriages. Nevertheless, our data also suggest that men's performance of housework improves their wives' sense of fairness, raises their wives' happiness with the marriage, and increases marital stability. Housework may be contested terrain in contemporary marriages, but the general benefits of sharing household labor equitably appear to be substantial for wives.

Decision Making and Marital Quality

In 1980 and well as in 2000, equal decision making (that is, reporting that neither the husband nor the wife had the final word most often) was associated with the highest levels of marital quality. In particular, people who reported equal decision making (compared with people who reported that one spouse made most of the decisions) reported more marital happiness, more interaction, less conflict, fewer problems, and less divorce proneness. Moreover, this trend held for husbands as well as wives. Figure 5.10 illustrates the associations between decision-making equality and marital quality. For each marital outcome, the gap between those who practiced equality and those who did not was about one-fourth of a standard deviation. Although these effect sizes were moderate, the consistency and pervasiveness of this factor across all dimensions of marital quality was impressive.

Some gender variations in the links between equality and marital quality were apparent. Husbands reported the most positive marital

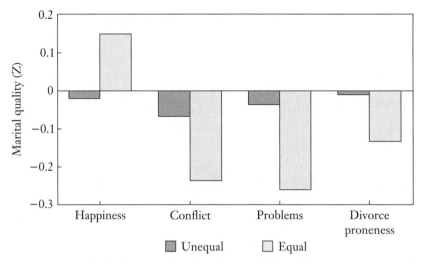

Figure 5.10 Adjusted mean level of marital quality by equal decision making, 2000

quality when decision making was equal, the second-highest level of marital quality when they had the most power, and the lowest level of marital quality when their wives had the most power. Women reported the highest marital quality when decision making was equal and low levels of marital quality when either they or their husbands had more power. The two genders differed, therefore, in how they reacted to male power; women were less comfortable than men when husbands made most of the decisions. Once again, these findings suggest that some husbands continue to value traditional male power within marriage. Women, in contrast, do not like the exercise of unilateral power in marriage, even if they are the dominant partner. Instead, wives prefer shared power and teamwork—an arrangement more consistent with the development of intimacy.

Our decomposition analysis revealed that the increase in the percentage of couples who reported overall equality in decision making was associated with positive changes in all five dimensions of marital quality. Between 1980 and 2000 the increase in decision-making equality was associated with a .03 increase in marital happiness (in standard deviation units), a .03 increase in marital interaction, a .03 decline in marital conflict, a .03 decline in marital problems, and a .02 decline in divorce proneness in the population. Although wives appeared to benefit from shared decision making more than husbands did, spouses of both genders benefited in absolute terms from the rise in decision-making equality.

Summary of Gender Relations and Marital Quality

In general, the changes in gender relations described in this chapter had mixed implications for marital quality. The increase in wives' percentage of family income appears to have had few consequences for marital quality, the shift toward less conservative views about gender and the increase in decision-making equality appear to have had positive consequences for marital quality, and the increase in men's share of housework appears to have negative consequences for husbands' marital quality and positive consequences for wives' marital quality. Despite these mixed results, the decomposition analysis revealed that these various changes, collectively, were associated with aggregate increases in marital quality. In particular, these changes were linked with an increase in marital happiness equivalent to .05 of a standard deviation, an increase in marital interaction equivalent to .08 of a standard deviation, and a decline in marital conflict equivalent to .04 of a standard deviation. These results support the view that the decline of the patriarchal breadwinner-homemaker model of marriage, and the rise of a more egalitarian, companionate form of marriage, has been good for marital quality. These findings also support the contention of some observers (Goode, 1980) that improvements in marriage will occur only when husbands are willing to give up some of their traditional male privileges and become more equal partners with their wives.

At this point it is useful to return to one of the key findings that emerged in Chapter 4. We noted there that the shift toward dual-earner marriages appeared to have improved marital quality among middle-class couples but lowered marital quality among working-class couples. In this chapter we found that middle-class couples, compared with working-class couples, hold more liberal views about gender and have a more egalitarian division of household labor. Both these factors are associated with enhanced marital quality, especially among wives. And although we did not relate the fact earlier in this chapter, we found that wives employed primarily to make ends meet (see Chapter 4) report less housework on the part of their husbands, more unfairness in the household division of labor, and less decision-making equality than do career-oriented wives. These findings provide more context for our conclusions about social class. Working-class employed wives, compared with middle-class employed wives, not only experience less job satisfaction and a greater desire to exit the labor force (as we reported in Chapter 4), but also receive less help from husbands with household chores and child care and have less decision-making power at home. Clearly, the movement of working-class wives into the paid labor force, although necessary to offset the stagnation (or decline) in working-class men's wages, resulted in a rise in marital tension for these women. Not all couples benefited equally from the shift toward dual-earner arrangements, and correspondingly, not all couples benefited equally from the shift toward more egalitarian gender arrangements in marriage.

Conclusions

Between 1980 and 2000 marriages in the United States became more egalitarian. These findings reflect the continuing shift from patriarchal, institutional marriage to a more egalitarian, companionate form of marriage. Despite some offsetting trends (and the concerns of some marital-decline theorists), changes in gender relations appear to have had generally positive implications for aggregate levels of marital quality in the U.S. population. As we noted earlier, Ernest Burgess believed that gender equality was essential for the development of companionate marriages—unions held together primarily by feelings of mutual attraction, understanding, and love. More recently, Francis Goldscheider and Linda Waite (1991) argued that the success of future marriages will require husbands and wives to work out a more equitable division of family and paid work. The findings in this chapter, therefore, allow for some cautious optimism about the future of marriage.

It would be a mistake, however, to conclude that contemporary marriages are thoroughly egalitarian. Some feminist scholars have pointed out that even among couples who claim to be egalitarian, gender inequality can be perpetuated by subtle, often latent processes. For example, although spouses may consult one another about major decisions, wives may still plan their days around their husbands' schedules, be more likely than husbands to focus on the family's emotional needs, and have less influence on the choice of everyday conversational topics. Given this possibility, we cannot conclude that all the couples who claimed to practice equality had thoroughly egalitarian marriages. And even in marriages in which husbands did half of the housework, wives may have taken the major responsibility for remembering that these tasks needed to be completed and delegating the work to husbands (Coltrane, 2000). These considerations suggest that we should be cautious not to overinterpret the results from our surveys.

Nevertheless, our data indicate a continuing trend toward gender equality—a trend that is entirely plausible, given the increase in wives' educational attainment, the growth of wives' labor-force participation, improvements in wives' earnings, and a rise in the proportion of family income contributed by wives. Hochschild (1989) referred to a "stalled gender revolution." But impatient observers run the risk of mistaking gradual change for no change at all. Social change often occurs through a process of cohort replacement, with younger generations (who contribute new ideas and practices) eventually replacing older generations in the population. Because cohort replacement is a slow process, social change typically occurs at a modest pace. In this sense, the notion of a stalled gender revolution is misleading, because social arrangements are rarely modified through sudden and dramatic shifts in thinking and behavior. Most social change is evolutionary rather than revolutionary. Even if one takes a cautious approach to the interpretation of the findings presented in this chapter, our results are consistent with the notion that slow but steady shifts in gender relations are gradually transforming marriage for the better.

6

Social Integration, Religion, and Attitudes toward Lifelong Marriage

$\mathscr{I}$N PREVIOUS CHAPTERS we described changes in demographics, employment patterns, economic well-being, and gender relations during the last two decades of the twentieth century, as well as how these changes were related to shifts in marital quality in the U.S. population. In this chapter we focus on three additional topics: social integration, religion, and attitudes toward lifelong marriage. Although these three topics differ in many respects, they share a central feature: each deals with people's links with and commitment to other individuals. Social integration refers to the number, quality, and durability of bonds that people have with other individuals. Religion is often seen as a set of deeply personal beliefs, but religion also has a social dimension. Like most sociologists, we see religion as an institution that brings like-minded people together and creates communities of believers. Indeed, religious participation can be viewed as a form of social integration. Finally, the norm of lifelong marriage refers to spouses' bonds with one another—bonds that are expected to persist even when spouses are dissatisfied with their relationships.

Changes in Social Integration

Marriage is a bond between two individuals, but it also connects spouses with other individuals (such as in-laws) and groups in the community (such as schools and religious congregations). For this reason, married individuals tend to be more socially integrated than are single individuals. Sociologists view social integration as both a source of support and a form of informal control. With respect to support, James Coleman (1988) used the term *social capital* to indicate that social relationships provide a variety of resources to individuals, including information, practical assistance, and emotional support. For these reasons, people with extensive and overlapping networks of friends and relatives tend to have better mental and physical health than do people who lack these resources (Mirowsky and Ross, 2003). With respect to control, social network members remind individuals of social norms and apply sanctions (such as disapproval) when these norms are violated. Consistent with this notion is the fact that young adults are less likely to engage in deviant behavior when they are integrated into social networks based on traditional institutions, such as marriage, employment, and religious congregations (Laub and Sampson, 2002). The beneficial effects of social integration have been documented for a wide range of other behaviors, including suicide (Durkheim, 1951), substance abuse (Umberson, 1987), and parental involvement with children (Wilcox, 2002).

Social integration also has been studied in relation to marital quality and stability. In this context, a successful marriage can be viewed as a union of both spouses' social networks. That is, in a well-functioning marriage, both spouses provide social contacts that can serve as important sources of social capital for the couple (including advice, information, and emotional support). Consistent with this view are studies showing that married couples with supportive networks of kin and friends, compared with relatively isolated married couples, tend to have more satisfying and less troubled marriages (Bryant and Conger, 1999; Julien and Markman, 1991; Julien, Markman, Leveille, Chartrand, and Begin, 1994; Oliker, 1989; Rubin, 1985). Two qualitative studies found that wives frequently discuss their marital problems with close friends, and these discussions tend to reinforce wives' marital satisfaction and commitment to their marriages (Oliker, 1989; Rubin, 1985). Similarly, Booth, Edwards, and Johnson (1991) found that social integration and support from network members lowers the likelihood of divorce, although this is true primarily during the first six years of marriage. Presumably, the early years of marriage are a period of change and adjustment—a time when social support is especially likely to reinforce marital stability.

Social support may strengthen marriage for several reasons. First, individuals with restricted social networks may rely extensively on their spouses to fulfill a wide variety of personal needs. For this reason, individuals with few social ties may place especially high demands on their marriages—demands that many (perhaps most) marriages cannot meet.

Second, close friends, especially when they are shared with spouses, can buffer married couples from the stress associated with occasional periods of marital discord. When spouses socialize with mutual friends, they spend leisure hours together, rather than pursuing individual pastimes. And although distressed spouses often treat their friends as confidants, friends are particularly likely to be helpful if they know both spouses well and, hence, have insight into the relationship dynamics and personalities of the couple. In contrast, nonshared friends may take one spouse's side or even provide advice that is detrimental to the stability of the marriage (for example, by encouraging the spouse to leave the relationship).

Third, following divorce, individuals tend to lose contact with married couple friends and relatives of the former spouse (Kalmijn and Bernasco, 2001; Milardo, 1987). For a couple contemplating divorce, the potential loss of close friends represents a barrier to ending the marriage. Correspondingly, network members (especially those who are close to both spouses) have an incentive to encourage spouses to stay together and to put them in contact with service providers (such as counselors or therapists) who may help to ameliorate the problem. Like purchasing a home and having children, mutual friends accumulated during the course of a marriage can be viewed as important forms of marriage-specific capital.

As we pointed out in Chapter 1, some observers believe that social participation has declined in American society. Putnam (2000) documented a trend during the last several decades for people to be less involved in social networks and community institutions, including civic organizations (such as community service groups), political parties, recreational groups (such as bowling teams), and religious social groups. Moreover, the continuing urbanization of American society means that people often do not know their neighbors, and high levels of residential mobility mean that people often live great distances from their families of origin and extended kin (Fischer, 1982). These trends suggest that married couples may be less integrated into supportive social networks today than they were in the recent past. Of course, not everyone agrees that social participation has declined in recent decades (Boggs, 2001). But if Putnam's claim is correct, and if social integration strengthens marriage, then marital quality may have declined correspondingly.

Number of Close Friends

The size of people's friendship networks represents a central dimension of social support and integration. To investigate this topic, we asked whether respondents had any "close friends" who were not family members. Overall, 87% reported having close friends—a figure that was identical in 1980 and 2000. For people who responded positively, we also asked about the number of close friends they had. People's responses to this question ranged from 1 to 60, although only 4% reported having 20 or more close friends. (The median was 5.) We assumed that people who provided unusually high numbers either were exaggerating or had misunderstood the question (perhaps by confusing acquaintances with close friends). For this reason, we truncated these responses to have a maximum value of 20. (Details on the variables described in this chapter are available in Table 8 in Appendix 2.)

Figure 6.1 shows the mean number of close friends in both surveys. People in the more recent survey reported fewer friends than did people in the earlier survey, which is consistent with the notion of a decline in social participation. Specifically, the mean number of close friends was 6.0 in 1980, compared with only 5.4 in 2000. (Because the distribution of friends was positively skewed, we checked this result after taking the logarithm of this variable and found a similar decline.) Spouses of both genders reported a decline in the number of friends, although the decline was more substantial for husbands than for wives (not shown).

Although close friends are an important source of social support for individuals, close friends are an especially important resource for marriages when they are shared by spouses. We asked two questions to determine the extent to which spouses had overlapping friendship networks. First we asked, "How well do your friends get along with your

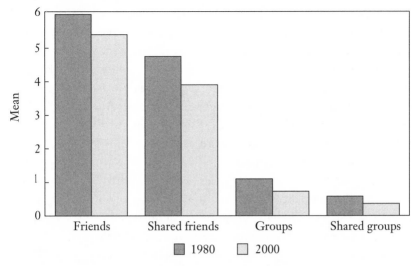

Figure 6.1   Indicators of social integration, 1980 and 2000

spouse?" Among individuals with at least one close friend, there was a significant decline between surveys in the percentage of people who reported that their friends got along "very well" with their spouses. In 1980, 77% gave this response, compared with 71% in 2000. Moreover, the magnitude of this decline was similar for husbands and wives.

Then we asked, "How many of your close friends also are close friends of your spouse?" (Although we did not ask this question of people who had no close friends, we assigned these individuals a score of zero. The means for 1980 and 2000 were 4.8 and 3.9, respectively—results that are consistent with those for the previous question. (See figure 6.1.) This decline, of course, may reflect the decrease in the size of people's friendship groups during this period. If people had fewer friends in 2000 than in 1980, then they also had fewer friends to share with their spouses. There was a strong correlation between the total number of friends and the number of friends shared with one's spouse ($r = .84$), which is consistent with this reasoning.

Another way to look at these data is to ask what *proportion* of a person's close friends are shared with the spouse. Consider two husbands, the first with two friends and the second with ten friends. The first husband has one friend in common with his wife, whereas the second husband has five friends in common with his wife. Although the second husband has substantially more friends, the proportion of shared friends is .5 in both cases. Because the proportion adjusts for the size of people's friendship networks, the correlation between the total number of friends and the proportion of friends shared with the spouse was weak ($r = .11$). On the basis of this measure, we found that the proportion of friends shared with the spouse was .76 in 1980 and .69 in 2000—a decline that was comparable for husbands and wives. In other words, husbands' and wives' friendship networks not only became smaller, but also became more separate during the last two decades of the twentieth century.

Numerous demographic variables were related to the number of close friends that people reported. For example, older individuals reported more friends than did younger individuals, whites reported more friends than did nonwhites, well-educated people reported more friends than did poorly educated people, people who cohabited before marriage reported fewer friends than did people who did not cohabit, and people in heterogamous marriages reported fewer friends than did people in homogamous marriages. Controlling for these (and other) demographic variables, however, did not affect the decline in the number of close friends between 1980 and 2000. This result indicates that the decrease in friends cannot be explained by shifts in the demographic composition of the married population. We also thought that the decline in the number of close friends might be related to the increase in work hours and work demands, which we described in Chapter 4, but these were not associated with the number of close friends. Husbands who worked long hours had as many friends as did husbands who worked fewer hours. And wives who worked long hours had as many friends as did wives who were full-time homemakers. The decline in close friendships, therefore, may have less to do with structural factors (such as employment patterns) or compositional factors (such as the demographic mix of the population) than with cultural factors (such as an increased desire for privacy and a preference to spend leisure time in solitary activities at home).

Like the total number of friends, the percentage of friends held in common with one's spouse also was related to several demographic variables. For example, husbands reported more shared friends than did wives. This gender difference may reflect a tendency for men to make friends through their wives' social networks (Thompson and Walker, 1991). Older couples had more shared friends than did younger couples—a difference that reflects either a tendency for spouses' friendship networks to converge later in life, or a cohort effect, whereby married couples were more likely to share friends in the past than in the present. In addition, whites had more shared friends than did nonwhites, and people in homogamous marriages had more shared friends than did people in heterogamous marriages. Changes in the demographic composition of the married population accounted for about one-fourth of the decline in shared friends between 1980 and 2000. But even after adjusting for changes in demographic composition, the decline in shared friends was still significant. For reasons that are difficult to pinpoint, husbands' and wives' friendship networks became more separate during the last two decades of the twentieth century. This trend is consistent with the general decline in marital interaction—especially the decline in spending time together with friends—that we reported in Chapter 2.

Organizational Involvement

Another dimension of social integration refers to people's involvement with formal and informal organizations. To assess this aspect of social integration, we asked: "Some people are members of organizations, such as church groups, unions or job-related groups, fraternal or civic groups, or recreational groups like bowling clubs or card clubs. Do you belong to any groups or clubs?" People's responses to this question provided further support for the notion of a decline in social participation. In 1980, 50% reported that they belonged to one or more groups, compared with only 38% in 2000.

We followed up by asking about the number of groups to which people belonged. Most people who belonged to organizations mentioned one or two affiliations, although a small number of people (6%) mentioned five or more. As Figure 6.1 shows, the mean number of groups declined from 1.1 to .73 between surveys. This decline was not due entirely to the larger number of people in 2000 who belonged to no organizations. Even among people who belonged to at least one group, there was a significant decrease in the mean number of memberships, from 2.2 in 1980 to 1.9 in 2000.

When people reported that they belonged to at least one group, we asked whether their spouses also were members. Contrary to our expectations, people were somewhat *more* likely to share at least one membership with their spouses in 2000 (52%) than in 1980 (45%). But because fewer people belonged to any organizations in 2000 than in 1980, the percentage of *all* couples who shared at least one membership declined from 29% to 24%. Figure 6.1 illustrates this trend in terms of the mean number of shared groups in each year, based on all individuals in the sample.

Like our earlier results for friends, the results for organizational involvement demonstrate a decline in general social participation. Between 1980 and 2000 a smaller proportion of married people participated in community groups, and people who belonged to community groups participated in a smaller number of groups. Although some observers have argued that wives are more likely than husbands to maintain the couple's social ties, the decline in group membership was similar for husbands and wives.

Organizational membership was less common among wives than husbands, although this was mainly because wives were less likely than husbands to be employed. Presumably, some of these organizational affiliations were work-related, such as labor unions. Membership also was positively associated with education and income, which indicates that participation in community organizations tends to be more of a middle-class than a working-class phenomenon. In addition, couples with children were more involved in organizations than were couples without children, which suggests that children help to connect parents with other groups in the community, such as schools, religious congregations, and sports leagues. Controlling for these demographic variables, however, did not account for any of the decline in membership between decades. In other words, the decline in organizational involvement was not due to shifts in the demographic composition of the population between surveys.

Putnam (2000) argued that the decline in social participation in recent decades is a cohort phenomenon. That is, more recently born individuals, compared with older individuals, have been socialized to be more individualistic and less involved with others in the community. To check on this interpretation, we conducted a decomposition analysis that separated social change into two components: change across cohorts and change within cohorts. (This analysis was comparable to the one described in Chapter 2.) For three forms of social integration—the percentage of shared friends, the number of organizational affiliations,

and the number of shared organizational affiliations—the change between decades was due entirely to cohort replacement. That is, earlier
cohorts had relatively high levels of social participation, but they were
replaced between 1980 and 2000 by more recent cohorts with lower
levels of social involvement. The pattern differed for the number of
friends. For this variable, the components for cohort replacement *and*
within-cohort change were significant, although these two processes
had contrary implications. Earlier cohorts had more friends, and these
individuals were replaced with more recent cohorts who had fewer
friends, which is consistent with other forms of social participation. At
the same time, however, individuals within the same cohort tended to
report more friends between surveys. This latter trend is probably an
aging effect (rather than a period effect), as older individuals tend to accumulate more friends over the life course.

To provide an example of cohort differences, we compared the affiliation patterns of individuals born in the 1940s (and interviewed in
1980) and individuals born in the 1960s (and interviewed in 2000).
These two groups had identical ages at the time of the interviews.
Compared to the more recent cohort, the earlier cohort had 51% more
friends, were 39% more likely to share friends with their spouse, had
168% more organizational memberships, and were 133% more likely
to share those affiliations with their spouse. Overall, our results support Putnam's (2000) assumption that the decline in social participation, at least among married individuals, has been driven primarily by a
process of cohort replacement.

Relations with In-Laws

Although marriage is a personal relationship between two individuals,
it also joins two families together. Even married individuals who live
far away from their in-laws are likely to spend time with them on holi-
days, birthdays, and other special occasions. For this reason, a strained
relationship with in-laws may be a source of tension for some couples. In contrast, assistance from in-laws—emotional support, advice,
practical help, or occasional economic assistance—can be an important
resource for spouses, particularly during the early years of marriage.
Timmer and Veroff's (2000) findings are consistent with this reasoning:
emotional closeness to in-laws was associated with greater marital happiness and a lower risk of divorce, especially for individuals who grew

up in divorced families. Another study (Bryant, Conger, and Meehan, 2001) found that increases in discord with in-laws was followed by declines in spouses' reports of marital satisfaction, commitment, and stability.

Our survey contained four questions on the respondent's and the spouse's relations with in-laws. The first question asked, "When you first got married, was either of your in-laws unhappy about the marriage?" A corresponding question asked, "When you first got married, was either of your parents unhappy with your choice of a husband/ wife?" Across both surveys, according to the respondents, the great majority of parents and in-laws were happy. During the 20-year interval between surveys, however, the percentage of respondents who reported that their in-laws were unhappy declined significantly, from 16% to 11%. Similarly, reports of parental unhappiness with the marriage declined significantly, from 17% to 13%. These results were comparable for husbands and wives.

As we reported in Chapter 3, between 1980 and 2000 increases occurred in the proportion of marriages preceded by cohabitation, the proportion of marriages that were heterogamous, and the proportion of marriages that were second unions following divorce. Given these trends, we expected declines (rather than increases) in the approval of in-laws and parents during this period. Presumably, some parents disapprove of their children cohabiting before marriage, marrying individuals of different races or religions, or marrying previously divorced individuals. In fact, respondents who cohabited before marriage were more likely than other respondents to report that their parents were unhappy with their spouses. Similarly, respondents in heterogamous unions reported greater unhappiness from parents as well as from in-laws. And although individuals in second marriages did not report less support from their own parents, they were especially likely to report that their spouses' parents were unsupportive.

Given these trends, why did the overall level of support from in-laws increase between surveys? The answer appears to be that between 1980 and 2000 spouses married at older ages and became better educated. Parents and in-laws were more likely to approve of marriages that occurred when offspring were older rather than younger. Similarly, parents and in-laws were more likely to approve of marriages that involved well-educated partners rather than poorly educated partners. Controlling for these two variables reduced the decline in parents' unhappiness with the marriage by about one-half and reduced the decline in unhappiness among in-laws by about three-fourths. Moreover, after controlling for these variables, the remaining differences between decades no longer were statistically significant. These results suggest that when offspring are older and better educated at the time of marriage, parents are more likely to trust and support their children's decisions about marriage partners.

As a follow-up question, we asked, "How about now? How well do you and your in-laws get along?" (1 = not too well, 2 = pretty well, 3 = very well). In both surveys 65% of people reported getting along very well with their in-laws, and only 4% reported not getting along well. Correspondingly, we asked, "How about now? How well do your parents and your spouse get along?" In both surveys 68% of people said that their parents got along well with their spouses, and only 3% said that their parents did not get along well with their spouses. These responses did not vary with decade or the gender of the respondents. In general, long-term friction between spouses and in-laws appears to be relatively uncommon.

Getting along well with in-laws was the norm, even among people who reported initial friction with in-laws. Among individuals who reported that their in-laws were not happy with the marriage initially, only 18% reported that they did not get along well with their in-laws at the time of the interview. Similarly, among individuals who reported that their own parents did not approve of the marriage initially, only 9% reported that their parents and spouses did not get along well at the time of the interview. Apparently, even when early tension exists between spouses and in-laws, these relationships improve over time—assuming that the marriage does not end in divorce. Consistent with this conclusion is the fact that the duration of marriage was associated with declines in respondents' reports that they (and their spouses) did not get along well with in-laws. Duration of marriage was not related to reports of initial disapproval from in-laws, however, which suggests that individuals were not "reconstructing" the past to make it consistent with the present.

Close Friends and Marital Quality

We argued earlier that close friends are important resources for married couples, especially when husbands and wives hold these friends in

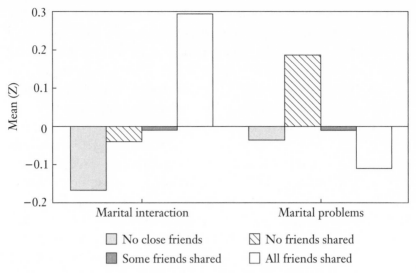

Figure 6.2   Adjusted mean level of marital quality by sharing friends with spouse, 2000

common. To assess this assumption, we examined the associations between our friendship measures and the five dimensions of marital quality. In 1980 as well as 2000 the number of close friends was related to all five dimensions of marital quality. People with many friends (compared to people with few friends) were happier with their marriages, interacted more with their spouses, engaged in less conflict, perceived fewer problems in their marriages, and were less divorce prone. These findings, however, did not take into account the high correlation between the total number of friends and the number of shared friends. Further investigation revealed that people with many friends tended to be in better-quality marriages mainly because they were especially likely to share at least some friends with their spouses. In fact, people who had only one or two close friends—but who shared these friends with their spouses—tended to be in high-quality marriages. In contrast, people who had many friends—but who did not share these friends with their spouses—tended to be in low-quality marriages.

Figure 6.2 provides further insight into this pattern. To create this figure, we placed people into four groups: those who had no close friends, those who had close friends but did not have any close friends in common with their spouses, those who had close friends and shared some of these friends with their spouses, and those who had close friends and shared all of these friends with their spouses. The marital quality of people in these four groups was comparable in both decades, although group differences were somewhat less pronounced in 2000 than in 1980 (but not significantly so). Figure 6.2 shows the results for marital interaction and marital problems in 2000.

Note that people who had no close friends reported the lowest level of marital interaction. Individuals who had close friends but did not have any friends in common with their spouses also reported a lower-than-average level of interaction. In contrast, individuals who had close friends and shared all of these friends with their spouses reported the highest level of marital interaction. Presumably, spouses with shared friends have more opportunities to engage in mutual interaction than do spouses with few or no friends in common. The difference between people who had friends but did not share these friends with their spouses and people who shared all of their friends with their spouses was about one-third of a standard deviation—a moderate effect size. The pattern for marital problems was somewhat different. For this outcome, individuals who had friends but did not share these friends with their spouses reported the largest number of problems. In contrast, people who shared all of their friends with their spouses reported the fewest problems. The difference between people in these two groups was about .30 of a standard deviation—another moderate effect size. The general pattern shown in Figure 6.2 was comparable for the other marital outcomes, although the overall differences between groups were not always statistically significant. Moreover, the links between friendship patterns and marital quality were similar for husbands and wives (as reflected in the absence of significant interactions between friendship patterns and gender in either survey).

As we noted earlier, we also asked how well respondents' friends got along with their spouses. Not surprisingly, people who reported that their friends did not get along well with their spouses tended to be in poor-quality marriages—an observation that was true in both decades. Of course, people who have friends in common with their spouses are unlikely to report that their friends don't get along with their spouses. (The correlation between the proportion of shared friends and how well friends and spouses got along was $-.65$ across both surveys.) As it turned out, the proportion of shared friends, rather than how well people's friends got along with their spouses, was the better predictor of marital quality.

These results are consistent with our reasoning that shared friends are an important marital asset. Of course, it also is probable that couples who do not get along well seek out separate friendship groups. Indeed, some couples on the verge of divorce may discover that their friends, previously held in common, have split into "his friends" and "her friends." Most likely, the direction of influence runs both ways. That is, overlapping networks of friends facilitate marital happiness and strengthen marital stability, but couples with seriously troubled relationships may be unable to maintain common friendships and prefer instead to seek out their own sources of social support.

How were changes in friendships related to changes in marital quality? Our decomposition analysis determined that the decrease in the number of friends (primarily shared friends) between 1980 and 2000 was associated with a decline in marital happiness in the population equivalent to .03 of a standard deviation. Similarly, the change in shared friends was associated with a decline in marital interaction (.03 of a standard deviation), an increase in marital conflict (.02 of a standard deviation), an increase in marital problems (.02 of a standard deviation), and an increase in divorce proneness (.02 of a standard deviation). These results suggest that the constriction of people's friendship networks between surveys, and the corresponding decline in the number of friends shared between spouses, had consistently negative consequences for marital quality.

Organizational Involvement and Marital Quality

There was a tendency for people who belonged to clubs and organizations to report higher levels of marital quality. In particular, club membership was positively associated with marital happiness and inteaction and negatively associated with marital problems and divorce proneness. As we noted earlier, the number of close friends was linked with marital quality, but only because having a large number of close friends was associated with having friends in common with one's spouse. The same pattern appeared for clubs and organizations. Belonging to the same groups as one's spouse, rather than simply belonging to groups, was the key variable. And like the results for friends, sharing affiliations with one's spouse was linked with better marital quality, whereas belonging to groups that one's spouse did not belong to was associated with poorer marital quality. This pattern, however, was more consistent in 2000 than in 1980.

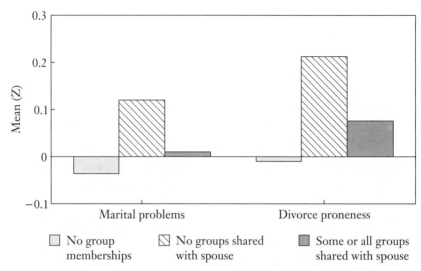

Figure 6.3   Adjusted mean level of marital quality by membership in clubs and organizations, 2000

Figure 6.3 illustrates this pattern using data from the 2000 survey. Note that marital problems and divorce proneness were elevated when couples belonged to clubs or organizations but did not share these affiliations with their spouses. Problems and divorce proneness were lower either when individuals had no group affiliations or when individuals shared some or all of their affiliations with their spouses. Overall, the pattern of results for organizational membership was similar to the pattern for friendship networks: participating in social groups but not sharing these affiliations with one's spouse was linked with problematic aspects of marriage. These results are consistent with the notion that shared organizational affiliations, like shared friendships, strengthen the marital relationship. Another possibility, of course, is that individuals in troubled marriages seek out separate organizational affiliations to get away from their spouses.

No matter how one interprets these findings, the decomposition analysis revealed that changes in people's memberships had modest implications for changes in marital quality. Overall, the change in the pattern of spouses' group affiliations between 1980 and 2000 was associated with a small increase in marital happiness (.01 of a standard deviation), a small decline in marital problems (.01 of a standard deviation), and a small decline in divorce proneness (.02 of a standard deviation). These modest improvements in marital quality occurred because the general decline in membership was balanced by a trend for people who belonged to groups to share these affiliations with their spouses.

Relations with In-Laws and Marital Quality

Earlier in this chapter we argued that the approval and support of parents and in-laws are important marital assets—an assumption supported by our data. People who reported that their in-laws or parents were unhappy with their marriages tended to have low levels of marital quality. Specifically, disapproval from in-laws was associated with more marital problems in both surveys, and disapproval from one's own parents was associated with higher levels of conflict, problems, and divorce proneness in 1980. Current relationships with in-laws, however, were stronger and more consistent correlates of marital quality. In particular, the extent to which respondents had good relations with in-laws was positively associated with marital happiness and negatively associated with conflict, problems, and divorce proneness in both surveys. Similarly, respondents who reported that their parents and their spouses got along well had relatively high levels of marital happiness and relatively low levels of problems and divorce proneness in both surveys.

Despite these significant associations, the decomposition analysis revealed that changes between 1980 and 2000 in relations with in-laws had no implications for aggregate levels of marital quality. Although disapproval from in-laws declined significantly between surveys, the magnitude of this decline was too small to have significant implications. And although getting along with in-laws was related to most dimensions of marital quality, relations with in-laws did not improve or decline between surveys.

Changes in Religion and Religiosity

The great majority of Americans report that religion is important in their lives, are members of religious organizations, and participate in religious services at least occasionally (Sherkat and Ellison, 1999). Although Americans are a religious people, some debate exists over whether religion became a weaker force in the United States during the last century. Some attitude surveys suggest that religion plays a smaller role in people's lives today than in the past (Glenn, 1987). Nevertheless, religious affiliation rates increased throughout most of the twentieth century, and in recent decades financial contributions to religious organizations increased, as did membership in conservative denominations (Finke, 1992).

Although data on objective trends (such as membership and contributions) are readily available, data on people's subjective feelings about religion are more difficult to obtain. To assess the role of religion in marriage, our surveys included a series of questions on people's religious affiliation, whether people had the same religious affiliation as their spouses, the extent to which religious beliefs influenced people's everyday lives, and how often people attended religious services with their spouses.

Religious Affiliation

We categorized people's responses on religious affiliation into five broad groups: Protestant, Catholic, Jewish, other faiths, and no affiliation. A significant shift in the relative sizes of these groups occurred between 1980 and 2000. In particular, the percentage of Protestants declined from 57% to 45%. Correspondingly, the percentage of Catholics increased from 28% to 31%, the percentage of people in the "other faiths" category increased from 6% to 11%, and the percentage of people reporting no religious affiliation increased from 7% to 11%. The percentage of Jewish respondents did not change (between 1% and 2%).

We originally assumed that shifts in the racial and ethnic composition of the married population were responsible for most of these changes. As we described in Chapter 3, the percentage of Latinos and people in the "other" ethnic category (Asians, Native Americans, and people of mixed heritage) increased between surveys. Moreover, the majority of Latinos in our surveys were Catholic, and nearly one-third of people in the "other" ethnic category had religious affiliations other than Protestant, Catholic, or Jewish. Our analysis indicated, however, that shifts in the racial and ethnic composition of the married population accounted for few of the changes in religious affiliation during this period. For example, only 13% of the decline in Protestantism was due to the increase in the percentage of Latino couples in the population.

We also asked whether respondents and their spouses shared the same religious affiliation. Overall, 80% reported that their spouses shared the same affiliation, and this figure was nearly identical in 1980 and 2000. Moreover, only minor differences were apparent among Protestants, Catholics, Jews, and people of other faiths in the extent of religious intermarriage. The one exception involved people with no religious affiliation. Nearly one-third of the people in this group had spouses who considered themselves to be members of some religion. Nevertheless, religious homogamy was the norm for the great majority of couples, irrespective of people's religious affiliations.

To assess the strength of people's religious feelings (henceforth referred to as religiosity), we asked: "In general, how much do your religious beliefs influence your daily life? Would you say very much, quite a bit, some, a little, or not at all?" The percentage of spouses who responded "not at all" was similar in both surveys. The percentage of spouses who reported "very much," however, increased from 32 in 1980 to 42 in 2000. Figure 6.4 displays this pattern. Although there were as many nonreligious respondents in 2000 as in 1980, there were a larger number of respondents who reported a high level of religiosity. (To simplify the figure, we combined respondents who reported "some" and "a little.")

To provide an overall measure of change in religiosity, we scored people's responses to the question of religious influence in the following manner: $1 =$ not at all, $2 =$ a little, $3 =$ some, $4 =$ quite a bit, and $5 =$ very much. On the basis of this scoring, the mean increased from 3.6 in 1980 to 3.8 in 2000. This difference reflects .13 of a standard deviation, which is a modest effect size. The amount (and direction) of change was similar for wives and husbands, older and younger individuals, people with high and low levels of education, and members of all racial and ethnic groups. The increase in religious influence, therefore, was modest but pervasive throughout the married population.

Finally, we asked how often people attended religious services with their spouses. We coded responses into the following categories: $1 =$ less than once a year or never, $2 =$ once a year or more but less than monthly, $3 =$ once a month or more but less than weekly, and $4 =$ weekly or more often. People reported attending services with their spouses somewhat more frequently in 2000 than in 1980, with the increase representing about one-tenth of a standard deviation—a weak

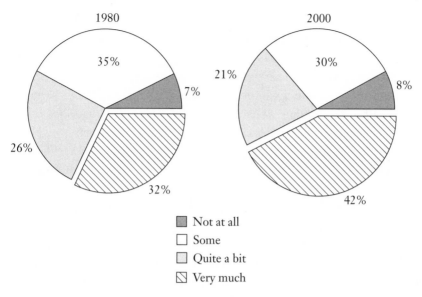

Figure 6.4   Extent that religion influences daily life, 1980 and 2000

effect size. For example, the percentage of people who reported weekly attendance increased from 34 to 37. As with religiosity, however, this modest change appeared across a wide variety of groups in the population.

Religiosity and Marital Quality

Earlier research indicates that people who are religious, when compared with those who are not religious, report more marital happiness, are more committed to their marriages, and have lower rates of divorce (Bramlett and Mosher, 2002; Dollahite, Marks, and Goodman, 2004; Lehrer, 2003; Mahoney, Pargament, Tarakeshwar, and Swank, 2001). Given these findings, the small rise in religiosity and attendance at services with spouses may have had positive implications for marital quality and stability in recent decades.

With respect to religious affiliation, few differences in marital quality were apparent between Protestants, Catholics, and Jews. People with no religious affiliation, however, scored higher on marital conflict, problems, and divorce proneness than did Protestants, Catholics, and Jews. We also found that people with other religious affiliations (that is, not Protestant, Catholic, or Jewish) scored relatively high on marital problems and divorce proneness. This latter finding is difficult to explain, because this group included people with diverse faiths: Buddhists, Muslims, Mormons—even pagans. People in this category did not differ from Protestants, Catholics, or Jews in how much religion influenced their daily lives, how often they attended religious services, or whether their spouses shared the same religious affiliation. Nevertheless, the increase in the size of this group between surveys, along with increase in the percentage of those without a religious affiliation, exerted modest downward pressure on marital quality in the population.

Consistent with earlier research is the fact that people who reported that religious beliefs influenced their daily lives a great deal tended to have high levels of marital happiness in 1980. People who were high on religiosity also tended to have elevated levels of marital problems and divorce proneness in 2000, however, which conflicts with earlier research. Why would religiosity be associated with high levels of problems and divorce proneness? One possibility is that religiosity influences marital quality only to the extent that it increases attendance at services, especially when both spouses attend together. Indeed, the correlation between religiosity and the frequency of attending services with one's spouse was moderately strong ($r = .48$). Moreover, attending services with one's spouse was a consistent predictor of marital quality in both surveys. Compared with people who did not, people who attended services together were happier with their marriages, interacted more frequently with their spouses, fought less often, perceived fewer problems in their marriages, and were less divorce prone.

Figure 6.5 shows the links between attending services together and marital interaction, marital problems, and divorce proneness, based on the 2000 sample. The associations are approximately linear, with greater levels of attendance being associated with improvements in marital quality. The gaps in marital quality between spouses who attended weekly and those who attended rarely or never were about one-fourth to one-third of a standard deviation, which represents moderate effect sizes. Presumably, people who hold strong religious beliefs tend to attend services more frequently. And attending religious services with one's spouse is a reflection of religious homogamy. For these reasons, attending services with one's spouse captures the two essential components noted earlier: having strong beliefs and sharing these beliefs with one's spouse.

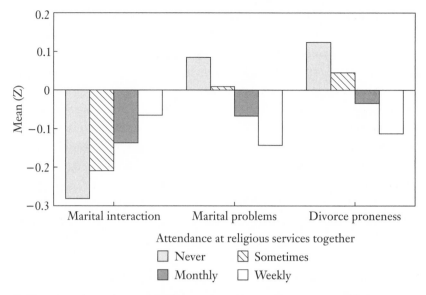

Figure 6.5   Adjusted mean level of marital quality by frequency of attendance at religious services together, 2000

These considerations cast some light on the finding that religiosity appeared to increase marital problems and divorce proneness. In both surveys reports that religious beliefs influenced one's life a great deal were associated with every dimension of marital quality in the expected direction in *bivariate* (rather than multivariate) analyses. That is, religiosity was positively associated with marital happiness and interaction and was negatively associated with conflict, problems, and divorce proneness. These significant associations did not change when we added the demographic and economic variables as controls. Adding attendance at services to the equation, however, reduced most of the associations to nonsignificance and changed the associations with marital problems and divorce proneness from negative to positive in 2000. This finding is consistent with our assumption that religiosity affects marital quality positively by motivating spouses to attend religious services together. Worshipping as a couple may strengthen the marital bond because it reinforces the fact that spouses have something important in common. Moreover, shared worship facilitates the integration of couples into social networks that are affiliated with religious congregations. Through attending religious services, as well as participating in congregation-sponsored social events, couples meet people with similar beliefs and values. Integration into a local community, as we argued earlier, is likely to promote marital happiness and satisfaction. This result also is consistent with a few other studies in suggesting that marital quality and stability are more strongly related to joint religious activities than to spouses' individual beliefs about religion (Clydesdale, 1997; Mahoney et al., 2001).

What is left when we statistically remove the effects of joint attendance at services from religiosity? People with strong religious beliefs who do not participate in religious activities with their spouses may be drawn to others who share their religious orientations. Religious individuals who do not share their practices with spouses are likely to attend religious services on their own, and the church may be a place where these individuals meet alternative partners who share their faith. If this is true, then religiosity may destabilize marriages among couples who do not practice their faiths together.

To check on this possibility, we separated couples into those who attended religious services together rarely or sometimes and those who attended religious services monthly or weekly. Among those who attended religious services together rarely or sometimes, the respondent's religiosity was associated with less marital interaction, more problems, and greater divorce proneness. In contrast, among spouses who attended religious services together monthly or weekly, religiosity was associated with greater marital happiness and less marital conflict.

These findings indicate that the estimated effects of religiosity depend on whether spouses participate in religious services together. When respondents were highly religious, not attending religious services with their spouses was associated with poorer marital quality. But when spouses attended religious services together, religiosity was associated with better marital quality. These findings make intuitive sense. When a person holds strong religious views, not being able to express these views through shared religious participation with one's spouse tends to weaken the marital relationship. But when a person holds deeply religious views, worshipping with the spouse tends to strengthen the marital relationship. These results indicate that strong feelings of religiosity can strengthen marriage or weaken marriage, depending on whether spouses participate together in religious activities.

Although religiosity and attendance at services both increased between 1980 and 2000, our decomposition analysis revealed that these increases had few implications for marital quality in the population.

Taken together, these two variables were associated with a modest rise in marital happiness—about .01 of a standard deviation—in the married population. Changes in religiosity and church attendance did not appear to influence any other dimensions of marital quality.

Changes in Attitudes toward Lifelong Marriage

Changes in Attitudes

Traditionally, marriage was seen as a lifelong union—an arrangement that could be broken only by the death of one spouse. Of course, some level of divorce always existed in American society. But lifelong marriage was the ideal and the goal to which most individuals aspired.

Most religions discourage divorce, and Americans, as we noted earlier, are a religious people. Moreover, because many people in the past viewed divorce as a form of deviance (or a sin), divorced individuals were, to a certain extent, stigmatized. Before the 1960s, for example, divorce was a campaign liability. Adlai Stevenson (who was divorced in 1949) served as the Democratic Party's candidate for president in 1952. During the campaign, Dwight Eisenhower (the Republican Party candidate) raised Stevenson's divorce as a campaign issue—an issue that resonated strongly among women voters (Rothstein, 2002). Partly for this reason, Stevenson lost the election.

People in the United States became more accepting of divorce after the 1960s. According to one survey, between 1965 and 1976 the percentage of respondents who felt that divorce laws were "too strict" increased modestly (Cherlin, 1992). In another study, the percentage of women who disagreed with the statement "When there are children in the family, parents should stay together even if they don't get along" increased from 51 in 1962 to 80 in 1977 (Thornton and Young-DeMarco, 2001). In contrast to Stevenson's candidacy in 1952, Ronald Reagan's run for the presidency in 1980 was successful, and his divorce did not become a campaign issue (Rothstein, 2002). By the end of the 1970s, the great majority of Americans viewed divorce as an unfortunate but common event, and the stigma of divorce, although still present, was considerably weaker than in earlier eras (Glenn, 1996).

One of our goals was to see if people's attitudes toward lifelong marriage changed between 1980 and 2000. To measure attitudes, we

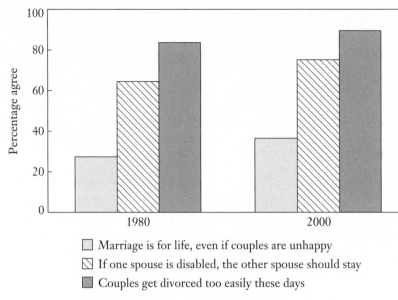

□ Marriage is for life, even if couples are unhappy
◻ If one spouse is disabled, the other spouse should stay
■ Couples get divorced too easily these days

Figure 6.6   Attitudes toward marriage, 1980 and 2000

asked whether people agreed strongly, agreed, disagreed, or disagreed strongly with a series of statements about marriage and divorce. Three of these statements reflected traditional views of marriage:

1. Marriage is for life, even if the couple is unhappy.
2. If one spouse becomes mentally or physically disabled, the other spouse should stay in the marriage, regardless of his or her own happiness.
3. Couples are able to get divorced too easily these days.

Figure 6.6 shows that the percentage of people who either agreed or agreed strongly with these statements increased between 1980 and 2000. These increases were from 27% to 36% (marriage is for life), from 64% to 75% (a person should stay with a disabled spouse), and from 83% to 89% (divorce is too easy). Contrary to the general trend since the 1960s, responses to these statements revealed a consistent shift toward more traditional views about marriage and divorce, at least among married individuals.

We also included three statements that reflected tolerant views of divorce:

1. The personal happiness of an individual is more important than putting up with a bad marriage.
2. In marriages where people fight a lot, children are better off if the parents divorce or separate.
3. It's okay for people to get married, thinking that if it does not work out, they always can get a divorce.

Responses to the first two statements changed significantly between surveys The percentage of people who disagreed with these statements increased from 26% to 36% (personal happiness is more important) and from 27% to 31% (children are better off if parents divorce). Responses to the final item did not change. Instead, the great majority of people disagreed with this statement in both years (83% overall). Despite this one exception, these results indicate growing support for the norm of lifelong marriage—and less support for divorce—among married individuals in the United States.

To summarize these data, we created a scale based on all six items. This scale, which measured support for the norm of lifelong marriage, increased by one-fourth (.24) of a standard deviation between 1980 and 2000—a moderate increase. The magnitude of this shift was similar for wives and husbands, for blacks and whites, for people with high and low levels of education, and for individuals in all age groups. It appears that a shift toward greater support for lifelong marriage was pervasive throughout the married population during this time.

Not surprisingly, people who reported a high level of religious influence in their daily lives also tended to report more support for the norm of lifelong marriage ($r = .30$). Similarly, attendance at religious services was positively associated with support for lifelong marriage ($r = .32$). These findings suggest that the increase in support for lifelong marriage may have been a reflection of the increase in religiosity during the same period (as we reported earlier). To check on this possibility, we used regression analysis to assess changes in attitudes before and after controlling for people's reports of religious influence and attendance at services. This procedure revealed that the increase in religiosity accounted for only 17% of the of the increase in support for lifelong marriage between 1980 and 2000. In other words, the rise in religiosity and the increase in support for the norm of lifelong marriage were largely independent phenomena.

A number of demographic variables were associated with people's support for lifelong marriage. In general, husbands had higher scores than wives, whites had higher scores than blacks or Latinos, people in first marriages had higher scores than people in second or higher-order marriages, people with children had higher scores than people without children, people with a low level of education had higher scores than people with a high level of education, and older individuals had higher scores than younger ones. To illustrate this pattern, a 25-year-old black woman, with a master's degree, in a second marriage, and with no children, would score a full standard deviation lower on this scale than a 50-year-old white man, with a high school diploma, in a first marriage, and with three children. Despite these differences, however, it is important to keep in mind that increases in support for the norm of lifelong marriage increased across most groups in the population.

Attitudes toward Marriage and Marital Quality

Why would we expect attitudes toward lifelong marriage to be associated with marital quality? Individuals with a strong belief in marital permanence are likely to invest a good deal of time and effort in trying to resolve marital disagreements and problems. In contrast, individuals who are tolerant of divorce may prefer to jettison an existing marriage (rather than invest more effort in it) and find greater happiness with a new partner. One longitudinal study that supports this reasoning found that individuals who adopted more favorable attitudes toward divorce tended to experience declines in marital happiness and increases in marital conflict (Amato and Rogers, 1999). This study also found that shifts in marital quality were not followed by changes in people's attitudes toward divorce. These findings suggest that an increase in support for the norm of marital permanence may have raised the aggregate level of marital quality in the population.

Our surveys revealed that people who held attitudes supportive of lifelong marriage tended to be in high-quality marriages. Specifically, support for lifelong marriage was associated positively with marital happiness and negatively with marital conflict, marital problems, and divorce proneness. For reasons that are not clear, however, the links between attitudes toward marriage and marital quality became somewhat weaker between surveys. That is, attitudes toward lifelong marriage did not predict marital quality as well in 2000 as they did in 1980.

Despite this decline in the strength of the link between attitudes and marital quality, the decomposition analysis revealed that the increase in support for lifelong marriage between 1980 and 2000 was associated with an increase in marital happiness (.02 of a standard deviation), a decline in marital conflict (.01 of a standard deviation), a decline in marital problems (.01 of a standard deviation), and a decline in divorce proneness (.01 of a standard deviation) in the population. Our findings, although modest, are consistent with the notion that increased support for the norm of lifelong marriage had beneficial consequences for marital quality.

Conclusions

We have explored in this chapter several factors that reflect the social bonds between people. As have other studies (Putnam, 2000), we found that married individuals had lower levels of social participation in 2000 than in 1980. Spouses in the later survey, compared with spouses in the earlier survey, reported having fewer friends and were less likely to be members of community organizations. More important, people in the later survey reported having fewer friends and group memberships in common with their spouses. The one exception to this pattern involved attending church with one's spouse—a form of social participation that increased slightly between decades. This decline in social participation was not due to shifts in the demographic composition of the married population or to changes in husbands' and wives' work schedules. It is more likely that this decline was due to cultural factors that are difficult to measure. Married individuals may value their privacy more these days than they did in the recent past, and they may prefer solitary activities, such as watching television or surfing the Internet, to socializing with friends and joining clubs (Robinson and Godbey, 1997).

Good reasons exist for believing that social integration generally strengthens people's marriages. Friends can provide emotional support, advice, and encouragement to married couples who are experiencing problems. In addition, friends, as well as organizations such as religious congregations, can reinforce norms of marital commitment. These benefits should be especially valuable when couples have friends and group memberships in common. Consistent with these assumptions is our finding that spouses who share close friends and belong to the same organizations tend to have higher-quality marriages. Of course, couples with chronically hostile relationships may find it difficult to form and maintain shared friendships. After all, who would want to be around these couples? But theory suggests that the direction of effect also runs from poorly integrated social networks to declines in marital cohesion. The decline in social integration, therefore, implies a corresponding decline in marital quality in the population. As this reasoning predicted, our decomposition analysis found that the decrease in the number of shared friends was associated with declines in both marital happiness and interaction and increases in conflict, problems, and divorce proneness between 1980 and 2000.

Although many forms of social participation are declining, religion seems to be an exception. Between surveys people reported a strengthening of religious influence and more frequent attendance at services with their spouses. Religious participation, more so than religious beliefs, was associated with positive marital outcomes, which is consistent with some earlier studies. Moreover, religious changes were accompanied by a modest increase in marital happiness in the population. But the amount of change in religious beliefs and practices was too small to have an appreciable effect on other dimensions of marital quality.

People also reported increased support for the norm of lifelong marriage. This finding indicates a reversal of the long-term increase (since the 1960s) in tolerant attitudes toward divorce. It would be a mistake, however, to assume that married people are strongly against divorce. Instead, they appear to be deeply ambivalent. For example, in the 2000 survey only a minority of people (17%) agreed with the statement "It's okay for people to get married, thinking that if it does not work out, they can always get a divorce." But at the same time, as we noted earlier, the majority of people continue to believe that "the personal happiness of an individual is more important than putting up with a bad marriage." Nevertheless, rising support for the norm of lifelong marriage suggests that people may be growing weary of a culture in which nearly half of all marriages end in divorce. Moreover, this change in attitudes was associated with modest improvements in several dimensions of marital quality in the population.

How do these findings relate to the deinstitutionalization of marriage? The trend for couples to have fewer close friends and organizational memberships in common represents a clear shift away from institutional marriage. Shared friendship networks and organizational affiliations help to reinforce traditional community norms and values.

To the extent that spouses are embedded within these structures, their behaviors are constrained and regulated by the expectations of others. In contrast, people with weak social ties have greater freedom to pursue individualistic interests, develop nontraditional relationships, and avoid obligations to others. The fact that couples have fewer friends and group memberships in common these days suggests that the institutional basis of marriage became even weaker during the last two decades of the twentieth century.

As we described in Chapter 1, marital-decline scholars believe that our culture has become increasingly individualistic since the 1960s. Similarly, Andrew Cherlin argued that contemporary unions have moved away from the companionate form of marriage described by Ernest Burgess during the middle of the last century and toward a more individualistic form of marriage. Our data on friends and group memberships support this view. The decline in shared social networks and the decrease in marital interaction (as described in Chapter 2) indicate a shift away from companionate marriage as well as institutional marriage. Moreover, the decline in social integration since 1980 appears to have had primarily negative consequences for marital quality. Consistent with the views of marital-decline scholars is our finding that increasing individualism appears to have had a corrosive effect on marital quality.

At the same time, however, we found that spouses had stronger religious feelings and were more likely to attend church with their spouses in 2000 than in 1980. Moreover, during this same period married people adopted attitudes that were less favorable toward divorce and more supportive of the norm of lifelong marriage. These trends contradict the notion of a monolithic shift toward greater individualism. Although some aspects of marital life became more individualistic, other aspects of married life became more traditional. Moreover, changes in religiosity, as well as greater support for the norm of lifelong marriage, were associated with modest improvements in marital quality between 1980 and 2000. Overall, our results provide some support for a marital-decline perspective, as well as some support for a modest "reinstitutionalization" of marriage. Combined with the results of previous chapters, these findings suggest a complex picture in which marriage became less institutionalized in certain respects but more institutionalized in others. In the next two chapters, we attempt to make sense of these contradictory trends.

℘ 7

How Our Most Important Relationships Are Changing

$\mathcal{B}$ETWEEN 1980 AND 2000—a relatively short period in historical terms—marriage in the United States changed significantly, both as a social institution and as a private relationship between spouses. During this time changes occurred in the demographic composition of the married population, the links between marriage and the workplace, the financial well-being of couples, gender relations within marriage, and the social integration of married couples. Many of these shifts were accompanied by increases or decreases in mean levels of marital quality in the population. In this chapter we summarize the main findings from our study. We organize this summary around the answers to four questions: (1) How did married individuals and their relationships change between 1980 and 2000? (2) How were these changes related to marital quality in each period? (3) How were changes in these variables between 1980 and 2000 associated with changes in marital quality? and (4) Did the pattern of change differ for husbands and wives?

After answering these questions, we turn to an alternative method —a person-centered approach rather than a variable-centered approach—to address similar issues. Throughout this book, we have focused on changes in one variable at a time. A person-centered approach, in contrast, focuses on groups of individuals who share common characteristics. In particular, we rely on cluster analysis to create groups of similar individuals, based on all the explanatory variables in our study. We then consider how the size of these groups changed over time, as well as how these groups differed in terms of marital quality.

How Did Marriage Change between 1980 and 2000?

The demographic composition of the married population changed in a variety of ways during the last two decades of the twentieth century. By 2000 this population was older, better educated, and more diverse than at any previous time in U.S. history. In particular, our two surveys revealed a number of trends that reflected growing individualism and personal choice in marriage:

- Men and women postponed marriage until later in life, as the mean age at first marriage increased by nearly three years.

- Cohabitation before marriage skyrocketed, rising from 16% of couples in 1980 to 41% by the end of the century—an increase of 250%.

- The percentage of marriages that were second or higher-order unions for one or both spouses increased. Correspondingly, the percentage of married-couple households with stepchildren increased.

- The percentage of married individuals who grew up with divorced parents increased. This change reflected the substantial rise in divorce rates that occurred a generation earlier, during the 1960s and 1970s.

- The percentage of heterogamous unions increased, as spouses became increasingly different from one another in terms of age, ethnicity, and marriage order.

Substantial changes also occurred during these two decades in the links between the home and the economy.

- The percentage of wives in the labor force increased substantially, from 58% to 75%. This increase occurred irrespective of women's race, ethnicity, age, or number of children.

- Husbands' labor-force participation declined slightly. Among employed husbands, however, time spent on the job did not change.

- Although husbands' job demands did not change, wives' job demands increased, especially those that involved attending evening meetings and going on overnight job-related trips.

- The percentage of people who felt that their jobs or their spouses' jobs interfered with family life increased between 1980 and 2000.

- Although wives' labor-force involvement increased substantially, many wives were not enthusiastic about their new economic role, and the percentage of employed wives who preferred "no job at all" increased between surveys. Regardless of decade, the modal choice of married women was a part-time job.

- In both decades the largest group of wives worked to help make ends meet rather than to have a career. Between decades, however, the percentage of wives who worked for careers *or* to make ends meet increased, and the percentage of wives who viewed employment as an escape from an unsatisfying home declined.

- Mean family income increased from $55,600 to $70,000 (adjusted for inflation). This change reflects wives' increased labor-force participation as well as increases in wives' earnings. Similarly, the average net worth of couples increased by 82%.

- Married couples' use of public assistance and perceptions of economic distress declined.

Overall, married couples were in better financial shape at the end of the twentieth century than they had been two decades earlier. This improvement came with the cost of greater work-family stress, however, especially for working-class wives married to men with relatively low earnings.

In addition to increasing economic resources, wives' growing labor-force participation fueled other changes in married life.

- The proportion of family income earned by wives increased from .21 to .32. By 2000 wives earned about one-third of all family income.

- The proportion of housework done by husbands increased from .27 to .35. By 2000 husbands performed about one-third of all housework.

- Spouses became less traditional in their beliefs about the division of labor by gender in marriage—a finding consistent with changes in behavior. In both surveys, however, wives were less traditional than husbands.

- In both decades wives were considerably more likely than husbands to believe that the household division of labor was unfair to them, but the percentage of wives who felt this way did not change between surveys. In contrast, the proportion of husbands who believed that the household division of labor was unfair to them increased significantly, although this proportion was small in absolute terms.

- Irrespective of decade, most spouses reported that they had the final word with respect to some family decisions and that their spouses had the final word with respect to other family decisions. More important, the percentage of couples who generally shared decision making equally increased from 49% to 64%.

Finally, several changes occurred in spouses' social integration, religiosity, and attitudes toward marriage.

- The number of close friends reported by husbands and wives declined. More important, the percentage of spouses who shared close friends declined, and the percentage of spouses with no close friends in common increased.

- Affiliations with clubs and community organizations declined. Individuals who belonged to organizations, however, were more likely to share these affiliations with their spouses in 2000 than in 1980.

- The percentage of respondents who claimed that their parents did not approve of their spouse at the time of marriage declined. This shift was largely due to increases in educational attainment and age at marriage. In both periods the majority of people reported having positive relations with their in-laws.

- People's reports that religion influenced their lives "a great deal" increased, as did reports of joint attendance at religious services.

- Husbands' and wives' support for the norm of lifelong marriage increased, and their attitudes toward divorce became more negative.

Married individuals had fewer friends and organizational affiliations in 2000 than in 1980, which reflects a marked decrease in social participation. At the same time, people's ties to traditional institutions, such as religious organizations and lifelong marriage, grew stronger. During this 20-year period some dimensions of social integration became weaker, whereas other dimensions of social integration became stronger.

Correlates of Marital Quality

Given that many aspects of married life changed between 1980 and 2000, the next step in our analysis was to ask how these factors were related to marital quality. Many of our findings are consistent with earlier studies on this topic (Glenn, 1990; Lewis and Spanier, 1979). For example, we found that people tended to have better-quality marriages if they married at older ages, shared a variety of demographic characteristics with their spouses, and attended religious services together regularly. We also found that people tended to have poorer-quality marriages if they lived together prior to marriage, grew up with divorced parents, or felt economically insecure, which is consistent with earlier research. In addition to replicating earlier findings, however, our surveys revealed associations that are relatively new in the research literature. For example, we found that individuals with high levels of marital quality tended to hold nontraditional attitudes toward the household division of labor, viewed the household division of labor as fair, shared decision making equally with their spouses, had close friends and organizational affiliations in common with their spouses, attended religious services frequently with their spouses, and expressed strong support for the norm of lifelong marriage. It also is of interest to note that some variables in our study were generally unrelated to marital quality, including education, marriage order, husbands' work demands, and wives' percentage of family income.

Period Differences in the Correlates of Marital Quality

Norval Glenn (1990) pointed out that it is difficult to account for marital quality statistically, partly because married individuals do not represent a "closed population." That is, because spouses can terminate marriages through no-fault divorce, individuals with the poorest marital quality tend to leave the married population relatively quickly. The loss of the most troubled couples from the population attenuates the strength of associations between explanatory variables and most dimensions of marital quality. As we noted in Chapter 2, the percentage of divorced individuals in the U.S. population was slightly higher in 2000 than in 1980. With more movement out of the married population, we might expect to find fewer significant correlates of marital quality, as well as lower R^2 values, in the second survey than in the first one.

Some of our results appear to support this assumption. For example, the 1980 regression equation for marital happiness identified 14 significant explanatory variables and produced an R^2 value of .26. (See Appendix 2.) In comparison, the 2000 regression equation for marital happiness identified only nine significant explanatory variables and produced an R^2 value of .21. In addition, between 1980 and 2000 four variables (gender, marriage order, family income, and shared friends) became weaker predictors of marital happiness, whereas only one variable (economic hardship) became a stronger predictor. These differences suggest that it became more difficult to identify significant correlates of marital happiness between 1980 and 2000.

Other results, however, contradict this notion. For example, the 1980 regression equation for marital problems yielded 12 significant predictors and produced an R^2 value of .23, whereas the corresponding 2000 regression equation yielded 17 significant predictors and produced an R^2 value of .25. (See Appendix 2.) And between 1980 and 2000 three variables (wives' employment, economic distress, and religiosity) became significantly stronger predictors of marital problems, whereas no variable became a significantly weaker predictor. Taking all five dimensions of marital quality into account, our results do not suggest that the small rise in the percentage of divorced individuals in the population between surveys restricted our ability to detect statistically significant correlates of marital quality. Of course, it is plausible that it was more difficult to identify correlates of marital quality between 1960 (before the rise in divorce rates) and 1980 (when divorce rates stabilized). Given the absence of large-scale surveys of marital quality before 1980, this hypothesis is difficult to test.

We also found that most of the regression coefficients in our analyses did not differ significantly across decades. For all five outcomes, our decomposition analysis generated a total of 190 pairs of regression coefficients. Of these pairs, only 20 (11%) differed significantly in the two surveys.

Did a common pattern underlie changes in the correlates of marital quality? As we noted in Chapter 3, the presence of stepchildren in the household was associated with less marital happiness, more marital conflict, and greater divorce proneness in 1980, but with more marital happiness, less marital conflict, and lower divorce proneness in 2000. These findings suggest that stepchildren, once considered to be a risk factor for poor marital quality, are no longer a source of marital tension for most married couples. Although economic distress was associated with lower marital happiness, less frequent interaction, more problems, and greater divorce proneness in both surveys, these associations became stronger over time—a finding we reported in Chapter 4. These results suggest that couples became more sensitive to financial insecurity, with perceptions of economic decline becoming increasingly corrosive of marital quality. Finally, wives' employment was associated with more conflict and a larger number of problems in 1980 but with less conflict and a smaller number of problems in 2000. This finding suggests that families are accommodating more successfully to having two earners these days. (Nevertheless, when wives spent long hours on the job in 2000, marital quality appeared to suffer. Apparently, the ease with which families can accommodate two earners without strain depends on the number of hours wives spend in the labor force.) No other regression coefficients that changed across decades did so for more than one marital outcome. These results do not suggest that changes in the correlates of marital quality between surveys were part of a general pattern. With a few exceptions, the predictors of marital quality were similar in magnitude and direction in both periods.

To quantify the overall degree of similarity between decades, we calculated the bivariate correlations between each of the five dimensions of marital quality and each of the explanatory variables separately for 1980 and 2000. Then, for each dimension of marital quality, we calculated the correlation between the 1980 correlations and the 2000 correlations. The resulting values indicate the extent to which the overall pattern of correlations between the 38 explanatory variables and the five dimensions of marital quality were similar across decades. This procedure revealed coefficients that were large and statistically significant for all five dimensions: .92 for marital happiness, .93 for marital interaction, .93 for marital conflict, .88 for marital problems, and .87 for divorce proneness. These results demonstrate that, with a few exceptions, the correlates of marital quality were remarkably similar in both periods.

"His" and "Her" Marriages: Gender Differences in the Correlates of Marital Quality

In an influential book, Jessie Bernard (1982) argued that husbands and wives experience marriage in fundamentally different ways, and that it is useful to distinguish "his" marriage from "her" marriage. Bernard's thesis has theoretical as well as methodological implications. Theoretically, this view assumes that gender is the central organizing principle in marriage, and that gender relations shape spouses' perceptions, feelings, and behaviors in basic—and perhaps irreconcilable—ways. Moreover, it is difficult to make generalizations about marriage, and researchers are on safer ground when they describe marriage as it is experienced separately by women and men. Methodologically, this view implies that one cannot reach conclusions about marriage by studying spouses of one gender only. Instead, it is necessary to interview spouses of both genders to determine their particular, and often clashing, understandings of the same marriage.

How does Bernard's thesis stand up against the findings in this book? In Chapter 2 we reported that wives scored lower than husbands on all five dimensions of marital quality, irrespective of the year of the survey. That is, wives reported less happiness, less interaction, more conflict, more problems, and greater divorce proneness than did husbands. These findings are consistent with Bernard's notion of "his" and "her" marriages. Although wives reported lower marital quality than did husbands, however, the differences were small. Averaged across all five dimensions of marital quality, wives scored .13 of a standard deviation below husbands in 1980 and .14 of a standard deviation below husbands in 2000. Most researchers would describe these effect sizes as weak rather than strong. (See our discussion of effect sizes in Appendix 1.)

We also considered gender differences in the correlates of marital quality. In Chapter 5 we reported that the links between decision-making equality and marital quality were stronger for wives than for husbands. (Nevertheless, decision-making equality was associated with better marital quality for spouses of both genders.) Similarly, we noted in Chapter 5 that husbands who claimed that they sometimes had the final word in family decisions reported no more marital conflict than did other husbands. In contrast, wive who claimed that their husbands sometimes had the final word reported more marital conflict than did other wives. This particular pattern, however, did not emerge for any other dimension of marital quality. Of all the marital characteristics that we considered in this book, only one—the husband's share of housework—operated in a consistently different manner for husbands and wives. This variable was associated with less marital happiness and greater divorce proneness among husbands but with more marital happiness and less divorce proneness among wives. To a certain extent, housework represents a zero-sum game; that is, the more housework husbands do, the less housework wives do, and vice versa. Consequently, doing a great deal of housework—especially doing more than one's fair share—tends to erode marital quality for husbands as well as wives. But with a few exceptions, our main conclusion is that the correlates of marital quality are quite similar for husbands and wives. This finding is surprising, given the large research literature on gender differences in romantic relationships and marriage (McGraw and Walker, 2004; Thompson, 1993; Thompson and Walker, 1991).

To demonstrate the overall degree of gender similarity, we calculated the bivariate correlations between the five dimensions of marital quality and each of the explanatory variables separately for husbands and wives. Then, for each dimension of marital quality, we calculated the correlation between the wives' correlations and the husbands' correlations. This procedure produced similarity coefficients that were moderately high and statistically significant for all five dimensions of marital quality: .77 for marital happiness, .87 for marital interaction, .90 for marital conflict, .91 for marital problems, and .89 for divorce proneness. These findings indicate a substantial convergence between husbands and wives in the overall pattern of associations between marital characteristics and marital outcomes. As far as marital quality is concerned, men and women react to the circumstances of married life in comparable ways.

The general similarity between husbands and wives suggests that researchers who develop causal models of marital processes will tend to get similar results, regardless of whether they rely on data from husbands or wives. To illustrate this notion, we return to the causal model shown in Figure 4.9 in Chapter 4. This model estimated the direct and indirect effects of wives' hours of employment and family income on five dimensions of marital quality. The results in the figure were based on the pooled sample of husbands and wives in 2000. In a second set of analyses (not shown), we estimated the model separately for husbands and wives. In one analysis we allowed the path coefficients to vary between husbands and wives, and in a second analysis we constrained the path coefficients to be identical for husbands and wives. The model with constrained coefficients fit the data as well as did the model with unconstrained coefficients. In other words, allowing the estimated causal paths to differ for husbands and wives did not improve the fit of the model to the data. It appears that the underlying causal processes linking wives' employment, family income, perceived economic distress, and marital quality are similar for husbands and wives.

Overall, we find some support for Bernard's theses of "his" and "her" marriages when we look at *mean* levels of marital quality. We find little support for Bernard's thesis, however, when we look at the *correlates* of marital quality. Although wives may be slightly less happy than husbands with their marriages, the factors that predict marital happiness and other dimensions of marital quality are basically similar for wives and husbands. In this sense, Bernard may have overestimated the extent to which gender shapes men's and women's experiences of marriage.

Changes in Marriage and Marital Quality between 1980 and 2000

Decomposition methods made it possible to determine how changes in the characteristics of married individuals between 1980 and 2000 were related to changes in mean levels of marital quality in the population. Detailed results of these analyses appear in Tables 9–13 in Appendix 2. To simplify the presentation of results, Figure 7.1 provides a summary of the key findings. In this figure the column labeled "Change in EV" indicates the direction of change in the explanatory variables between surveys—that is, whether these variables increased, decreased, or

Figure 7.1 Associations between changes in explanatory variables (EV) and changes in mean levels of marital quality between 1980 and 2000: decomposition analysis summary

		Change in marital quality variables				
Explanatory variable	Change in EV	Marital happiness	Marital interaction	Marital conflict	Marital problems	Divorce proneness
Demographic factors						
Age	+	−	−	−	−	ns
Age at current marriage	+	ns	+	ns	−	−
Black respondent	ns	ns	ns	ns	ns	ns
Latino respondent	+	ns	ns	ns	ns	ns
Other race respondent	+	ns	+	ns	ns	−
Premarital cohabitation	+	ns	−	+	+	+
Education of respondent	+	ns	ns	ns	ns	ns
Remarried respondent	+	ns	ns	ns	ns	ns
No. of children < 19	−	ns	+	ns	ns	ns
Any stepchildren	+	ns	ns	ns	ns	ns
Heterogamy index	+	−	−	+	+	+
Parental divorce	+	ns	ns	+	+	+
Employment and income						
Husband employed	−	ns	ns	ns	ns	ns
Husband's weekly hours	ns	ns	ns	ns	ns	ns
Wife employed	+	ns	ns	ns	ns	ns
Wife's weekly hours	+	−	ns	ns	ns	ns
Husband's job demands	ns	ns	ns	ns	ns	ns
Wife's job demands	+	ns	ns	ns	ns	ns
Family income	+	+	ns	ns	ns	ns
Public assistance	−	ns	ns	ns	−	−
Economic distress	−	+	+	−	−	−
Gender relations						
Wife's share of income	+	ns	ns	ns	ns	ns
Hsbd's share of housework	+	ns	+	ns	+	ns
Housework unfair to hsbd.	+	−	ns	+	+	+
Housework unfair to wife	ns	ns	ns	ns	ns	ns
Traditional gender views	−	+	+	ns	−	ns
Equal decision making	+	+	+	−	−	−
Husband has last word	−	ns	ns	ns	ns	ns
Wife has last word	ns	ns	ns	ns	ns	ns
Social integration						
Shared friends	−	−	−	+	+	+
Shared group affiliations	−	+	ns	ns	−	−
Religiosity	+	+	ns	ns	+	ns
Attendance at services	+	ns	ns	ns	ns	ns
Support lifelong marriage	+	+	ns	−	−	−

+ = Increase between 1980 and 2000 ($p \leq .05$)
− = Decrease between 1980 and 2000 ($p \leq .05$)
ns = No change between 1980 and 2000 ($p > .05$)

did not change significantly. For example, the plus sign (+) following "Age" in the first row indicates that the mean age of married individuals increased during this 20-year period. The columns labeled "Change in marital quality variables" show the direction of the association between changes in each of the explanatory variables and each dimension of marital quality. For example, the negative sign (−) under "Marital happiness" in the first row indicates that the rise in the mean age of married couples was associated with a significant decline in marital happiness in the population. Similarly, the negative signs in the rest of this row indicate that the increase in age was associated with a decline in marital interaction, a decline in marital conflict, and a decline in marital problems. In the following section, we summarize the results for each dimension of marital quality separately.

Marital Happiness

Our decomposition analysis revealed that changes in several variables were related to declines in marital happiness between 1980 and 2000. These changes included the increase in age, the increase in marital heterogamy, the increase in wives' weekly hours of employment, the increase in husbands' perceptions of unfairness in the division of labor, and the decline in shared friends. Taken together, these changes were associated with a decline in marital happiness in the population equivalent to .11 of a standard deviation.

Despite these problematic trends, our decomposition analysis revealed several changes associated with improved marital happiness: the increase in family income, the decline in perceived economic hardship, the decline in traditional gender attitudes, the increase in decision-making equality, the increase in religiosity, and the increase in support for the norm of lifelong marriage. Curiously, the decline in shared organizational affiliations was associated with more (rather than less) marital happiness. This occurred because, although the proportion of individuals who belonged to organizations declined overall, individuals who belonged to organizations were more likely to share these affiliations with their spouses in 2000 than in 1980. Correspondingly, individuals who belonged to organizations but did not share these affiliations with their spouses (the group with the lowest level of marital happiness) declined. Overall, changes in these variables were associated with an increase in marital happiness in the population equivalent to .13 of a standard deviation.

These results demonstrate that positive changes essentially offset negative changes, which resulted in no net difference in marital happiness between surveys. Table 9 in Appendix 2 leads to the same conclusion, albeit in a more detailed way. With all variables in the decomposition equation, the difference in intercepts between surveys was $-.06$, which was not statistically significant. (The difference in intercepts is the same as the b coefficient for decade in an equation with pooled data from both surveys.) In other words, the small difference in intercepts indicates no net change between decades in the mean level of marital happiness in the population.

Marital Interaction

Several changes were associated with declines in marital interaction between 1980 and 2000. These changes included the increase in age, the growing popularity of cohabitation before marriage, the rise in heterogamy, and the decline in the number of shared friends. In addition, although it is not shown in Figure 7.1, the increase in wives' hours of employment was associated with a decline in marital interaction at a marginally significant level. Taken together, changes in these variables were associated with a decline in marital interaction in the population equivalent to .13 of a standard deviation.

Offsetting these declines were other trends that appeared to raise the level of marital interaction in the population: the increase in age at marriage, the growth of the number of "other nonwhites" in the population, the decline in the number of children in the household, the drop in perceived economic distress, the increase in the husband's share of housework, the erosion of traditional gender attitudes, and the increase in shared decision making. Taken together, these variables were associated with a rise in marital interaction in the population equivalent to .12 of a standard deviation.

Once again, the changes that we tracked during this 20-year period resulted in no net change in marital interaction. As we noted in Chapter 2, however, the mean level of marital interaction in the population declined by about one-third of a standard deviation between 1980 and 2000. Despite the fact that the variables in our analysis essentially offset each other, the drop in marital interaction between surveys continued to be significant in our decomposition analysis. Nevertheless, our analysis indicates that if the positive changes described above had not occurred, the decline in marital interaction would have been even greater, approaching one-half of a standard deviation. Although we cannot explain the decline in marital interaction with our survey data, this trend may reflect a cultural shift toward greater individualism in American society, as Putnam (2000) and others have claimed. This trend also may reflect a desire for some spouses to retain elements of a single lifestyle in their marriages. The finding that couples had fewer friends in common in 2000 than in 1980 is consistent with this interpretation.

Marital Conflict

Several changes appeared to exacerbate the level of discord in marriage, including the growing popularity of cohabitation before marriage, the rise in heterogamy, the increase in parental divorce, the increase in husbands' perceptions of unfairness in the household division of labor, and the decline in shared friends. Taken together, these variables were associated with a rise in marital conflict in the population equivalent to .11 of a standard deviation. Offsetting these factors were other changes, including the increase in age, the decline in perceived economic distress, more decision-making equality, and growing support for the norm of lifelong marriage. Taken together, these variables appeared to lower the mean level of marital conflict in the population by .08 of a standard deviation. Once again, these positive and negative changes largely offset each other.

We noted in Chapter 2 that the mean level of marital conflict in the population declined by .15 of a standard deviation between 1980 and 2000. As Table 11 in Appendix 2 indicates, the decline in marital conflict continued to be significant, even with all explanatory variables in the decomposition analysis. The value of $-.169$ represents the mean change that would have occurred if there had been no differences between decades in the means and slopes of the explanatory variables included in the model. In other words, we were unable to account for the lower level of conflict in 2000. Nevertheless, our results indicate that if cohabitation, heterogamy, and parental divorce had not increased, the decline in conflict would have been even greater than we observed (about one-fourth rather than one-seventh of a standard deviation). Correspondingly, if there had been no increases in age, decision-making equality, and support for the norm of lifelong marriage, and if there had been no decline in economic distress, then the drop in marital conflict would have been much smaller than we observed.

Marital Problems

Several trends between 1980 and 2000 were associated with increases in reports of marital problems, including the rise in cohabitation before marriage, the increase in heterogamy, the increase in parental divorce, the increase in husbands' share of housework, the increase in husbands' perceptions of unfairness in the household division of labor, the decline in the number of shared friends, and the increase in religiosity. The positive link between religiosity and marital problems was puzzling, but it may reflect the fact that shared attendance at religious services was included in the model. Holding strong religious beliefs but not attending services with one's spouse may lead to problems in the marriage, as we noted in Chapter 6. This finding also may reflect a selection effect, as some religious spouses may choose not to divorce, despite problems in the marriage. Taken together, these variables were associated with an increase in marital problems in the population equivalent to .13 of a standard deviation. Offsetting these trends were the increase in age, the increase in age at marriage, the decline in use of public assistance, the decline in perceived economic hardship, the adoption of more liberal gender attitudes, the growth of shared decision making, the increase in support for the norm of lifelong marriage, and changes in group affiliations. Taken together, these variables were associated with a decline in marital problems in the population equivalent to .14 of a standard deviation.

As we reported in Chapter 2, people's reports of marital problems declined by about one-tenth of a standard deviation between 1980 and 2000. After taking all explanatory variables into account, the difference between decades remained significant. In other words, we were unable to explain why marital problems declined during this period using the variables in our decomposition model. This result means that some unmeasured factors lowered people's perceptions of problems in their marriages during this period. Nevertheless, our analysis suggests that, on the one hand, if cohabitation, heterogamy, and parental divorce had not increased, the decline in marital problems would have been more than twice as large as we observed, or about one-fourth of a standard deviation. On the other hand, if other changes had not occurred, such as the increase in age at marriage, the shift toward more egalitarian gender attitudes, and the increase in shared decision making, then the mean level of marital problems in the population would not have declined at all.

Divorce Proneness

Several explanatory variables were linked with a rise in divorce proneness between decades, including increases in cohabitation before marriage, heterogamy, parental divorce, and husbands' perceptions of unfairness in the household division of labor, as well as the decrease in shared friends. In addition, the increase in wives' work demands was associated with greater divorce proneness at a marginally significant level. Taken together, these variables were associated with a rise in divorce proneness in the population equivalent to .12 of a standard deviation. Offsetting these trends were the increase in age at marriage, the growth in the size of the "other nonwhite" category, the drop in welfare use, the decline in perceived economic hardship, the increase in decision-making equality, growing support for the norm of lifelong marriage, and changes in patterns of group affiliations. Taken together, these variables were associated with a decline in divorce proneness equivalent to .13 of a standard deviation. Overall, these positive and negative changes were approximately equal in magnitude, resulting in no net change in divorce proneness in the population.

Gender Differences in Decomposition Results

In addition to the decomposition analyses summarized in Figure 7.1, we conducted separate decompositions for husbands and wives. These analyses revealed a number of differences between husbands and wives, although most of these differences were a matter of degree rather than of substance. For example, the increase in the average age of couples appeared to lower marital happiness by .05 of a standard deviation for wives but by only .01 of a standard deviation for husbands. This difference was due to the fact that age was related to marital happiness more strongly among wives than among husbands. In other words, as couples grew older, wives tended to become less happy with their marriages more quickly than did husbands. Another example refers to family income. The increase in family income between decades was associated with an increase in marital happiness equivalent to .04 of a standard deviation for wives but less than .01 of a standard deviation for husbands. This result reflected the fact that family income was related to marital happiness more strongly among wives than husbands. These gender differences for age and income, however, did not appear for other dimensions of marital quality.

Only two variables consistently operated differently for husbands and wives, one of which was decision-making equality. The increase in decision-making equality was associated with an increase in marital happiness equivalent to .06 of a standard deviation for wives and .01 of a standard deviation for husbands. Similarly, the increase in decision-making equality was associated with an increase in marital interaction equivalent to .04 of a standard deviation for wives, compared with .02 of a standard deviation for husbands. With respect to marital conflict, the increase in decision-making equality was associated with a decline of .04 of a standard deviation for wives and .02 of a standard deviation for husbands. Corresponding declines were .05 of a standard deviation for wives and .01 of a standard deviation for husbands (for marital problems), and .04 of a standard deviation for wives and .01 of a standard deviation for husbands (for divorce proneness). These results reflect the fact that decision-making equality was related more strongly to dimensions of marital quality among wives than among husbands. This pattern makes sense, given that a shift from patriarchal to equal decision making should benefit wives more than husbands. Even though the results for decision-making equality were consistently stronger for wives than for husbands, however, the direction of change was similar for both genders.

The only variable that produced opposing results for husbands and wives was the husband's share of housework. The increase in this variable between 1980 and 2000 was related to general improvements in marital quality among wives and to general declines in marital quality among husbands. The results for this variable (expressed in standard deviation units) were .03 for wives and −.07 for husbands for marital happiness, .00 for wives and .04 for husbands for marital conflict, .00

for wives and .06 for husbands for marital problems, and −.02 for wives and .06 for husbands for divorce proneness. In other words, as husbands increased their share of housework, wives became happier with their marriages and reported less divorce proneness. In contrast, as husbands increased their share of housework, men reported less happiness, more conflict, more problems, and greater divorce proneness. These results clearly indicate that housework has the potential to be a contentious issue in many marriages. But despite the results for this one variable, the overall pattern of results from the decomposition analysis revealed that social change had similar implications for the marital quality of husbands and wives. This conclusion is consistent with our finding, noted above, that the correlates of marital quality were generally similar for men and women.

Are Changes in Marital Quality Substantively Important?

Most of the associations between changes in marital characteristics and changes in aggregate levels of marital quality appear to be relatively weak. For example, we indicated that changes in some of our explanatory variables between 1980 and 2000 were associated with a rise in divorce proneness in the married population equivalent to .12 of a standard deviation. Correspondingly, we reported that changes in other variables were associated with a decline in divorce proneness equivalent to .13 of a standard deviation. Although these estimated changes are modest, it is important to note that even modest differences can be substantively important when applied to large populations.

To provide a clearer understanding of these changes, it is useful to think in terms of successful (or unsuccessful) outcomes in the population (Rosenthal, 1994). Assume that a successful outcome is present in 50% of the population. In the present context, this would occur if we split the divorce proneness scale at its median into *low* and *high* groups. Given that half of all marriages end in divorce, and given that our divorce proneness scale is an excellent predictor of divorce, the 50% figure is not unreasonable. We could then describe change as the proportion of cases in 1980 and 2000 that fell into these two groups. Under these circumstances, the effect size would be equivalent to twice the difference in the proportion of cases in the high group between surveys.

For example, if we assume that half of all marriages were divorce

prone in 1980, then factors that increased the level of divorce proneness in the population during the next two decades would have shifted
the proportion of divorce-prone marriages from .50 in 1980 to .56
in 2000. (The difference of .06 is one-half the effect size, which was
.12.) Although a .06 increase may not seem large, we need to consider the size of the population to which it applies. In 2000 there were
approximately 60,050,000 married couples in the United States (U.S.
Census Bureau, 2002). Given the size of this population, the increase
in divorce proneness would have raised the number of married couples at risk for divorce from 30,025,000 to 33,628,000—an increase of
3,603,000 couples. This did not happen, of course, because other social
changes (such as the rise in age at first marriage and the decline in perceived economic hardship) had offsetting effects. Correspondingly, if
the factors that *decreased* divorce proneness during this period had not
been offset by other trends (such as the increase in marital heterogamy
and parental divorce), then there would have been 3,603,000 *fewer* couples at risk of divorce in 2000. Given that these numbers represent
7,206,000 individual husbands and wives, and given that most divorces
also involve children, the total number of people involved is large indeed. In other words, even small effect sizes, when applied to large
populations, reflect changes in the lives of many people.

Summary of Changes in Marital Quality

Across all five dimensions of marital quality, a similar story appears:
some social changes appear to strengthen marriage, and other social
changes appear to weaken marriage. Our findings are consistent with
the general assumptions that we stated in Chapter 1. We argued that
social change during any particular era is unlikely to have consistently
positive or negative implications for individual or family well-being.
Instead, economic, social, cultural, and demographic changes often
have contradictory and offsetting effects. This assumption applies particularly well to our results for marital happiness and divorce proneness. Our research suggests that between 1980 and 2000, a balance
of positive and negative forces kept these two dimensions of marital quality in a state of equilibrium. Although merely looking at the
means (which were nearly identical in each decade) suggests that not
much was going on, our more detailed analyses revealed a great deal of

churning "beneath the surface." Stability, like change, is problematic and requires an explanation. Although we found changes in three other dimensions of marital quality—marital interaction, conflict, and problems—the extent of change might have been larger or smaller if certain social processes had not been operating.

We also assumed that the effects of single variables are almost always weak—an assumption that reflects a substantive rather than a methodological point. Because social relationships are shaped by a large number of contextual forces, no single variable is likely to have a major impact on aggregate levels of marital quality. Moreover, if marriage is shaped by a large number of variables with small and often contradictory effects, then large-scale changes in marital quality will tend to occur gradually, rather than quickly, during most historical periods.

Readers should be aware of several limitations of our methods. First, a decomposition analysis is not the same as a causal analysis. Although methods such as path analysis and structural equation modeling estimate the direct and indirect effects of the explanatory variables, decomposition analysis estimates only the direct effects. This difference has implications for how one interprets the role of our explanatory variables. For example, consider remarriage. Compared with first marriages, remarriages are more heterogamous and more likely to be preceded by cohabitation. If one views remarriage as a cause of heterogamy and cohabitation, then the decomposition analysis omits the indirect effects of remarriage (through heterogamy and cohabitation) on marital quality. Consequently, the decomposition analysis underestimates the total effect (direct effect + indirect effect) of remarriage. In addition, our analysis was not able to consider reciprocal relationships between explanatory variables and marital quality. For example, although wives' long hours of employment may put a strain on some marriages, it also is possible that some wives in troubled marriages seek out long hours of employment. Given the large number of variables in the current analysis, testing specific causal models must await future research. Nevertheless, decomposition analysis is a useful approach for taking a first pass through the data to locate the most promising variables for further investigation (Firebaugh, 1997).

Another limitation involves our use of single items to measure some explanatory variables, such as religiosity and decision-making equality. Measurement error associated with single-item indicators generally attenuates correlations and can lead researchers to underestimate the strength of associations between variables in the population. Moreover, although we examined five dimensions of marital quality, our list was not exhaustive, and it is possible that different trends would have appeared if we had included other dimensions of marital relationships, such as commitment to one's partner. Furthermore, the availability of only two time points makes it impossible to know the true shape of marital trajectories. For example, it is possible that marital happiness rose (or fell) after 1980 but returned to its earlier level by 2000, which would result in the mistaken conclusion that no change had occurred. Finally, our analysis was based primarily on a variable-centered approach, in which we considered each variable individually. Of course, society consists of individuals, not variables, and each person and marriage can be thought of as a unique cluster of traits and characteristics. We attempt to deal with this limitation in the following section.

A Person-Centered Approach

Throughout this book we have focused on individual variables. For example, in Chapter 6, we presented information sequentially on people's close friends, organizational affiliations, relations with in-laws, religiosity, and attitudes toward marriage. We did not attempt to combine these variables in a single analysis to see if people with high levels of social integration also tended to be religious or to hold certain attitudes toward marriage. An alternative approach is to search for groups of individuals with similar profiles of scores across a range of variables. This way of looking at the data, often referred to as a "person-centered" approach, combines individuals into groups on the basis of characteristics that these individuals have in common. A person-centered approach provides an alternative way of investigating the data and can yield insights that complement a variable-centered approach. Despite the appeal of this approach, especially for exploratory work, these methods have rarely been used by marital researchers. (For an exception, see Hetherington and Kelly, 2002.)

To accomplish this goal, we relied on cluster analysis, a general set of statistical techniques that combines individuals into groups (clusters) on the basis of multiple characteristics. Statisticians have developed a variety of clustering algorithms, and our preliminary analyses explored several different methods (Arabie, Hubert, and De Soete, 1996; Bailey, 1994). To determine the optimal number of clusters, we relied on statistical criteria as well as the interpretability of each solution. (See Appendix 1 for more details.) We settled on a straightforward, parsimonious categorization of married individuals into five groups, with people assigned to the cluster that best matched their particular mix of characteristics. This solution appeared to be stable; that is, the same clusters emerged irrespective of decade or the gender of the respondent. These clusters were based on *all* the explanatory variables described in this book

Five Types of Marriage

Cluster 1 reflected *disadvantaged, young, single-earner marriages.* Of the five groups, respondents in this cluster had the lowest level of education, earned the least income, reported the fewest financial assets, experienced the highest level of economic distress, and were most likely to have used public assistance during the previous three years. One-fifth of individuals in this group did not have high school diplomas. Moreover, the majority of husbands were relatively low-status workers, such as unskilled laborers or industrial operatives, which involved few job demands. More than one-fourth of these husbands had been unemployed during the previous three years, and at the time of the survey more than one-fifth of husbands did not have jobs (because of either unemployment or a disability). These individuals were young (mainly in their twenties and thirties) and had married at relatively early ages. About three-fourths of these couples had preschool children in the household. These marriages followed a traditional pattern: most wives were not employed (and if they were employed, they held part-time rather than full-time jobs), husbands did relatively few household chores, and spouses held conservative views about gender. These couples were struggling to get by, but their traditional attitudes and division of labor prevented wives from realizing their income-earning potential.

We refer to the second cluster as *working-class, young, dual-earner marriages.* These individuals were relatively young (mainly in their twenties and thirties)—not much older than individuals in the first group. Although they married at relatively early ages, many had lived together before marrying. These couples had slightly more education than did couples in the first cluster. The majority of husbands held blue-collar jobs, although one-fourth held lower-level professional or managerial positions. As was the case in cluster 1, unemployment was relatively common in this group; about one-sixth of husbands had been unemployed in the previous three years. These couples had below-average family incomes, relatively few assets, and elevated levels of perceived economic distress. These couples were not as badly off as were couples in the first cluster, however, because the great majority of wives were in the labor force. Most of these wives were employed full-time, mainly to help make ends meet. These wives typically held clerical or sales jobs or were employed in the service sector. Although wives contributed about one-third of family income, they were especially likely to feel that the household division of labor was unfair to them.

We refer to the third cluster as *working-class / middle-class, traditional, single-earner marriages*. This cluster included couples with average levels of education, income, and assets. Although most husbands held blue-collar jobs, more than one-third held professional or managerial positions. Compared with those in the other clusters, couples in this group had the largest number of children. The great majority of wives were full-time homemakers, and husbands did few household chores. This group had the lowest level of decision-making equality. In addition, these couples held traditional attitudes toward gender, were religious, attended religious services frequently, and reported strong support for the norm of lifelong marriage. With respect to attitudes as well as behavior, this was the most conservative of all clusters.

Cluster 4 reflected *middle-class, egalitarian, dual-earner marriages*. Members of this cluster were older (mainly in their thirties and forties), had married at older ages, and were better educated than were members of the first three clusters. All wives in this cluster held jobs, and the great majority were employed full-time. About half of the husbands and wives held professional or managerial positions. Spouses held liberal attitudes toward gender, husbands in this group performed the largest share of household chores, and these couples reported the highest level of decision-making equality. These couples also had fewer children than did couples in the other clusters.

Finally, cluster 5 referred to *upper-middle-class, prosperous, mostly dual-earner marriages*. Like those in cluster 4, members of cluster 5 tended to be older (mainly in their thirties forties). Members of this group also had married at relatively late ages. Husbands and wives were well educated, the great majority being college graduates. Most of husbands held demanding professional or managerial positions. Nearly one-third of wives were full-time homemakers. When wives were employed, however, they tended to be in professional or managerial positions. Of all clusters, these couples had the largest annual income, the highest rate of home ownership, and the most financial assets. (The mean was greater than $500,000.) Not surprisingly, perceptions of economic distress were rare among this group. Like those in cluster 4, these individuals held liberal attitudes toward gender, although husbands performed only an average proportion of household chores—perhaps because their wives contributed a smaller share of family income. Although decision-making equality was high, most husbands and wives had the final word with respect to certain decisions, which suggests that spouses had separate spheres of influence.

Given that these five clusters appeared in both surveys, the next step was to see if the size of these groups differed in 1980 and 2000. Figure 7.2 provides this information. In 1980 working-class, young, dual-earner marriages were the largest group and represented 32% of all marriages. Working-class / middle-class, traditional, single-earner marriages were the second largest group, at 30%. Disadvantaged, young, single-earner marriages and middle-class, egalitarian, dual-earner marriages represented 18% and 14% of the total, respectively. Upper-middle-class, prosperous, mostly dual-earner marriages were relatively uncommon at 6%.

The distribution of these five groups differed considerably in 2000. Between surveys, working-class, young, dual-earner marriages declined by six percentage points and no longer represented the largest group. Three trends—the rising age at marriage, the increase in spouses' educational attainment, and the growth in wives' earnings (in constant dollars)—were responsible for the decline in the relative size of this group. The second largest group in 1980, working-class / middle-class, traditional, single-earner marriages, declined by 12 percentage points between surveys. Several trends eroded the size of this group, including the growing labor-force participation of wives, the decline in family size, the increase in husbands' share of housework, and the increase in decision-making equality. Curiously, this cluster de-

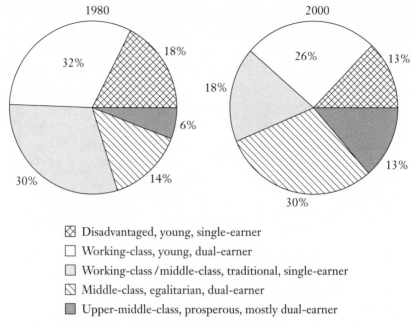

Figure 7.2   Five types of marriage based on cluster analysis

clined in size despite the fact that religiosity and religious service attendance increased. The category comprising disadvantaged, young, single-earner marriages declined by five percentage points, owing largely
to increases in education, wives' labor-force participation, wives' earnings, and age at marriage.

The most dramatic change between 1980 and 2000 was the increase
in the percentage of middle-class, egalitarian, dual-earner couples. In
2000 this group represented the most common type of marriage, rising
from only 14% of all couples in 1980 to 30% of all couples in 2000—
more than doubling in size. Several changes during this period were responsible for the growing dominance of this group, including the increase in educational attainment, the rise in wives' earnings, the decline
in family size, and the general cultural shift toward gender egalitarianism (as spouses shared breadwinning, housework, and decision making). The fifth group, upper-middle-class, prosperous, mostly dual-
earner couples, also more than doubled in size, increasing from 6% of
all couples in 1980 to 13% in 2000. The change in the size of this
group reflects the growth of the U.S. economy during the 1990s, which
propelled many couples to higher levels of affluence.

In general, changes in the size of these groups in the population reflected the broad social trends that shaped marriage during the last two decades of the twentieth century. Married couples became more prosperous, largely because of the expansion of the economy during the 1990s, along with the increase in wives' education, labor-force participation, and wages. At the same time, married couples became more egalitarian, as is reflected in shared breadwinning, family work, and decision-making power. Of course, these two trends are related, as changes in wives' economic position fueled the cultural shift toward more egalitarian arrangements in marriage.

Marriage Clusters and Marital Quality

All five dimensions of marital quality varied significantly across marriage clusters. Because the patterns were very similar in 1980 and 2000, we pooled the data from the two surveys. Figure 7.3 shows how mean levels of marital happiness, interaction, conflict, problems, and divorce proneness varied across the five types of marriages. Disadvantaged, young, single-earner couples tended to have a comparatively high level of marital interaction and approximately average levels of marital happiness, conflict, problems, and divorce proneness. It is not difficult to understand why marital interaction was high in this group. A substantial minority of these husbands did not have jobs (because of unemployment or disabilities), some husbands worked less than full-time, and almost all wives were full-time homemakers. Consequently, spouses in this cluster had more opportunities to engage in shared activities than did spouses in the other clusters. More surprising is the fact that conflict, problems, and divorce proneness were not noticeably elevated in this group. Despite the economic hardship experienced by these couples, the stress of having to make ends meet may have been offset by the high level of interaction between spouses. A few studies have shown that spouses who spend more time together tend to experience high levels of marital quality (White, 1983; Zuo, 1992). Consequently, frequent interaction may have reinforced the cohesiveness of these couples in the face of other difficulties.

Working class, young, dual-earner couples appeared to be the most troubled, with a below-average level of marital happiness and modestly elevated levels of marital conflict, problems, and divorce proneness. These couples lacked the economic resources that help to strengthen

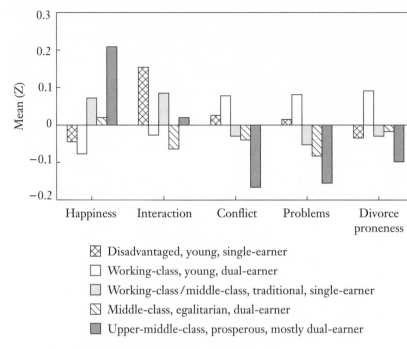

☒ Disadvantaged, young, single-earner
☐ Working-class, young, dual-earner
▨ Working-class / middle-class, traditional, single-earner
◩ Middle-class, egalitarian, dual-earner
▰ Upper-middle-class, prosperous, mostly dual-earner

Figure 7.3   Marital quality profiles by marriage type

marital relationships, and they did not have the benefit of a high level of marital interaction, as did couples in the first cluster. In addition, many of these individuals were in the early years of marriage—a time that requires the greatest adjustment on the part of spouses. Moreover, most of these wives were in the labor force because their husbands had modest earnings—not because they held jobs that were intrinsically rewarding. In fact, many of these wives preferred not to be employed or to be employed fewer hours. Correspondingly, husbands in this group often complained that their wives came home from work tense and irritable or that their wives' jobs interfered with family life. Moreover, these husbands were less supportive of their wives' jobs than were husbands in clusters 4 or 5 (the other two dual-earner groups). Finally, wives in this group were especially likely to feel that the household division of labor was unfair.

Working-class / middle-class, traditional, single-earner couples had slightly above-average levels of marital happiness and interaction, and approximately average levels of conflict, problems, and divorce proneness. The elevated level of marital interaction is probably due to the fact that wives were not employed, and husbands' jobs did not involve substantial demands, such as long hours, working in the evenings, or taking overnight trips. Their average scores on other dimensions of marital quality may reflect a balance between strengths and weaknesses. On the one hand, these couples had an adequate level of family income and reported relatively little economic distress. Moreover, a strong religious orientation, combined with frequent attendance together at religious services, tends to promote positive marital quality. On the other hand, the patriarchal nature of these families (as reflected in traditional views on gender and the dominance of the husband in decision making) is linked with lower levels of marital quality—especially among wives. Taken together, these offsetting influences may have resulted in approximately average levels of conflict, problems, and divorce proneness.

Middle-class, egalitarian, dual-earner couples had the lowest level of marital interaction of any group, presumably because most husbands and wives had demanding jobs. These couples also had average to slightly below-average levels of marital conflict, problems, and divorce proneness. The strong economic foundation of this group (in which two well-educated spouses had full-time careers) meant that money was rarely a source of stress. This group also benefited from decision-making equality and held liberal attitudes toward gender issues—two factors associated with positive marital outcomes. And the dual-earner arrangement was consistent with both spouses' preferences: Most wives in this group wanted to have careers, and most husbands had few concerns about their wives' employment. At the same time, however, the stress of managing a dual-career household may have eroded some of these benefits, given that these wives worked longer hours than did wives in any other group.

Individuals in the upper middle-class, prosperous, mostly dual-earner group had the most positive profile of marital quality scores. Despite the fact that these couples had an average level of marital interaction, they had a higher level of marital happiness and lower levels of marital conflict, problems, and divorce proneness than did other couples. This group's high level of economic well-being provided a strong foundation for marital success and stability. And although not as egalitarian as the couples in cluster 4, these couples held liberal attitudes toward gender and practiced a high level of decision-making equality—traits that promote the marital quality of both spouses.

Only two gender differences appeared when we examined the links between marriage clusters and marital quality. Husbands reported more marital happiness than did wives in the working-class / middle-class, traditional, single-earner group. This gender difference probably reflects the fact that these households involved a traditional division of labor and had a relatively low level of decision-making equality. Presumably, the patriarchal tilt of these marriages provided more benefits to husbands than to wives. In addition, wives reported less marital happiness than did husbands in *working-class, young, dual-earner households*. As we noted earlier, most of these wives were employed because their husbands earned relatively little income, and most preferred to be working fewer hours or not at all—factors that tend to erode wives' marital happiness. With these two exceptions, however, the links between marriage cluster and marital quality were similar for husbands and wives.

Summary of Cluster Analysis

Our adoption of a person-centered approach represented an attempt to go beyond the one-variable-at-a-time approach that we have followed throughout most of this book. We relied on cluster analysis to identify broad groups of individuals who shared (or differed on) multiple characteristics. This analysis revealed that most people could be categorized reasonably well into five groups. Although these groups varied in many respects, they were differentiated largely on the basis of social class, wives' employment, age, and traditional versus egalitarian gender relations.

Our analysis revealed a substantial increase in the size of two groups: middle-class, egalitarian, dual-earner couples and upper-middle-class, prosperous, mostly dual-earner couples. Taken together, these two groups represented only 20% of the population of married couples in 1980 and 43% of the population of married couples in 2000. The ascendance of these groups reflects the movement of wives into the paid labor force, the growing affluence of dual-earner families, and the shift toward egalitarian gender relations, especially among well-educated couples. The other three clusters declined over time. Of the five groups, upper-middle-class, prosperous, mostly dual-earner couples had the most positive marital quality profile. Economic security combined with gender equality appears to be a good recipe for ensuring marital success.

Readers should keep in mind that cluster analysis has a number of limitations. For example, the identification of groups depends entirely on the variables included in the analysis. If we had used a different set of explanatory variables, different groups would have emerged from the analysis. Moreover, different clustering algorithms produce different solutions, so this method rarely produces a single, "true" identification of groups in the data. Nevertheless, this method has a great deal of heuristic value, and the five groups produced through our analysis represent a plausible typology of married couples. We suggest that other researchers explore these methods as an alternative to the variable-centered procedures that dominate family research.

♺ 8

Implications for Theory, Future Research, and Social Policy

$\mathcal{R}$ECENT CHANGES in the nature of marriage and the well-being of contemporary marital unions are of interest to large numbers of people. Social scientists wish to understand, at a theoretical level, the adaptability of marriage as a social institution in a time of rapid social change. Policy makers are concerned about the current state of marriage because they wish to fashion programs that promote the well-being of families and children. Counselors and therapists who work with married couples and their children need to base their interventions on knowledge of marital relationships as they exist today, not as they were a generation ago. And individual men and women want to know "what's happening" to marriage as they grapple with private decisions about cohabitation, marriage, parenthood, and divorce.

In this concluding chapter we consider the broad implications of the research described in this book. We begin by returning to the marital-decline and marital-resilience perspectives—two strongly contested views that we introduced in Chapter 1. As we argue below, although both perspectives contain some truth, the current status of marriage is more complex than either perspective acknowledges. We then focus our attention on another topic introduced in Chapter 1: the historical transformation of marriage from a social institution to a private relationship. We propose that contemporary marriages are moving in two contradictory directions. On the one hand, some aspects of marriage are becoming increasingly private and individualistic. On the other hand, we see modest signs of a reversal in the long-term trend of marital deinstitutionalization. Following this discussion, we make some methodological suggestions for future studies of marital quality. We then turn to policy issues and provide some ideas, based on our research, for interventions to strengthen marriage. We finish this chapter with some thoughts on the future of marriage.

The Marital-Decline and Marital-Resilience Perspectives Revisited

In Chapter 1 we described the marital-decline perspective. Although advocates of this perspective hold a variety of views, they share a few basic assumptions. According to these scholars, American culture has become increasingly individualistic in recent decades, and the unrestricted pursuit of self-interest, once condemned as selfish and irresponsible, is now accepted as a legitimate basis for organizing one's life. To maximize self-interest, people reject traditional institutions (such as marriage and religion) that place constraints on individual behavior and emphasize obligations to others. Because of this cultural shift, many spouses are unwilling to make the sacrifices that are necessary to ensure that their marriages are successful, and they see little value in remaining together through the hard times that inevitably occur in all relationships. Scholars who adopt this perspective believe that greater selfishness and the corresponding weakening of marital commitment have resulted in a decline in marital quality and stability in the American population (Blankenhorn, 1990; Glenn, 1996; Popenoe, 1988, 1993, 1996; Waite and Gallagher, 2000; Whitehead, 1993, 1996; Wilson, 2002).

Some of our findings are congruent with a marital-decline perspective. For example, two trends that we discussed in Chapter 3—the increase in premarital cohabitation and marital heterogamy—can be viewed as reflections of greater individualism and freedom from traditional constraints. These freedoms come at a cost, however, because heterogamous marriages and marriages preceded by cohabitation tend to be more conflicted and unstable than other marriages. Similarly, the increase in the percentage of spouses who grew up in divorced families indicates that many parents are modeling behaviors for their children that emphasize personal happiness over commitment to marriage as an institution. Our study shows that growing exposure to parental divorce in one generation was followed by an increase in marital conflict, marital problems, and divorce proneness in the next generation, which is consistent with this view.

In addition, the large-scale movement of wives into the paid labor force has generated a degree of "social disorganization" in some homes. As we described in Chapter 4, the percentage of husbands and wives who reported that their spouses' jobs interfered with family life increased between 1980 and 2000, as did the percentage of husbands who complained about the household division of labor. Both trends appear to have had problematic consequences for marital quality.

As we noted in Chapter 6, the decline in friendship networks and group affiliations is consistent with the notion of growing individualism and the general erosion of community bonds in American society (Putnam, 2000). Shared friends and group ties are important sources of marriage-specific capital. Our study revealed a decline in the number of friends and group affiliations shared by spouses. Similarly, people were less likely in 2000 than in 1980 to report that their friends get along well with their spouses. These changes were linked with pervasive negative shifts in marital quality in the population, which is consistent with a marital-decline perspective.

The general decline in marital interaction that we noted in Chapter 2 also is troubling. People may be bowling alone these days, as Putnam (ibid.) argued, but married couples increasingly are eating alone. The mean level of marital happiness did not change between surveys, which suggests that most couples are reasonably satisfied with their marriages, despite the decline in interaction. Perhaps the general increase in the pace of life noted by some authors (Robinson and Godbey, 1997) has led couples to lower their expectations for spending time together. Nevertheless, previous studies have found that a low level of marital interaction eventually leads to a decline in marital happiness (White, 1983; Zuo, 1992) and is a risk factor for divorce (Booth, Johnson; White, and Edwards, 1985; Hill, 1988). The drop in marital interaction between 1980 and 2000, therefore, may be a harbinger of future problems for American marriages. For example, we know that marital interaction tends to decline with age and duration of marriage. What will happen to the couples that we studied in 2000 as they age and as their level of marital interaction—already low by 1980 standards—declines even further?

Finally, although the mean level of divorce proneness did not change, the percentage of couples with highly unstable marriages increased. As we noted in Chapter 2, high expectations for personal fulfillment, combined with the relative ease of divorce these days, may mean that couples progress relatively quickly from thinking that their marriages might be in trouble to taking more active steps to end their marriages (such as discussing divorce with their spouses or consulting with an attorney). The decline in the number of shared friends (who often serve as barriers to divorce) may have exacerbated this trend.

In contrast to the marital-decline perspective, some scholars have articulated a marital-resilience perspective (Bengtson, Biblarz, and Roberts, 2002; Coontz, 1992, 2000; Demo, 1992; Hackstaff, 1999; Scanzoni, 2001; Skolnick, 1991; Stacey, 1996). Advocates of this perspective reject the assumption that Americans have become more individualistic and selfish in recent decades, along with the assumption that marriages are more troubled today than in the past. In an earlier era, people remained in dysfunctional marriages because divorces were difficult to obtain and because divorced individuals were stigmatized. Today, however, people are free to leave flawed marriages and find happiness with new partners. Moreover, divorce frees many children from high-conflict households and allows them to grow up in more peaceful alternative family forms. Rather than view the current high rate of divorce and the declining centrality of marriage as social problems, these scholars believe that recent changes have improved the lives of large numbers of adults and children. In particular, the decline of the patriarchal breadwinner-homemaker family has resulted in greater equality within marriage—an outcome that is likely to have improved women's happiness with marriage.

Some of the findings from our study support a marital-resilience perspective. Four changes in particular appear to have had generally positive consequences for multiple dimensions of marital quality: an improvement in the economic well-being of married couples (as reflected in an increase in family income, a decline in the use of public assistance, and a drop in people's perceptions of economic distress), the adoption of less traditional views about gender arrangements in marriage, the increase in decision-making equality between husbands and wives, and greater support for the norm of lifelong marriage. More-over, as we reported in Chapter 2, marital conflict—especially reports of marital violence—declined during this period, as did reports of marital problems involving interpersonal behavior, such as getting angry easily, being domineering, and being critical of one's spouse. If the state of marriage is declining, then why are spouses getting along better these days than in the recent past?

In general, our findings do not provide consistent support for either the marital-decline or the marital-resilience perspective. Instead, some recent changes appear to have eroded marital quality and stability, whereas other changes appear to have strengthened marital quality and stability. Other changes appear to have had mixed or contradictory implications. For example, the increase in the mean age of married couples was associated with declines in marital happiness and interaction, as well as declines in marital conflict and problems. Similarly, the increase in religiosity was associated with greater marital happiness as well as more marital problems. In other words, it is possible to support either a decline or a resilience perspective by citing evidence selectively. A more balanced view, however, reveals a complex pattern: marriages have become stronger and more satisfying in some respects and weaker and less satisfying in other respects. This conclusion is consistent with our assumption (stated in Chapters 1 and 7) that during any particular historical era, some social changes may strengthen marriage whereas other may undermine marriage. This assumption is related to another—that is, that marital quality is affected by a large number of social factors, each of which has only a small effect. Given a large number of factors with small effects, there are likely to be multiple offsetting trends at any given time.

Institutional and Individualistic Aspects of Contemporary Marriage

In the first chapter we described the theoretical perspective of Ernest Burgess, a sociologist who wrote extensively on marriage and family life around the middle of the twentieth century (Burgess and Cottrell, 1939; Burgess, Locke, and Thomes, 1963; Burgess and Wallin, 1954). Burgess argued that marriage in the United States was slowly transforming from a formal social institution into a private arrangement based on mutual affection and companionship. Because of environmental constraints and limited economic development early in American history, the nuclear family was essential for survival. For these reasons, society had a stake in ensuring family stability, and marriage was regulated by social norms, public opinion, law, and religion. Parents and kin monitored young adults' interactions with members of the other sex, and parental approval was expected before marriage. Once married, spouses were expected to conform to traditional standards of behavior and to sacrifice their personal feelings, if necessary, for the sake of their marriages. Moreover, the community frowned on divorce, and the legal dissolution of marriage was possible only if one partner had seriously violated the marriage contract, for example, by engaging in physical abuse, desertion, or adultery. Through marriage men and women participated in an institution that was larger and more significant than themselves.

According to Burgess, changes in American society during the nineteenth and early twentieth centuries weakened the institutional basis of marriage. Individuals came to have more control over their marriages, because of greater geographical mobility (which freed individuals from the influence of parents and the larger kin group), the rise of democratic institutions (which increased the status and power of women), and a decline in religious control (which resulted in more freedom to adopt unconventional views and behaviors). Later in the twentieth century, the growth of the service sector enhanced economic opportunities for women—opportunities that gave daughters more economic independence from parents and wives more economic independence from husbands. As parents, religion, community expectations, and patriarchal traditions exerted less control over individuals, marriage came to be based on the individual preferences of spouses. And because social constraints on the selection of partners became weaker, young adults experienced greater freedom to marry whomever they pleased.

The deinstitutionalization of marriage continued well after Burgess wrote his major works. In the 1960s effective contraception (especially the birth control pill) made it possible for single individuals to engage in sexual activity without the complications of unwanted pregnancies. As people's attitudes toward nonmarital sex became more liberal, increasing numbers of men and women chose to live together in sexually bonded relationships outside marriage. Since the 1970s the legal system has shifted from viewing married couples as a single legal entity (in which wives are dependent on their husbands) to a contractual relationship between two equal individuals (Mason, Fine, and Carnochan, 2004). Moreover, the shift to no-fault divorce during the 1970s made it relatively easy for individuals to leave unsatisfying unions. The continuing movement of wives into the paid labor force, coupled with real increases in women's wages, further undermined patriarchal control of marriage. And the decline in marital interaction and the number of friends held in common, as our study demonstrates, suggests that the lives of husbands and wives have become increasingly separate and disconnected.

As men and women gained greater freedom to engage in multiple sexual relationships before marriage, marry whomever they pleased, negotiate their own marital roles, and leave unsatisfactory unions, people came to focus increasingly on whether potential spouses would be good companions, emotionally supportive mates, and satisfying sexual partners. Expectations for marriage became even higher after the cultural upheavals of the 1960s and 1970s. Currently, many people expect their spouses to be soul mates, sources of deep personal fulfillment, and facilitators of personal growth (Bellah et al., 1985; Furstenberg and Cherlin, 1991). Andrew Cherlin (2004) argued that the current emphasis on marriage as a vehicle for self-development represents a qualitative shift in the nature of marriage, as individualistic marriage replaces companionate marriage as the cultural ideal.

Some observers believe that current expectations for marriage are so high that many—perhaps most—unions are incapable of meeting people's perceived psychological and emotional needs. According to this perspective, the inevitable disappointment that occurs when people's expectations meet reality, combined with a weak commitment to the norm of lifelong marriage, has resulted in widespread marital instability (Glenn, 1996; Popenoe, 1988). There is little doubt that the shift away from institutional marriage was bound up with the long-term rise in divorce in American society since the mid nineteenth century. Burgess was aware of this connection, and he believed that marriages held together by mutual satisfaction were intrinsically less stable than were marriages held together by community expectations, legal requirements, and religious restrictions. In this context he stated:

Marriage no longer has its permanence guaranteed by custom and public opinion . . . It has entered upon a precarious existence, with its future dependent more than ever before in human history upon the affection, the temperamental compatibility, and the common objectives of husband and wife. Love and companionship are the personal ties that are replacing the communal and customary bonds which formerly held husband and wife together . . . Each couple . . . is on its own in marriage. The roles of husband and wife are no longer clearly defined, and each couple must work out its own patterns of relationship (Burgess and Cottrell, 1939, p. vii)

Despite these concerns, Burgess believed that the rise in divorce during the first half of the twentieth century was a temporary phenomenon—a social dislocation due to the normative ambiguity surrounding the emergence of the new system of marriage. As he stated, the "increase in family disruption as evidenced by divorce seems to have reached a plateau. It is probable that there will be no radical increase in divorce in the new future" (Burgess, Locke, and Thomes, 1963, p. 539). According to Burgess, marriages would become more stable once people learned the attitudes and interpersonal skills necessary to make companionate marriage succeed. Burgess assumed that marriage counseling and marriage education, which emerged as professional fields during the first half of the twentieth century, would ease the transition from institutional to companionate marriage. He also believed that empirical research conducted by family scholars would be essential to inform the work of practitioners.

Burgess did not anticipate the dramatic increase in marital dissolution that began during the second half of the 1960s and continued throughout the 1970s. Burgess also failed to anticipate another consequence of the deinstitutionalization of marriage: the general decline in the centrality of marriage in people's lives. As social constraints weakened, and as personal choice expanded, alternatives to marriage became increasingly common. After the 1960s nonmarital cohabitation became popular, the percentage of nonmarital births increased, adults postponed marriage to increasingly later ages, the percentage of unmarried people in the population increased, and the percentage of people who remarried following divorce declined (Cherlin, 1992). Increasing numbers of individuals searched for personal fulfillment outside marriage, and the number of years that individuals spent in marriage in their lives dropped substantially (Casper and Bianchi, 2002). So many changes occurred in marriage between the late 1970s and the end of the century that the historian Stephanie Coontz (2005) referred to this period as a "perfect storm" (p. 263).

These considerations lead to a troubling theoretical possibility. Successful and stable marriages may require a strong institutional foundation, including a high level of support and guidance from the kin group, religion, the local community, and the state. Cut free from institutional moorings, unions based entirely on private choice and the pursuit of individual happiness may be inherently and intractably unstable. In this cultural climate it may seem entirely reasonable for spouses with an amicable and cooperative relationship to divorce, merely because the relationship no longer promotes their search for self-growth—a decision that would have made little sense in an earlier era. Indeed, the institutional basis of marriage may have degenerated to the point where marriage has become a fragile and unstable arrangement for the majority of people.

Although there may be some truth in this notion, an alternative and less pessimistic interpretation is possible. Our surveys reveal a modest rise in personal feelings of religiosity, the percentage of couples who attend services together regularly, and support for the norm of lifelong marriage. Religion provides a formal, institutional framework for marriage, and a shift toward greater religious participation suggests that the influence of religion on marriage may be growing stronger. Similarly, increasing support for the norm of lifelong marriage suggests that people are becoming more wary of divorce and more accepting of the notion that a stable marriage is an important goal in its own right, irrespective of the happiness of individual spouses. These trends suggest a modest reversal of the view that personal choice and autonomy are more important than social expectations and institutional structures in guiding married life.

This conclusion is not specific to our particular study. Data from the General Social Survey reveal a similar shift in married people's views about marriage and divorce. In most years between 1974 and 2000, respondents were asked the following question: "Should divorce in this country be easier or more difficult to obtain than it is now?" Figure 8.1

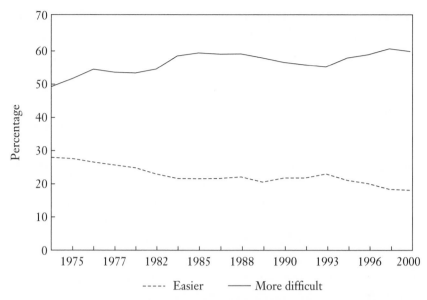

Figure 8.1   Percentage of married people reporting that divorce should be more difficult to obtain: General Social Survey, 1974–2000

shows the percentage of people who responded "easier" or "more difficult" in each year. (People who reported "the same" are not shown in the figure, although they were included in the calculation of percentages.) To provide a clearer picture, we used three-year moving averages to smooth fluctuations between survey years. This figure reveals a gradual increase in the percentage of married individuals who said that divorce should be more difficult to obtain and a corresponding decline in the percentage of people who said that divorce should be easier to obtain. This finding—based on an entirely different data set from our own—is consistent with our suggestion that married individuals are becoming increasingly hesitant to advocate divorce as the solution to relationship problems.

It is not clear what caused the shift toward greater religiosity and more conventional views about marriage between 1980 and 2000. One possibility is that individuals have become increasingly uncomfortable with—and perhaps overwhelmed by—the large number of choices in contemporary society. Religious traditions and shared norms (such as the norm of marital permanence) provide clear guidelines for dealing with ambiguity. Many individuals may be willing to give up a degree of freedom and the expectation of deep personal fulfillment in exchange for greater stability and security in their family lives.

We have discussed institutional and individualistic marriage as if they were two distinct forms, but we should point out that marriage always has contained institutional as well as individualistic elements. In the past many couples married for pragmatic reasons and stayed married because of social custom, religion, and legal restrictions on divorce. But many—probably most—of these marriages also had companionate features. Many husbands and wives were in love, provided emotional and practical support to their spouses, and enjoyed each other's company. Correspondingly, contemporary marriages still contain some institutional elements. For example, the majority of people marry in religious settings and make vows in front of parents, kin, and friends. Moreover, the state continues to register marriages and to confer special legal rights and responsibilities on married couples. And marriage is still guided by social norms. For example, the norm of sexual fidelity continues to be one of the central, defining elements of marriage (Nock, 1998), and the great majority of people condemn extramarital sex (Thornton and Young-DeMarco, 2001). The public nature of weddings, the legal regulation of marriage, and the continuing influence of social norms indicate that marriage (unlike cohabitation) is not a completely private arrangement between two individuals.

In recent years the community and the state have begun to take a greater interest in the stability and well-being of married couples. For example, the Marriage Movement—a loosely knit affiliation of academics, therapists, educators, policy makers, and religious leaders—gained strength in the United States during the 1990s. Members of this movement have suggested a variety of strategies to improve the quality of marriage and to reduce the rate of divorce (Ooms, 2001; Parke and Ooms, 2002). Three states (Louisiana, Arizona, and Arkansas) implemented Covenant Marriage—a form of marriage in which spouses vow to seek counseling if their marriages are in trouble and to refrain from seeking a no-fault divorce. In 2000 Oklahoma established the Oklahoma Marriage Initiative and trained hundreds of individuals to provide free premarital education to thousands of people planning to marry. Other states adopted alternative strategies to strengthen marriage, such as incorporating relationship skills and conflict resolution courses into high school curricula, distributing information on marriage to newlyweds, and funding public education campaigns to promote the value of marriage.

During the 1990s the federal government became more involved in marriage. The most prominent manifestation of this trend was the 1996 welfare reform legislation, the Personal Responsibility and Work Opportunities Reform Act (PRWORA). This act replaced the older Assistance to Families with Dependent Children (AFDC) program with Temporary Assistance to Needy Families (TANF) block grants to the states. Although most of the media attention to this new program focused on new rules for single mothers on public assistance (such as stringent work requirements and time limits for public assistance), the act also had much to say about marriage. In particular it included goals to promote marriage, reduce the incidence of nonmarital births, and encourage the formation and maintenance of two-parent families (Ooms, 2001). Only a few states (such as Oklahoma, Arizona, Michigan, and Utah) spent TANF funds to develop policies that were consistent with these pro-marriage goals, perhaps because it was unclear how to implement such programs. In 2001 President Bush announced plans to direct more than $1 billion over five years to promote the formation and maintenance of healthy, married-couple families. This proposal was controversial, and it was stalled in Congress for several years, largely because of a disagreement between Republicans and Democrats over child-care funding. In February 2006, however, the president signed the Deficit Reduction Act of 2005, which reauthorized the TANF program. The act allocates $150 million a year for five years on programs to promote healthy marriage and responsible fatherhood. Although less than pro-marriage supporters had hoped for, this amount is sufficient to fund a variety of marriage-promotion activities across the country, and diverse organizations currently are applying for funding. These recent moves on the part of the federal and state governments to improve marital quality and stability represent clear attempts to reinstitutionalize marriage.

Policies to strengthen marital quality and stability are based on consistent evidence that happy and stable marriages promote the health, psychological well-being, and financial security of adults (Marks and Lambert, 1998; Waite, 1995; Williams, 2003) as well as children (Amato and Booth, 1997; McLanahan and Sandefur, 1994). Moreover, recent research suggests that a large proportion of marriages that end in divorce are *not* deeply troubled, and that many of these marriages might be salvaged if spouses sought assistance for relationship problems, remained committed to their unions, placed their children's well-being ahead of their own, and stayed the course through difficult times (Amato, 2001). By providing social and economic resources to married couples, recent social policies have the potential to revitalize marriage and decrease the number of unnecessary divorces in the United States—a trend that would have positive implications for children's long-term well-being

Many people are skeptical about the value of these steps, and a debate has emerged about the appropriate role of government in promoting and strengthening marriage. Some individuals and groups are opposed to these measures because they believe that marriage is a private rather than a public matter—a perspective consistent with an individualistic view of marriage. But there is also a growing recognition among policy makers, as well as the general public, that marriage is not a strictly private relationship between two individuals, and that the broader community has an interest in increasing the proportion of healthy and stable marriages, especially those with children. Other people are suspicious that pro-marriage policies imply a return to a patriarchal authority structure and a traditional gender division of labor. It is true that members of some conservative religious groups want to see a return to the patriarchal, strictly regulated marriages of the past. Other marriage advocates, however, believe that contemporary unions should be based on the norm of gender equality, and that couples should be free to choose a division of homemaking, breadwinning, and child-care responsibilities that best meets their particular needs.

In short, we may be witnessing a shift toward a new view of marriage that values the institutional basis of marriage but also recognizes the importance of companionate and individualistic elements—a form of marriage in which individual happiness and obligations to the larger society are in balance. We return to this theme in the book's conclusion, where we comment on the possible future of marriage.

Suggestions for Future Research on Marital Quality

As we noted in Chapter 2, most sociological studies of marital quality have focused on either marital adjustment—a single variable that combines information on multiple relationship dimensions, such as happiness, conflict, and interaction—or marital happiness (or satisfaction) and ignored other relationship characteristics. In contrast, we defined marital quality as a set of conceptually distinct but empirically correlated dimensions. To assess these dimensions, our surveys included separate measures of happiness, interaction, conflict, problems, and divorce proneness—five relationship characteristics that distinguish "good" marriages from "bad" marriages. Given the complexity of this topic, however, our measures provide a limited view of the marital relationship.

We make two basic points in this chapter. First, survey research would benefit from building on the work of family psychologists during the last two decades. Family psychologists—using largely observational methods with small samples—have produced a rich set of constructs related to marital functioning, and many of these constructs are good predictors of divorce. The development of survey-based measures of these constructs, and the application of these measures to large probability samples, would substantially enrich our understanding of marriage. Second, we argue that the construct of marital commitment is still underdeveloped, both theoretically and empirically. Moreover, the study of commitment may prove to be as central to our understanding of marital quality as the study of marital happiness has been.

Interpersonal Behavior in Marriage

Most psychological studies of marital interaction are based on observations of married couples discussing a problem in their marriage. Researchers typically videotape these interactions, and teams of independent coders later rate spouses' behaviors using objective coding schemes that often include categories for communication content (disagreement, showing support), tone of voice, and facial expressions. Some labs also include physiological measures, such as respiration and heart rate. The ability to study sequences of behavior makes it possible to identify recurring patterns of interaction that distinguish happily married couples from unhappily married couples. Moreover, these studies demonstrate that observations of interaction early in marriage can predict subsequent divorce with a reasonably high level of accuracy. (For a review, see Gottman and Notarius, 2000.)

Longitudinal research by John Gottman (1994) has identified four corrosive behaviors that are good predictors of later marital disruption. One behavior involves expressing *contempt*, which includes insults, mockery, sarcasm, and hostile humor. Contempt can be communicated through facial expressions and tone of voice, as well as through verbal content. The second behavior is *criticism*, especially criticism that is harsh in tone. The third behavior is *defensiveness*, which involves an attempt to ward off or protect oneself from perceived criticism. Defensiveness can take the form of denying responsibility for a problem, engaging in counterattacks, or whining. Whining involves statements like "Why are you always picking on me? I didn't do anything wrong." The final behavior is *stonewalling*, that is, avoiding disagreements by emotionally or physically withdrawing from one's spouse.

Not surprisingly, spouses headed for divorce tend to exhibit relatively high levels of negative affect during marital interactions. Moreover, distressed couples tend to engage in long chains of reciprocal negativity (for example, responding to anger with anger). Gottman, Murray, Swanson, Tyson, and Swanson (2002) pointed out that all couples—even happily married couples—engage in cycles of reciprocal negativity. Nondistressed couples, however, use repair attempts to de-escalate negative exchanges. Repair mechanisms include using humor, exchanging information, sharing information about feelings, finding areas of common ground, and appealing to larger expectations about the marriage (for example, we are in this for the long term). De-escalation attempts are most likely to succeed early in a disagreement, when negativity is still at a relatively low level.

For distressed couples, in contrast, reciprocal negativity tends to be an absorbing state that, once entered, is difficult to leave. Spouses in distressed marriages become so focused on negative affect that they are unresponsive to other possibilities, even when their spouses try to use repair strategies. In addition, distressed couples tend to escalate (rather than de-escalate) negative affect during episodes of conflict. Escalation often reflects a rejection of influence on the part of one (or both) partners, although research indicates that husbands tend to reject influence more often than do wives. For example, when one spouse engages in criticism, the second partner may angrily reject the point or engage in countercriticism. In many distressed marriages, the escalation of negativity during conflict can be viewed as a power struggle between spouses.

In addition to the escalation of reciprocated negativity, spouses in troubled marriages often exhibit a *demand-withdrawal* or *pursuer-distancer* pattern (Gottman, 1994; Hetherington and Kelly, 2002). In these marriages, one spouse (more often the wife) is habitually critical of the other spouse's behavior. In response, the other spouse (more often the husband) denies the existence of the problem and physically or emotionally withdraws from the interaction. Withdrawal leads many wives to intensify their criticism, the result being even more withdrawal on the part of husbands. Eventually, some wives grow tired of this routine and become contemptuous of their husbands (Gottman, Coan, Carrere, and Swanson, 1998).

Most observational studies have focused on negative interactions, on the assumption that these behaviors are better predictors of divorce than are positive interactions. In fact, during interactions happily married couples tend to exhibit about five positive behaviors for every negative behavior. Unhappily married couples, in contrast, exhibit roughly equal numbers of negative and positive behaviors (Gottman et al., 2002). These findings suggest that it takes five positive comments to make up for the damage inflicted by one negative comment. Nevertheless, some observational studies show that the provision of social support within marriage (showing affection, expressing agreement, and providing practical assistance) predicts subsequent marital outcomes, even after controlling for negative behaviors (Pasch, Bradbury, and Davila, 1997). Indeed, some researchers believe that existing research has underestimated the importance of positive interactional processes in predicting the long-term success of marriages (Bradbury, Fincham, and Beach, 2000).

One question that arises from observational research is whether the interpersonal behaviors that erode marital happiness are reflections of stable personality traits that individuals bring to their marriages or specific relationship patterns that develop within marriage. A number of studies have shown that certain personality traits, such as neuroticism or a tendency to engage in antisocial behavior, are good predictors of marital discord and divorce (Capaldi and Patterson, 1991; Karney and Bradbury, 1995; Kurdek, 2002). Given these findings, we can expect that personality problems may be responsible for some of the corrosive interpersonal behaviors that characterize troubled marriages. A longitudinal study by Johnson and Booth (1998), which followed people through two marriages, is relevant to this issue. This study found that the frequency of disagreements in the first marriage did not predict the frequency of disagreements in the second marriage. The Johnson and Booth study also found, however, that people's reports of specific marital problems that they (rather than their spouses) caused (such as getting angry easily or being critical) were similar in both marriages. Taken together, these results suggest that some problematic marital behaviors reflect individual traits that generalize across marriages, whereas other problematic marital behaviors reflect dyadic traits that are specific to a particular marriage.

Although the results of observational studies are intriguing, these data are time-consuming and expensive to collect. For example, it takes months to train a team of coders to rate behaviors with an acceptable level of reliability. Furthermore, once trained, coders require about one hour to code about ten minutes of interaction (Rogge and Bradbury, 1999). Although observational methods are well suited to identify problematic interpersonal dynamics associated with poor marital outcomes, applying these methods on a large scale is not practical.

Given these constraints, some family psychologists have attempted to measure marital behaviors using questionnaires focusing mainly on styles of communication and methods of problem solving. A few longitudinal studies indicate that questionnaire measures of interaction predict subsequent marital outcomes about as well as do observational measures (Hill and Peplau, 1999; Larsen and Olson, 1989). For example, Rogge and Bradbury (1999) directly compared the predictive utility of observational and self-report measures of marital interaction. They found that self-report measures and observational measures were equally successful in predicting marital happiness and stability over a four-year period. This finding suggests that survey researchers would profit from including interview items that tap interactional features of marriage.

In summary, previous research suggests the utility of adapting or developing survey questions to measure constructs such as contempt, criticism, defensiveness, withdrawal, cycles of escalating reciprocal negativity, and the pursuer-distancer pattern. Measures of social support and positivity within marriage also may prove to be useful. Few survey data sets, however, contain items that measure more than a small subset of the constructs that have emerged from observational studies. Including measures of these constructs in future large-scale surveys will make it possible to determine the extent to which these problematic interpersonal behaviors are linked to larger structural, cultural, and economic factors.

Marital Commitment

Marital commitment can be defined as the extent to which people hold long-term perspectives on their marriages, make sacrifices for their relationships, take steps to maintain and strengthen the cohesiveness of their unions, and stay with their spouses even when their marriages are not rewarding. Commitment implies an obligation to others—an obligation that can be abandoned only under extreme circumstances. Implicit in the notion of marital obligation is the sense that marriage has value that extends beyond the happiness of the individual spouses.

As we noted in Chapter 2, many researchers define marital quality primarily in terms of marital happiness or satisfaction (Bradbury, Fincham, and Beach, 2000; Glenn, 1990). According to this view, marital happiness is the sine qua non of a high-quality marriage. Other dimensions of marriage, such as spending time together, the frequency of conflict, or perceptions of relationship problems, are *causes* of marital quality rather than *forms* of marital quality. A good argument can be made, however, that commitment is as central to what we mean by marital quality as is happiness. Consider a marriage in which both spouses are reasonably happy, but one spouse decides to leave the marriage because he or she has found an even more attractive partner. Most observers would not consider this to be a successful marriage. Now consider a marriage in which both spouses are unhappy with the relationship but want their marriage to work, reject the option of divorce, and decide to attend counseling with the goal of improving the relationship. Most observers probably would consider the second marriage to be in better shape than the first one, despite the fact that spouses in the second marriage are unhappy. It is likely that the current focus among family scholars on marital happiness as the central defining characteristic of high-quality marriages reflects the culture of expressive individualism and self-growth that has become pervasive in American society since the 1960s (Bellah et al., 1985). Seen in this light, a focus on commitment as a central feature of marital quality represents a necessary corrective to the individualistic and hedonistic slant of much contemporary research on marriage.

Exchange theory recognizes that stability and happiness are different relationship dimensions (Levinger, 1976). For example, Johnson, Caughlin, and Huston (1999) distinguished among three forms of commitment. *Personal commitment* is based on the rewards that partners receive from their relationships. When partners enjoy each other's company and obtain multiple benefits from being together, relationship cohesion is strengthened. *Moral commitment* is based on feelings of obligation—moral beliefs that one should remain in a relationship despite the existence of problems. Finally, *structural commitment* is based on constraints—that is, the existence of barriers to leaving the relationship and the absence of good alternatives to the current partner. Even when spouses are unhappy, they may remain together because of barriers to leaving (for example, not wanting to give up their homes, concerns about their children's well-being) or because no viable alternative partners are available. From this perspective, rewards, moral beliefs, barriers, and the absence of alternatives are all factors that promote relationship commitment. One can question, however, whether it makes sense to say that people are "committed" to relationships only because they feel constrained to remain in them. Although Johnson, Caughlin, and Huston's (ibid.) categories are useful for understanding why some couples remain together and other couples break up, this perspective is more applicable to the study of relationship stability than to the study of commitment. As we see it, actions that reflect commitment are engaged in willingly and reflect more than the existence of internal or external constraints on leaving a relationship. Moreover, commitment implies more than staying in a relationship because it meets one's personal needs.

Commitment to a relationship requires what the psychologist Caryl Rusbult calls *accommodative behavior* (Rusbult, Bissonnette, Arriaga, and Cox, 1998). Accommodative behaviors are actions in which partners sacrifice their short-term well-being for the long-term stability of their relationships. Accommodation can take a variety of forms, such as watching boring television programs that one's spouse enjoys, dealing with unpleasant in-laws, accepting faults in one's partner without criticism, forgiving one's partner for transgressions, or inhibiting an urge to retaliate when one's partner is annoying.

Sometimes people are said to have "accommodating" personalities, but this is not what we mean by the term. Although some people may have a general predisposition to be cooperative in interpersonal relationships, accommodation between spouses is driven by a strong belief in the value of the relationship. This tendency may be strengthened by religious beliefs, positive experiences in the family of origin, or an awareness that compromises are required to maintain strong relationships. Although accommodative behavior involves sacrificing short-term self-interest, it does not mean that people are motivated to maximize their partner's interests at the expense of their own. Being accommodating is not the same as being submissive or obsequious. Instead, accommodative behaviors benefit the relationship, rather than the individual partners. In short, people engage in accommodative behavior because they are committed to and value their relationships.

The measurement of commitment as we define it is not well developed. Researchers have developed several commitment scales that include items such as "How likely is it that your relationship will be permanent?" (Lund, 1985), "To what degree do you feel committed to maintaining your marriage?" (Rusbolt et al., 1998), and "I want this relationship to stay strong, no matter what rough times we may encounter" (Stanley and Markman, 1992). These scales usually are highly correlated with measures of relationship happiness, however, which suggests they are measuring the same construct. These studies demonstrate that commitment is difficult to disentangle from happiness when people's relationships are progressing smoothly. Under these circumstances, people will say that they are committed to their partners because their relationships are rewarding.

It is only when relationships are troubled, and spouses are unhappy with their marriages, that commitment comes into sharp focus. When confronted with unhappiness or tension in a relationship, people can respond in four ways. One possibility is to leave the relationship—a response that reflects the absence of commitment. A second strategy—one that reflects a minimal level of commitment—is to remain in the marriage but to disengage from one's partner or deny the existence of problems. A third strategy (which reflects a stronger level of commitment) is to stand by one's partner and optimistically wait, trusting that the relationship eventually will improve. The final strategy, and one that reflects the highest level of commitment, is for couples to work actively on their disagreements with the goal of making their marriages satisfying again. In other words, commitment is reflected primarily in how couples react to stress in their marriages. (See Rusbult et al., 1998, for a discussion.)

Seen in this light, commitment implies that people have a sense of efficacy about their relationships. We argue that people hold implicit theories about marriage. One implicit theory is that relationships (and people) are difficult to change, and that a successful marriage depends largely on a good match with the right partner—and perhaps a certain amount of luck. People who hold this view are unlikely to invest substantial amounts of time and energy attempting to solve marital problems. Instead, these individuals are likely to jettison troubled relationships relatively quickly and search for new partners. Another implicit theory is that relationships (and people, to a certain extent) are changeable, and that a successful marriage depends largely on learning how to adapt to one another and to the changing circumstances of married life. When confronted with marital problems, people who hold this view are likely to take steps to improve the situation, even if the process is time-consuming. In a relevant study, Myers and Booth (1999) examined people's marital locus of control, that is, the belief that what happens in marriage is largely under one's personal control. They found that people's scores on a scale measuring this construct were positively correlated with measures of marital quality. This finding is consistent with the notion that commitment—and in the long run, marital stability—is strengthened when people believe that they can influence marital outcomes.

To illustrate the difference between stability and commitment, we turn to data from our 1980 survey. When marital happiness was high (in the top half of the distribution), no one reported talking about divorce. After all, why should they? In contrast, among those in the bottom quartile, 10% had talked with their spouses recently about divorce. The interesting question is why the figure was as low as 10%. Some people may not have wanted to admit during the interview that they had discussed divorce with their spouses. Other individuals may have felt constrained to stay in their marriages, either because of barriers (such as religious beliefs) or the lack of good alternatives. But other people were not considering divorce because they were committed to their marriages.

What happened to these relatively unhappy individuals three years later? By 1983, some of these people—mainly those who were thinking about divorce—had ended their marriages. Among those who stayed together, two-thirds were still unhappy with their marriages. But one-third were happier at the next interview, and 10% shifted from the bottom quartile of the happiness distribution to the top 50%. One hypothesis is that unhappily married individuals who remained unhappily married were stuck in their marriages because of perceived barriers or the lack of good alternatives. Correspondingly, those who experienced improvements in happiness may have engaged in accommodative behaviors associated with high levels of commitment. That is, these individuals expressed loyalty to their partners and waited patiently for the bad times to pass, made sacrifices for their relationships, or actively sought solutions to their problems. It is not possible to test these ideas with our data. But the hypothesis that commitment provides a mechanism not only to maintain marital stability, but also to recover from periods of unhappiness, is one that could be explored in future research. In other words, just as happiness can strengthen commitment, commitment also can strengthen happiness over the long haul.

In summary, the next generation of survey research on marriage would benefit from developing and incorporating measures of relationship interaction and commitment. Observational studies have revealed patterns of interaction that are good predictors of subsequent marital unhappiness and divorce. And the construct of relationship commitment has been underdeveloped, both theoretically and empirically. Incorporating valid and reliable measures of these variables into future data sets should make it possible to describe the mechanisms that link specific demographic variables (such as age at marriage or divorce in the family of origin) to specific marital outcomes. Taking these steps would not only promote a better dialogue between family sociologists and family psychologists, but also provide a stronger basis for interventions to strengthen marriage—an important concern in an era in which promoting marital quality and stability has become an explicit goal of social policy.

Implications for Social Policy

Our research suggests a number of intervention points for policies to strengthen marital quality and stability. For example, a number of studies have shown that financial distress increases the risk of marital discord and divorce (Bramlett and Mosher, 2002; Conger et al., 1990; Fox, Benson, DeMaris, and Van Wyk, 2002; Lehrer, 2003). Our study is consistent with this research in that it also shows that economic well-being is linked with multiple dimensions of marital quality. Our study also shows, however, that perceptions of economic hardship became a stronger predictor of marital quality between 1980 and 2000. On a positive note, the financial well-being of married couples increased substantially between 1980 and 2000, and this trend appears to have contributed to higher levels of marital quality in the population. But these benefits were not distributed equally among all couples. During the last few decades, men—especially young men with relatively little education—experienced deteriorating work opportunities because of declines in the manufacturing, mining, and construction sectors (Farley, 1996; Levy, 1995). As we showed in chapter 4, the economic well-being of breadwinner-homemaker families, especially those in which husbands did not have a college degree, declined during this period.

Given the links between financial hardship and marital quality, policies to strengthen marriage should include a focus on the economic security of poor and near-poor married couples. Although most state and community interventions have emphasized marriage education, economically disadvantaged couples would benefit from job training, employment assistance, and the removal of financial disincentives to marry and stay married. With respect to the last point, poor couples who marry are often penalized by losing benefits, such as Medicaid or food stamps. Allowing poor couples to retain these benefits after marriage would help to get these couples off to a better start. The Earned Income Tax Credit (EITC) is an example of a current policy that benefits many working poor couples, and raising the minimum wage would strengthen marriage among disadvantaged populations. More generally, policy makers should recognize that any initiative that improves the financial security and well-being of married couples is a pro-marriage policy.

Our study also shows that married couples with supportive networks of kin and friends tend to have more satisfying and less troubled marriages—a conclusion also supported by other studies (Bryant and Conger, 1999; Julien and Markman, 1991; Julien et al., 1994). Yet our study indicates that spouses' social networks are becoming smaller and increasingly disconnected. Although most marital education programs focus on topics such as communication and conflict resolution, shared social networks are important resources that should be considered in attempts to strengthen marriage. Some existing programs match young couples with senior marriage mentors—couples who have been in stable marriages for many years. Most mentoring programs have a religious basis, presumably because the church provides a ready supply of couples willing to serve as mentors. Nevertheless, it should be possible to create mentoring programs in secular settings. The assumption underlying these programs is that mentors share insights and practical experience with younger couples and, more generally, act as positive role models. In addition, mentors can refer troubled couples to professional counselors when necessary. Some mentors keep in contact with couples for years by, for example, sending cards on anniversaries or other special occasions.

Although mentoring programs provide social resources to married couples, marriage education programs could incorporate information on the importance of shared networks along with suggestions for constructing them. For example, recently married individuals could be encouraged to get to know each other's friends and family members and to make new, shared friends. Couples also could be encouraged to join clubs or organizations together. In addition, when marital educational is offered in a group setting, opportunities for socializing could be built into the program, and couples could be encouraged to share telephone numbers or e-mail addresses to keep in touch when the program ends. Some of these contacts may evolve into friendships, with possibly beneficial consequences for the couples involved.

Another point of intervention involves people's understanding of social norms and expectations for marriage. In Chapter 6 we reported that people's support for the norm of lifelong marriage became stronger between 1980 and 2000. This would appear to be a positive development, because these attitudes are positively associated with multiple dimensions of marital quality. One longitudinal study (Amato and Rogers, 1999) suggested that the direction of influence is primarily from attitudes to marital quality. That is, individuals who strongly support the norm of lifelong marriage tend to experience increases in marital happiness and decreases in marital conflict over time. In contrast, individuals who are accepting of divorce tend to experience declines in marital happiness and increases in marital conflict. Presumably, people who believe strongly in lifelong marriage are motivated to work on marital problems and find ways to resolve them. Other studies have shown that people who hold favorable views toward divorce are more likely to see their own marriages end in divorce, all things being equal (Amato, 1996).

These findings suggest that people's attitudes about marriage and divorce influence their future marital success. Although people's attitudes have not been a traditional focus of marital education interventions, it may be useful to incorporate material on how people view marriage. Couples participating in educational programs can learn more effective ways of communicating and resolving conflict, but they may be unwilling to exercise these skills if they feel that it is easier to jettison an unhappy relationship than to expend energy trying to improve it. In contrast, people who recognize the emotional and financial costs involved in obtaining a divorce will be motivated to invest time and energy in improving their relationships.

Programs to strengthen marriage could incorporate a normative component by including material on the value of strong marriages—not only for adults, but also for children. Programs also could incorporate material on the difficulties experienced by people who choose to divorce. Although divorce is often the best outcome for seriously dysfunctional marriages (especially marriages that involve violence or psychological abuse), marital dissolution also exacts a toll in terms of emotional hardship, disruption of social networks, and declines in standard of living—especially for women. Correspondingly, fathers are often distressed to discover that divorce makes it difficult to maintain close ties with their children. (For a review of stressors associated with divorce, see Amato, 2000.) Providing realistic information about the costs of divorce, along with the benefits of stable, long-term marriage, may help couples to make informed decisions about splitting up if their relationships become troubled.

Another relevant social norm refers to people's expectations for the division of labor in marriage. Several decades ago most Americans believed that it is better for the husband to be the breadwinner and the wife to be in charge of housework and child care. As we noted in Chapter 5, however, people have become increasingly supportive of wives' and mothers' participation in the labor force. Correspondingly, people now believe that husbands should do a greater share of housework and child care, especially when their wives are employed. Currently, a range of views exist; some people prefer a breadwinner-homemaker model, and others prefer a model that emphasizes role sharing and equality between husbands and wives. The former model, however, is in decline, whereas the latter model has become dominant.

We also reported in Chapter 5 that egalitarian attitudes toward gender arrangements are associated with better marital quality among husbands as well as wives. Wives reported especially high levels of marital quality when their husbands did a substantial proportion of housework and child care and when spouses had equal input in decision making. Of course, the shift toward role sharing and gender equality within marriage has generated a certain amount of normative confusion among couples, as wives often press for more change than husbands are willing to concede. A number of studies have shown that disagreements between spouses over these issues tend to lower marital quality and increase the risk of divorce (Greenstein, 1996; Hochschild, 1989). Similarly, our study indicates that wives' feelings of unfairness over the division of household labor represents one of the most consistent correlates of poor marital quality. For these reasons, incorporating discussions of the division of household labor into marriage education programs would be useful. By improving communication and conflict-resolution skills, existing programs make it easier for couples to discuss these issues and to reach mutually satisfying agreements. Nevertheless, directly covering material on the division of household labor (perhaps through group discussion or role-playing exercises) could be useful. Although educational programs should not necessarily attempt to change people's values, a nudge in the direction of greater equality (and more sharing of housework and decision making) may benefit many couples. Men, in particular, need to be made aware of the importance that wives attach to their husbands' contributions to household labor and child care. To the extent that American society is becoming more egalitarian with respect to gender, couples who organize their marriages around shared roles and decision making are likely to experience less strain and higher levels of marital quality.

What Is the Future of Marriage?

Social scientists do not have a particularly good record of forecasting social change. This modest record is due partly to the relatively young age of our discipline, and partly to the complexity of understanding how and why society changes. Research generally indicates that people's experiences and behavior are affected by a large number of factors that interact in ways that are difficult to conceptualize and model statistically. For example, the decision to divorce is affected by experiences in the family of origin (such as parental divorce), personality traits (such as neuroticism), interpersonal skills (such as conflict-resolution skills), demographic variables (such as age at marriage), economic factors (such as education, employment, and earned income), exposure to stressors (such as unemployment), social integration and social support (such as the number of close friends, especially friends shared with one's spouse), and attitudes about marriage and divorce (Bramlett and Mosher, 2002; White, 1990). Given this complexity, it is risky to make bold predictions about marriage, or about any other family-related behavior. Nevertheless, we can propose some general possibilities on the basis of existing knowledge.

One issue that we have not discussed thus far, partly because it lies beyond the scope of our data, involves same-sex marriage. Early in the new millennium, this issue became a hot topic not only in the United States, but also in a variety of other countries. Several countries now recognize same-sex marriage, including the Netherlands, Belgium, Spain, and Canada. Currently, Massachusetts is the only state in this country that recognizes marriages between same-sex couples.

Although legal recognition of same-sex marriage is rare, a large number of countries, as well as several U.S. states (including California, Connecticut, Hawaii, Maine, New Jersey, Vermont, and Washington, D.C.), recognize civil unions (or domestic partnerships), which confer certain legal rights on gay and lesbian couples. In many cases, these rights (and responsibilities) are nearly identical to those of heterosexual married couples.

In many European countries, the majority of the population support the right of same-sex couples to marry. In contrast, opinion polls reveal that most people in the United States do not support marriage between same-sex couples. In fact, 19 states have passed the Defense of Marriage Act, which explicitly forbids marriage between same-sex couples. Despite this opposition, the Massachusetts Supreme Court ruled in 2003 that the denial of marriage to same-sex couples was unconstitutional. Since then, hundreds of same-sex couples have been married in that state.

Given the current antipathy toward same-sex marriage in the United States, we do not believe that widespread legal marriage between same-sex couples is likely in the near future. Nevertheless, we expect that an increasing number of states will recognize civil unions between gay and lesbian couples. The term *marriage* however, will be reserved exclusively for heterosexual couples, although in many cases this distinction will have more symbolic than legal implications.

As we noted earlier, marriage became a less central institution in American life during the last century, and it is difficult to imagine that marriage will regain the monolithic status that it once had. Effective contraception made it possible for single individuals to engage in sexual activity outside marriage without the complications of unwanted pregnancies. People today value the right to live together without being married, and single women value the freedom to bear children. After marriage, if spouses believe that their relationship problems are irreparable, husbands and wives demand access to no-fault divorce. History demonstrates that once people have obtained certain rights and privileges, they are unwilling to give them up. It is impossible to undo the past, and it seems likely that alternatives to mandatory lifelong marriage are here to stay.

These considerations do not imply, however, that marriage will continue to dwindle in importance to the point where it becomes irrelevant to most people. Surveys continue to show that the great majority of young adults want to marry and value the benefits of marriage (Glenn, 1996). And as Andrew Cherlin (2004) pointed out, marriage continues to be a marker of prestige and status in American society. A reasonable projection for the near future is that alternatives to marriage will continue to be accepted and widespread. People will have sexual relationships before marriage, live together without being married, have children outside marriage, avoid marriage completely, and divorce if their unions are flawed. At the same time, however, most people will view marriage as the gold standard for relationships and the best context for raising children.

What will marital quality be like in the near future? If the trend toward individualism continues unabated, then marital interaction will decline even more, and spouses' friendship networks, group affiliations, and leisure pursuits will become even more disconnected.

Spouses will operate as autonomous individuals who contract to stay together as long as their needs for personal growth and self-fulfillment are met. These relationships may be satisfying and even stable over long periods of time. But if the terms of the contract are not met, and if people's psychological rewards from the relationship are less than expected, individuals will dissolve their unions relatively quickly to seek out more promising opportunities with new partners. Serial marriage, punctuated by periods of being single and cohabitation, may meet the emotional needs of some adults reasonably well. Serial marriage, however, is unlikely to meet children's deep-seated needs for stability and long-term emotional bonds with both parents.

Another possibility, which we alluded to earlier in this chapter, is that a new equilibrium will emerge in which marriage is expected to meet societal as well as personal needs. As we noted earlier, some institutional features of marriage, such as shared attendance at religious services and support for the norm of lifelong marriage, are increasing. Correspondingly, many state and local governments view strengthening the institutional foundations of marriage as a legitimate policy goal. Of course, achieving the right balance between institutional and individualistic elements, between fulfilling obligations to others and meeting one's own needs, will be difficult. Nevertheless, we see some hints of what these new unions might be like.

Relations between husbands and wives will be egalitarian—an arrangement that facilitates intimacy and mutual feelings of closeness. Although some spouses will prefer to remain outside the labor force (especially when young children are in the household), most couples will share breadwinning and homemaking responsibilities over the life course—an arrangement that not only maximizes economic security, but also facilitates the personal development of wives as well as husbands. Although dual-earner marriages are more likely than single-earner marriages to experience tension over household chores and a degree of work-family conflict, the sharing of breadwinning and homemaking roles also offers greater possibilities for mutual understanding between spouses. At the same time, spouses—especially those with children–will recognize that marriage implies a commitment to a cause more important than the short-term satisfaction of two individuals. In particular, they will recognize that a stable, two-parent family is the arrangement best suited for raising the next generation of youth to become healthy, competent, and well-adjusted adults. People also will recognize that stable, two-parent families make positive contributions to the communities in which they live. Compared with single individuals, married couples are less likely to move (thus lowering residential turnover), are more likely to establish ties with neighbors, schools, and civic organizations (thus increasing social capital); and are more likely to monitor public spaces and keep an eye on neighborhood children and adolescents (thus increasing public safety and lowering crime). Many spouses will prefer the stability of their unions to be grounded in shared religious convictions and participation in religious events. Our study demonstrates that the most successful marriages combine gender equality, two incomes, shared social ties, and a strong commitment to marital permanence. After being in a state of flux for half a century, contemporary marriage may be moving toward a new synthesis of institutional, companionate, and individualistic features, with generally positive consequences for women, men, and children.

Appendix 1
Study Methodology

The 1980 and 2000 Marriage Surveys

Our 1980 data come from the first wave of the Marital Instability over the Life Course study (Booth, Johnson, White, and Edwards, 1981). In 1980 telephone interviewers used a random-digit dialing procedure to locate a national sample of 2,034 married persons (not couples) 55 years of age and under who were living with their spouses. Interviewers used a second random procedure to select the husband or wife as the respondent. After ten callbacks at different times of the day and on different days of the week, 17% of targeted telephone numbers could not be reached. Of those individuals contacted, 78% provided complete interviews, which resulted in an overall response rate of 65%. This response rate compares favorably with other studies that have used random-digit dialing (Booth and Johnson, 1985). Because the focus of the 1980 interview was on employment and marriage, we did not interview people if they (or their spouses) were over 55 years of age and, hence, were close to entering the retirement years.

Our 2000 data come from the Survey of Marriage and Family Life. As in the 1980 study, telephone interviewers contacted a random sample of households and randomly selected the husband or wife to serve as the respondent. The overall response rate for the survey (including

refusals and failures to locate targeted respondents) was 63%. The total sample consisted of 2,100 individuals who met the same sampling
criteria used in 1980; that is, respondents were married, respondents'
spouses lived in the household, and both spouses were 55 years of age
or less.

Inspection of data from the 1980 and 2000 U.S. Census revealed that
our samples were representative of the U.S. married population (age
55 or under) in many respects. Both samples, however, contained the
usual survey biases: Men, young adults, racial and ethnic minorities,
poorly educated individuals, and people residing in metropolitan areas
were underrepresented. For this reason we weighted the 1980 sample
to represent the 1980 U.S. population of married individuals (age 55
or under) with respect to gender, age, race (white, black, Latino, and
other), years of education, metropolitan status, and household size.
Correspondingly, we weighted the 2000 sample to represent the 2000
U.S. population of married individuals (age 55 or under) on the same
characteristics. For example, although the percentage of wives was
60% in the 1980 survey and 55% in the 2000 survey, we weighted the
data files so that the percentage of wives was 50% in each year.

Analytic Procedures

We use regression techniques for most of the analyses. We relied on
ordinary least squares (OLS) regression when the dependent variable
was ordered (for example, a scale of marital happiness) and logistic regression when the dependent variable was dichotomous (for example,
whether individuals cohabited before marriage). To describe change
across decades, we relied on decomposition analysis. Although regression methods are widely understood, decomposition methods are less
commonly used, so we provide a description for readers who are not familiar with this method.

DECOMPOSITION ANALYSIS

To identify overall changes in marriage between 1980 and 2000, we
compared the means of the explanatory variables (age at marriage, family income, husbands' share of housework, etc.) and the marital quality
variables (happiness, interaction, divorce proneness, etc.) across the
two surveys. Next, we regressed the three measures of marital quality

on the explanatory variables separately for 1980 and 2000. We then conducted a decomposition analysis for each marital quality variable, following procedures described by Firebaugh (1997) for analyzing social change. In the equation below, $\bar{x}$ represents a vector of means and b represents a vector of regression coefficients. Using subscripts to denote time (1 = 1980, 2 = 2000), change in the mean level of marital quality can be expressed as:

$$\bar{x}_2 - \bar{x}_1 = (a_2 + \bar{x}_2\, b_2) - (a_1 + \bar{x}_1\, b_1)$$

$$= a_2 - a_1 + \bar{x}_1(b_2 - b_1) + b_1(\bar{x}_2 - \bar{x}_1) + (\bar{x}_2 - \bar{x}_1)\,(b_2 - b_1)$$

$$= \Delta a + \bar{x}_1 \Delta b + \Delta \bar{x} b_1 + \Delta \bar{x} \Delta b.$$

The equation partitions the change in $\bar{x}$ (a dimension of marital quality) into four components: change in the intercepts of the two regression equations (Δa), changes in the effects of the explanatory variables ($\bar{x}_1 \Delta b$), changes in the levels (means) of the explanatory variables ($\Delta \bar{x} b_1$), and joint changes in the levels and effects of the explanatory variables ($\Delta \bar{x} \Delta b$). The first component can be thought of as the residual effect of time with all explanatory variables controlled. The second component represents the effects of changes in the b coefficients, assuming no changes in the means of the explanatory variables. The third component reflects the effects of changes in the means of the explanatory variables, assuming no changes in the b coefficients. The fourth component captures the interaction between changes in the means and changes in the b coefficients. Combining the second, third, and fourth components for each explanatory variable provides a measure of the overall contribution of each explanatory variable to change in the aggregate level of marital quality in the population.

All independent variables were grand mean centered (centered on the mean of the pooled samples) in the regression models used in the components analysis. Centering is a method used in the multilevel modeling literature (Bryk and Raudenbush, 1992) to solve the problem of arbitrary intercepts found in components models with interval-level variables that have no true zero value. (For a discussion of this issue, see Firebaugh, 1997, pp. 36–39). After conducting decomposition analyses for the entire sample, we considered whether these patterns differed for husbands and wives by conducting separate decomposition analyses for each gender.

Although our use of weights ensured that the two samples matched the population of married people in 1980 and 2000 on key variables, weighting also tends to increase the standard errors of sample estimates. For this reason, we used the survey data module in Stata 6.0 (StataCorp, 1999) to take sample weights into account when calculating standard errors. Across most of the variables described in this book, the design effect for means (which reflects the increase in error due to weighting when estimating the means of variables in the population) ranged from 1.17 to 2.23, with a mean value of 1.34. In other words, weighting the data increased the variance of the estimated means (the square of the standard error) by about 34%, on average. Adjusting the standard errors for weighting minimizes the possibility of concluding that a finding is statistically significant when it is not.

We present details for the key findings (such as regression equations) in Appendix 2. In describing our results in the text, however, we omit most statistics and simply describe how variables are associated. Readers should assume that if we say that two variables are associated, we mean that the association is statistically significant at the .05 level of probability or less. Occasionally, we state that two variables are marginally associated. This means that the association is marginally statistically significant ($.10 > p > .05$). We always rely on two-tailed tests of statistical significance.

MISSING DATA

In any survey, data are missing because some respondents refuse to answer certain questions, or because some respondents do not know the answer to certain questions. To deal with this problem, some researchers rely on listwise deletion of missing cases—a simple procedure in which cases with missing data on any variable are excluded from the analysis. This procedure is problematic for two reasons, however. First, it requires the researcher to throw away a good deal of useful data. For example, a researcher might exclude from all analyses a husband who does not provide information on his income, even though the husband provided useful information on his age, race, education, and occupation. Second, if respondents with missing data tend to differ from respondents with complete data (which is likely), then listwise deletion of missing cases biases estimates of population parameters. For example, if people who fail to report their incomes tend to have relatively high incomes, and if we exclude these missing cases from the analysis, then our estimate of the mean level of income in the population will be too low.

Rather than delete cases with any missing data, a preferable solution is for researchers to impute values on the basis of other information in the data. We used two procedures for dealing with missing data. In preliminary analyses we imputed values for all variables using the expectation maximization (EM) algorithm. This procedure has been shown to generate accurate maximum likelihood estimates with up to 50% missing data (Acock, 1997; Allison, 2001). If the amount of missing data is large, however, EM may underestimate standard errors, as it does not take into account variability (error) introduced by the imputation procedure itself. The level of missing data in the present study, however, was small. Most variables were missing less than 1% of observations, with the largest occurring for total family income (8.7%) and wives' portion of family income (8.8%).

To check on the possibility that EM imputation downwardly biased the standard errors, we relied on multiple imputation (MI) as an alternative method for dealing with missing data (Allison, 2001). Using Schafer's (1999) NORM software, we simulated missing data five times, producing five alternative but plausible versions of the complete data. We then conducted separate analyses for each of these data sets, with variation in results across data sets reflecting uncertainty due to imputation. We then combined these results into a single set of estimates and standard errors, using rules described by Rubin (1987). Across several preliminary OLS multiple regression analyses, standard errors for 70 parameters were, on average, only 1% higher when using imputation based on MI rather than the EM method. Because the increase in standard errors due to EM imputation was trivial, we relied on EM methods for all analyses reported in this book.

EFFECT SIZES

For ease of presentation, we show many of the key results in each chapter graphically. When dependent variables have an inherent meaning (for example, age at first marriage or years of education), we present the results using the original metric of the variable. When dependent variables are scale scores (such as a scale of marital happiness or traditional attitudes toward gender roles), we standardized the distributions to have means of zero and standard deviations of one before presentation. Given that the unit of measurement in most scales is arbitrary, this procedure results in little loss of information. More important, the use of standardized scores makes it possible to report effect sizes: that is, differences between groups expressed as a proportion of the standard deviation of the dependent variable. By providing a common metric, effect sizes allow meaningful comparisons between outcomes that involve different scales of measurement. Effect sizes also provide a convenient way of interpreting the strength of associations. We assess effect sizes using the following conventions: effect sizes of .19 or less (that is, less than one-fifth of a standard deviation difference between groups) are weak, effect sizes between .20 and .39 are moderate, effect sizes between .40 and .59 are strong, and effect sizes of .60 or more are very strong.

To provide a clearer grasp of the magnitude of associations expressed as effect sizes, it is useful to rely on the Binomial Effect Size Display (Rosenthal, 1994). Assume that a successful outcome is present in 50% of the population. In the present context, this would occur if we pooled our 1980 and 2000 data and split the marital happiness scale at its median into low and high groups. We could then describe change as the proportion of cases in each survey year that fell into these groups. Under these circumstances, the effect size has a simple interpretation; that is, the effect size is equivalent to twice the difference in proportions between groups. For example, if an explanatory variable appeared to increase the proportion of people in the high-happiness group from .45 to .55, then this change would represent an effect size of .20. Correspondingly, an effect size of .40 would represent an increase from .40 to .60, and an effect size of .60 would represent an increase from .35 to .65.

Thinking in terms of effect sizes is useful in interpreting the results of our decomposition analyses. When describing how change in an explanatory variable (such as the increase in the mean age at marriage in the population) is associated with change in a marital outcome (such as the mean level of marital happiness in the population), we express the association in terms of proportions of a standard deviation. For example, in Chapter 4 we point out that the increase in family income between 1980 and 2000 was associated with an increase in the mean level of marital happiness in the population equivalent to .02 of a standard deviation, which is equivalent to an effect size of .02. This example is not atypical. Most of the associations between specific explanatory variables and marital quality outcomes that we present in this book are weak, based on the rule of thumb that we described earlier. Readers should keep in mind, however, that explanatory variables do not act in isolation, and the combined effects of multiple changes on marital quality can be substantial.

For example, in Chapter 3 we report that the increase in premarital cohabitation, parental divorce, and marital heterogamy between 1980 and 2000 increased divorce proneness in the general population by .08 of a standard deviation. If we translate these findings into a binomial effect size display, then the increase in these three factors increased the share of divorce-prone marriages from 48% in 1980 to 52% in 2000. This difference may seem small in absolute terms, but if we consider the number of married couples in the population, it is profound.

In 2000 there were nearly 49 million married couples with children in the United States (U.S. Census Bureau, 2001). The increase in premarital cohabitation, parental divorce, and marital heterogamy, therefore, shifted about 1 million couples from the low-divorce-risk category to the high-divorce-risk category. This estimate indicates that even a modest change in effect size, when multiplied by the large number of married couples in the population (in this case, couples with children), results in a substantial change in the absolute number of people at risk of divorce or serious marital dysfunction. In other words, even small effect sizes can affect the stability and well-being of a large number of families.

CLUSTER ANALYSIS

In Chapter 7 we report the results of a cluster analysis. The goal of cluster analysis is to find a parsimonious number of categories into which cases can be classified, on the basis of a variety of attributes of these cases. Methodologists have developed a variety of clustering algorithms that rely on different statistical assumptions (Arabie, Hubert, and De Soete, 1996; Bailey, 1994). We explored several algorithms in preliminary analyses, and we settled for a straightforward solution based on k-means clustering—one of the most commonly used clustering methods (Hartigan and Wong, 1979). The algorithm begins by randomly assigning cases to k clusters. (The user specifies the number of clusters.) Subsequent steps reassign the cases to new clusters on the basis of the distances between the cases and the cluster centers. These iterations are repeated until the amount of improvement is minimal.

We generated solutions based on 2, 3, 4, 5, 6, 7, and 8 clusters. We relied on three criteria to determine the optimal number of clusters. First, we looked at the number of explanatory variables (age at marriage, wives' employment, religiosity, etc.) that differed significantly across the clustering solutions. Second, we looked at the ability of the clustering solutions to explain variance in five dimensions of marital quality. And third, we looked at the decline in the mean distance of all cases from their respective cluster centers. (As the number of clusters increases, the mean distances decline, but there is a point at which further increases result in minimal declines in distance.) All three of these procedures suggested that the optimal solution involved five clusters, as we describe in Chapter 7.

Selection Effects

Glenn (1990) pointed out a recurring difficulty in the study of marital quality: the population of married individuals is not "closed." In other words, people choose to marry and hence enter the married population. Similarly, people decide to divorce and hence leave the married population. The fact that the married population is not closed raises several important conceptual and methodological issues in studying changes in marital quality. We refer to these potential problems as "selection into marriage" effects and "selection out of marriage" effects.

SELECTION INTO MARRIAGE

If the traits that lead people to marry are related to marital quality, and if these traits have changed over time, then selection factors may be partly responsible for aggregate shifts in marital quality. For example, suppose that low-income couples were less likely to marry in the two decades preceding 2000 than in the two decades preceding 1980. A decrease in the proportion of low-income couples who marry might come about because, facing a precarious and uncertain future, these couples might prefer to cohabit rather than marry. We know from other re-

search that low-income couples are more likely than economically secure couples to have troubled marriages (Conger et al., 1990; White,
1990). A decline in the percentage of low-income couples who marry,
therefore, would raise the mean level of economic well-being among
married couples, and correspondingly, the mean level of marital quality. In this example, the increase in marital quality between decades
would be due to a tendency for risky couples to avoid marriage, rather
than to some factor intrinsic to marriage itself.

Testing for selection-into-marriage effects is difficult, and we do not
pursue this strategy in this book. This is not a serious limitation, however, because the great majority of people in the United States marry.
Current projections indicate that about 90% of all adults will marry,
compared with about 95% of all adults earlier in the twentieth century
(Cherlin, 1992). It seems unlikely that a small decline in the percentage
of people who marry would have substantial effects on aggregate levels
of marital quality in the population. Moreover, even if selection effects
are present, our estimates of changes in aggregate levels of marital
quality still describe the population accurately.

SELECTION OUT OF MARRIAGE

Selection out of marriage is potentially problematic, because a single
cross section of married people necessarily excludes a large group of
unhappily married people who divorced before the time of data collection. For this reason, any cross-sectional study that attempts to understand the correlates (and causes) of marital quality omits some of
the most important cases—people with unhappy, short, unstable marriages.

Our conclusions would be threatened if changes in marital quality
were driven primarily by differential selection out of marriage. Because
divorce rates reached a plateau in 1980, there probably was more selection out of marriage between 1980 and 2000 than in the two decades
preceding the first survey. Consistent with this view is the fact that census data from 1980 and 2000 indicate that of all adults who had ever
been married, 13% were divorced or separated in 1980, compared with
19% in 2000. (These percentages exclude widows and widowers.) With
increased selection out of troubled marriages, one might expect remaining marriages to be of higher quality in 2000 than in 1980. If this
is true, then the apparent stability in marital happiness and divorce

proneness between surveys that we report in Chapter 2, for example, would represent a decline in the real level of these variables over time.

To see if the increase of 6 percentage points in the divorced population affected our results, we adopted two strategies. First, we restricted our comparisons to marriages of less than two years. Because these marriages are at risk of divorce for a relatively short time, movement out of these marriages through separation and divorce is minimal. Indeed, only about 7% of first marriages end in divorce within the first two years (Bramlett and Mosher, 2002). For individuals married less than two years ($n = 200$ in 1980 and 146 in 2000), the mean differences between 1980 and 2000 were .08 for happiness, $-.31$ for interaction, $-.28$ for conflict, .08 for marital problems, and $-.01$ for divorce proneness. Of the five comparisons, the mean differences for interaction and conflict were significant. These calculations indicate that changes in marital quality for individuals in marriages of short duration were similar to the changes observed in the full sample (see Chapter 2). The one exception involved marital problems. For this variable, the decline between 1980 and 2000 observed in the full sample was not present in the sample restricted to individuals in short-term marriages. This finding suggests that the decline in marital problems between surveys may have been due partly to greater movement out of marriage through divorce in the latter period.

Second, we estimated how marital quality would have changed if there had been no selection out of marriage through divorce in 1980 and 2000. Our 1980 sample was the first wave of a longitudinal study, with additional interviews occurring in 1983, 1988, 1992, and 1997. In marriages that ended in divorce during the study, it was possible to examine marital quality prior to dissolution. We used data on happiness, interaction, conflict, problems, and divorce proneness (drawn from the interview preceding disruption) from 305 individuals who divorced between 1980 and 1997. Not surprisingly, married respondents who were on the verge of divorcing, compared with those who remained continuously married, reported lower marital happiness, less interaction, more conflict, more problems, and greater divorce proneness. We added these predisruption means to the observed means in 1980 and weighted the predisruption means by .13 and the obtained means by .87, based on the percentage of people who had ever been divorced in the 1980 population. We followed the same procedure for 2000 but weighted the predisruption means by .19 and the obtained means by .81, based on the proportion who had ever been divorced in the 2000 population. These weighted means represent estimates of marital quality in 1980 and 2000 if no individuals had left the marriage population through divorce.

This procedure, of course, decreased the mean levels of marital happiness and interaction and increased the mean levels of conflict, problems, and divorce proneness in both survey years. The resulting differences in marital quality between surveys, however, were not substantially different from those we report in Chapter 2. For example, the differences between 1980 and 2000 were −.05 for marital happiness, −.29 for interaction, and .00 for divorce proneness. The relatively minor differences between these figures and those we report in Chapter 2 are due to the fact that movement out of marriage was only slightly higher in 2000 than in 1980. This procedure suggests that the increase in divorce did not substantially affect our estimates of changes in marital quality.

Appendix 2
Tables

Table 1 Correlations between measures of marital quality in 1980 and 2000

	Dimensions of marital quality				
	Happiness	Interaction	Conflict	Problems	Divorce proneness
Happiness	—	.451	−.457	−.527	−.512
Interaction	.443	—	−.208	−.294	−.261
Conflict	−.488	−.249	—	.497	.477
Problems	−.471	−.297	.551	—	.586
Divorce proneness	−.533	−.324	.550	.613	—

Note: Correlations for 1980 are below the diagonal, and correlations for 2000 are above the diagonal.

$N = 2,034$ in 1980; $N = 2,100$ in 2000.

All correlations are significant at $p < .001$.

Table 2 Means and standard deviations for marital quality variables in 1980 and 2000

	Husbands		Wives		Probability		
	1980	2000	1980	2000			
	x̄ (S)	x̄ (S)	x̄ (S)	x̄ (S)	Year	Gender	Year × gender
Happiness	.144 (.900)	.064 (.979)	−.143 (1.067)	−.066 (1.021)	.965	.000	.023
Interaction	.194 (.905)	−.106 (.982)	.125 (1.008)	−.203 (1.044)	.000	.016	.699
Conflict	.062 (.977)	−.157 (.887)	.094 (1.068)	.005 (1.041)	.000	.005	.058
Problems	−.015 (.900)	−.115 (.979)	.109 (1.067)	.024 (1.021)	.010	.000	.827
Divorce proneness	−.064 (.943)	−.102 (1.008)	.077 (1.000)	.090 (1.031)	.711	.000	.456

Table 3 Linear decomposition of change in marital quality between 1980 and 2000

	Marital quality				
	Marital happiness	Marital interaction	Marital conflict	Marital problems	Divorce proneness
Total change (1980–2000)	−.002	−.315**	−.154**	−.092**	−.013
Source of change					
Within-cohort change	.026	−.382**	−.453**	−.278**	−.236**
Cross-cohort change	−.027	.067*	.299**	.186**	.223**

* $p < .05$.   ** $p < .01$.

Table 4 Within-cohort change and total change in marital conflict between 1980 and 2000

| Birth cohort | Year of survey | | | | |
	1980	(N)	2000	(N)	Change
1920–1929	−.213	(189)	—	—	—
1930–1939	−.093	(552)	—	—	—
1940–1949	.101	(581)	−.325	(221)	−.426
1950–1959	.277	(667)	−.180	(725)	−.457
1960–1969	.168	(45)	−.018	(761)	−.185
1970–1979	—	—	.145	(393)	
All cohorts	.078	(2,034)	−.076	(2,100)	−.154

Table 5 Descriptive statistics for demographic variables in 1980 and 2000

Variable	Range	$\bar{x}_{1980}$	S_{1980}	$\bar{x}_{2000}$	S_{2000}	$\bar{x}_{2000} - \bar{x}_{1980}$
Female	0–1	.50	.50	.50	.50	0.00
Black respondent	0–1	.07	.26	.09	.28	0.02
Latino respondent	0–1	.06	.23	.11	.32	0.06**
Other race respondent	0–1	.02	.14	.06	.24	0.04**
Education of respondent	0–28	12.93	2.81	13.85	2.84	0.92**
Age of respondent	16–55	36.16	9.69	39.12	8.64	2.96**
Age at current marriage	13–54	22.90	5.55	25.86	6.71	2.96**
Respondent remarried	0–1	.15	.35	.20	.40	0.05**
Premarital cohabitation	0–1	.16	.37	.41	.49	0.24**
Number of children < 19	0–8	1.40	1.26	1.30	1.18	−0.10**
Any stepchildren	0–1	.06	.24	.11	.32	0.05**
Parental divorce respondent	0–1	.16	.36	.25	.43	0.09**
Heterogamy index	0–4	.61	.76	.86	.90	0.17**

$* p < .05$ $** p < .01$ (two-tailed)

Table 6 Descriptive statistics for economic variables in 1980 and 2000

Variable	Range	$\bar{x}_{1980}$	S_{1980}	$\bar{x}_{2000}$	S_{2000}	$\bar{x}_{2000} - \bar{x}_{1980}$
Husband employed	0–1	.95	.23	.92	.26	−.03*
Husbands' weekly hours	0–80	48.41	16.17	48.45	17.78	.04
Wife employed	0–1	.58	.49	.75	.43	.17**
Wives' weekly hours	0–80	22.25	21.12	30.09	20.78	7.84**
Husbands' job demands	0–4	1.35	1.11	1.37	1.19	.02
Wives' job demands	0–4	.46	.84	.68	.98	.22**
Family income (in 000s)	2.5–271.8	55.60	26.93	70.00	34.27	14.40**
Public assistance	0–1	.11	.31	.07	.26	−.04**
Economic distress	0–1	.22	.41	.17	.37	−.05**

$* p < .05$ $** p < .01$ (two-tailed)

Table 7 Descriptive statistics for gender relations variables in 1980 and 2000

Variable	Range	$\bar{x}_{1980}$	S_{1980}	$\bar{x}_{2000}$	S_{2000}	$\bar{x}_{2000} - \bar{x}_{1980}$
Wives' proportion of earnings	0–1	.21	.22	.32	.21	.11**
Traditional gender attitudes	1–4	2.42	.46	2.26	.43	−.16**
Husbands' proportion of housework	0–1	.27	.18	.35	.19	.08**
Division of labor unfair to husband	0–1	.05	.21	.08	.27	.03**
Division of labor unfair to wife	0–1	.27	.45	.28	.45	.01
Husband sometimes has last word	0–1	.73	.44	.68	.47	−.05**
Wife sometimes has last word	0–1	.66	.47	.67	.47	.01
Equal decision making	0–1	.49	.50	.64	.48	.15**

$* p < .05$ $** p < .01$ (two-tailed)

Table 8 Descriptive statistics for measures of social integration, religiosity, and attitudes toward lifelong marriage

Variable	Range	$\bar{x}_{1980}$	S_{1980}	$\bar{x}_{2000}$	S_{2000}	$\bar{x}_{2000} - \bar{x}_{1980}$
Friendship networks						
No close friends	0–1	.13	.34	.13	.34	.00
No shared friends	0–1	.08	.27	.11	.31	.03**
Some friends shared	0–1	.28	.45	.34	.47	.06**
All friends shared	0–1	.52	.50	.41	.49	−.11**
Organizational membership						
No memberships	0–1	.50	.50	.62	.49	.12**
No shared memberships	0–1	.21	.41	.14	.35	−.07**
Some/all memberships shared	0–1	.29	.45	.24	.43	−.05**
In-laws unhappy with marriage	0–1	.17	.37	.13	.33	−.04**
Parents unhappy with spouse	0–1	.16	.36	.11	.32	−.05**
Get along with in-laws now	1–3	2.73	.50	2.72	.51	−.01
Parents get along with spouse now	1–3	2.68	.56	2.67	.56	−.01
Influence of religion on life	1–5	3.64	1.24	3.81	1.29	.17**
Attendance at services together	1–4	2.54	1.21	2.63	1.21	.09*
Support for lifelong marriage	1–4	2.62	.41	2.73	.43	.10**

Note: $N = 2,034$ in 1980, 2,100 in 2000.
* $p < .05$ ** $p < .01$ (two-tailed)

Table 9 Decomposition analysis of 1980 to 2000 change in marital happiness with mean centered explanatory variables

Explanatory variable	$\bar{x}_1$ 1980	$\bar{x}_2$ 2000	$\bar{x}_2 - \bar{x}_1$	b_1 1980	b_2 2000	$b_2 - b_1$	Slope $\bar{x}_1\Delta b$	Level $\Delta\bar{x}b_1$	Joint $\Delta\bar{x}\Delta b$	Sum
Demographics										
Female	0.000	0.000	0.000	−0.225**	−0.067	0.158*	0.000	0.000	0.000	0.000
Black	−0.010	0.009	0.019	−0.189	−0.089	0.099	−0.001	−0.003	0.002	−0.003
Latino	−0.028	0.027	0.055**	0.000	−0.078	−0.078	0.002	0.000	−0.004	−0.002
Other race	−0.021	0.021	0.042**	−0.218	0.015	0.234	−0.005	−0.009	0.010	−0.004
Education	−0.478	0.475	0.953**	−0.011	0.005	0.017	−0.008	−0.011	0.016	−0.003
Age	−1.532	1.459	2.991**	−0.009**	−0.006	0.003	−0.005	−0.027**	0.009	−0.023**
Age married	−1.511	1.462	2.973**	−0.001	0.002	0.003	−0.005	−0.004	0.010	0.001
Remarried	−0.027	0.026	0.053**	0.260**	0.018	−0.241*	0.007	0.014*	−0.013	0.008
Premarital cohabitation	−0.124	0.120	0.244**	0.054	−0.052	−0.106	0.013	0.013	−0.026	0.000
Number of children	0.050	−0.051	−0.101**	−0.061**	−0.062**	0.000	0.000	0.006	0.000	0.006
Any stepchildren	−0.027	0.026	0.053**	−0.197	0.157*	0.354*	−0.010*	−0.010	0.019*	−0.001
Parental divorce	−0.048	0.047	0.095**	0.075	0.019	−0.056	0.003	0.007	−0.005	0.005
Heterogamy index	−0.128	0.123	0.251**	−0.084*	−0.060*	0.024	−0.003	−0.021*	0.006	−0.018**
Employment and income										
Husband employed	0.011	−0.011	−0.022*	−0.249**	−0.151	0.098	0.001	0.005	−0.002	0.004
Husband's hours of work	−0.022	0.025	0.047	0.002	0.002	−0.001	0.000	0.000	0.000	0.000
Wife employed	−0.089	0.085	0.174**	0.061	0.085	0.024	−0.002	0.010	0.004	0.013
Wife's hours of work	−3.977	3.827	7.804**	−0.003	−0.004*	−0.001	0.003	−0.026	−0.005	−0.029*
Husband's work demands	−0.011	0.010	0.021	−0.001	0.002	0.003	0.000	0.000	0.000	0.000
Wife's work demands	−0.113	0.108	0.213**	−0.003	−0.015	−0.012	0.001	−0.001	−0.003	−0.002
Family income	−7.300	7.101	14.401**	0.003**	0.000	−0.003**	0.023**	0.042**	−0.046**	0.019*
Use of public assistance	0.019	−0.019	−0.038**	−0.109	−0.004	0.105	0.002	0.004	−0.004	0.002
Economic distress	0.025	−0.024	−0.049**	−0.098	−0.468**	−0.370**	−0.009*	0.005	0.018**	0.014*

	C1	C2	C3	C4	C5	C6	C7	C8	C9	C10
Gender relations										
Wife's share of income	−0.057	0.054	0.111**	0.038	0.181	0.143	−0.008	0.004	0.016	0.012
Traditional gender attitudes	0.182	−0.178	−0.360**	−0.049	−0.094**	−0.045	−0.008	0.018	0.016	0.026**
Husband's share of housework	−0.042	0.041	0.083**	0.114	−0.162	−0.276	0.011	0.009	−0.023	−0.002
Division of labor unfair to husband	−0.016	0.016	0.032**	−0.547**	−0.385**	0.162	−0.002	−0.017*	0.005	−0.014**
Division of labor unfair to wife	−0.007	0.000	0.007	−0.515**	−0.578**	−0.063	0.000	−0.003	0.000	−0.003
Husband final word sometimes	0.027	−0.027	−0.054**	−0.098	−0.014	0.084	0.002	0.005	−0.004	0.003
Wife final word sometimes	−0.006	0.005	0.011	0.005	−0.032	−0.037	0.000	0.000	−0.001	0.000
Decision-making equality	−0.076	0.074	0.015**	0.251**	0.173**	−0.079	0.006	0.038**	−0.012	0.032**
Social integration										
No shared friends	−0.017	0.017	0.034**	−0.486**	−0.163	0.323*	−0.006	−0.017	0.011	−0.011*
Some shared friends	−0.033	0.031	0.064**	0.009	−0.043	−0.053	0.002	0.001	−0.003	−0.001
All friends shared	0.055	−0.053	−0.108**	0.123	0.135	0.011	0.001	−0.013	−0.001	−0.014*
No shared affiliations	0.037	−0.035	−0.072**	−0.113	−0.116	−0.003	0.000	0.008	0.000	0.008*
Some or all affiliations shared	0.025	−0.024	−0.049**	−0.081	0.066	0.147	0.004	0.004	−0.007	0.000
Religiosity	−0.086	0.082	0.168**	0.049*	0.030	−0.019	0.002	0.008	−0.003	0.007*
Attendance at services	−0.046	0.041	0.087*	0.078**	0.027	−0.051	0.002	0.007	−0.004	0.005
Support for lifelong marriage	−0.053	0.051	0.104**	0.307**	0.151**	−0.156	0.008	0.032**	−0.016	0.024**
Regression constant				0.040	−0.021					
R^2				0.260**	0.211**					
Sum of components	0.002	0.000					0.021	0.078*	−0.041	0.058*

Means of marital happiness:

$$\bar{x}_2 - \bar{x}_1 = \Delta a + \Sigma \bar{x}_1 \Delta b + \Sigma \Delta \bar{x} b_1 + \Sigma \Delta \bar{x} \Delta b$$

Decomposition of mean difference:

$$-0.003 = -0.061 + 0.021 + 0.078 + -0.041$$

* $p < .05$ ** $p < .01$

Table 10 Decomposition analysis of 1980 to 2000 change in marital interaction with mean-centered explanatory variables

Explanatory variable	$\bar{x}_1$ 1980	$\bar{x}_2$ 2000	$\bar{x}_2 - \bar{x}_1$	b_1 1980	b_2 2000	$b_2 - b_1$	Slope $\bar{x}_1\Delta b$	Level $\Delta\bar{x}b_1$	Joint $\Delta\bar{x}\Delta b$	Sum
Demographics										
Female	0.000	0.000	0.000	−0.014	−0.013	0.001	0.000	0.000	0.000	0.000
Black	−0.010	0.009	0.019	−0.355**	−0.201*	0.154	−0.002	−0.007	0.003	−0.005
Latino	−0.028	0.027	0.055**	0.050	0.248*	0.199	−0.005	0.003	0.011	0.008
Other race	−0.021	0.021	0.042**	0.226	0.214*	−0.011	0.000	0.009	0.000	0.009*
Education	−0.478	0.475	0.953**	−0.022*	−0.007	0.015	−0.007	−0.021	0.014	−0.014
Age	−1.532	1.459	2.991**	−0.011**	−0.013**	−0.002	0.002	−0.034**	−0.005	−0.036**
Age married	−1.511	1.462	2.973**	0.013*	0.005	−0.008	0.012	0.038*	−0.024	0.026*
Remarried	−0.027	0.026	0.053**	0.138	0.124	−0.014	0.000	0.007	−0.001	0.007
Premarital cohabitation	−0.124	0.120	0.244**	−0.187*	0.005	0.192*	−0.024*	−0.046*	0.047*	−0.023*
Number of children	0.050	−0.051	−0.101**	−0.091**	−0.094**	−0.003	0.000	0.009*	0.000	0.009*
Any stepchildren	−0.027	0.026	0.053**	0.063	0.031	−0.032	0.001	0.003	−0.002	0.002
Parental divorce	−0.048	0.047	0.095**	0.040	0.008	−0.031	0.002	0.004	−0.003	0.002
Heterogamy index	−0.128	0.123	0.251**	−0.091*	−0.041	0.050	−0.006	−0.023*	0.013	−0.017**
Employment and income										
Husband employed	0.011	−0.011	−0.022*	0.061	0.268	0.207	0.002	−0.001	−0.005	−0.004
Husband's hours of work	−0.022	0.025	0.047	−0.005*	−0.005*	0.000	0.000	0.000	0.000	0.000
Wife employed	−0.089	0.085	0.174**	−0.042	−0.075	−0.033	0.003	−0.007	−0.006	−0.010
Wife's hours of work	−3.977	3.827	7.804**	−0.001	−0.005*	−0.004	0.014	−0.011	−0.028	−0.025
Husband's work demands	−0.011	0.010	0.021	−0.006	−0.016	−0.010	0.000	0.000	0.000	0.000
Wife's work demands	−0.113	0.108	0.213**	−0.063	−0.014	0.049	−0.006	−0.014	0.011	−0.009
Family income	−7.300	7.101	14.401**	0.001	0.000	−0.001	0.009	0.018	−0.017	0.010
Use of public assistance	0.019	−0.019	−0.038**	−0.070	−0.222*	−0.152	−0.003	0.003	0.006	0.005
Economic distress	0.025	−0.024	−0.049**	−0.057	−0.317**	−0.260**	−0.007	0.003	0.013*	0.009*

Gender relations

Wife's share of income	-0.057	0.054	0.111**	0.113	0.272	0.160	-0.009	0.012	0.018	0.021
Traditional gender attitudes	0.182	-0.178	-0.360**	-0.057*	-0.062*	-0.005	-0.001	0.020*	0.002	0.021**
Husband's share of housework	-0.042	0.041	0.083**	0.545**	0.465**	-0.079	0.003	0.045**	-0.007	0.041**
Division of labor unfair to husband	-0.016	0.016	0.032**	-0.126	-0.213*	-0.087	0.001	-0.004	-0.003	-0.005
Division of labor unfair to wife	-0.007	0.000	0.007	-0.341**	-0.309**	0.032	0.000	-0.002	0.000	-0.002
Husband final word sometimes	0.027	-0.027	-0.054**	-0.022	-0.050	-0.029	-0.001	0.001	0.001	0.002
Wife final word sometimes	-0.006	0.005	0.011	0.044	-0.026	-0.070	0.000	0.001	-0.001	0.000
Decision-making equality	-0.076	0.074	0.015**	0.260**	0.073	-0.187**	0.014*	0.039**	-0.028*	0.025**

Social integration

No shared friends	-0.017	0.017	0.034**	-0.383**	0.017	0.400**	-0.007	-0.013*	0.014*	-0.006
Some shared friends	-0.033	0.031	0.064**	-0.002	0.158	0.161	-0.005	0.000	0.010	0.005
All friends shared	0.055	-0.053	-0.108**	0.105	0.460**	0.356**	0.019*	-0.011	-0.038**	-0.030**
No shared affiliations	0.037	-0.035	-0.072**	-0.113*	-0.048	0.065	0.002	0.008	-0.005	0.006
Some or all affiliations shared	0.025	-0.024	-0.049**	-0.063	0.087	0.150	0.004	0.003	-0.007	-0.001
Religiosity	-0.086	0.082	0.168**	-0.001	-0.013	-0.012	0.001	0.000	-0.002	-0.001
Attendance at services	-0.046	0.041	0.087*	0.070**	0.069**	-0.001	0.000	0.006	0.000	-0.001
Support for lifelong marriage	-0.053	0.051	0.104**	0.115	-0.015	-0.131	0.007	0.012	-0.014	0.005

Regression constant				0.185	-0.165					
R^2				0.187**	0.176**					
Sum of components							0.016*	0.051	-0.033	0.034
Means of marital interaction	0.161	-0.155								

Decomposition of mean difference

$$\bar{x}_2 - \bar{x}_1 = \Delta a + \Sigma \bar{x}_i \Delta b + \Sigma \Delta \bar{x} \bar{b}_1 + \Sigma \Delta \bar{x} \Delta b$$

$$-0.316 = -0.350 + 0.016 + 0.051 + -0.033$$

* $p < .05$ ** $p < .01$

Table 11 Decomposition analysis of 1980 to 2000 change in marital conflict with mean-centered explanatory variables

Explanatory variable	$\bar{x}_1$ 1980	$\bar{x}_2$ 2000	$\bar{x}_2 - \bar{x}_1$	b_1 1980	b_2 2000	$b_2 - b_1$	Decomposition component Slope $\bar{x}_1\Delta b$	Level $\Delta\bar{x}b_1$	Joint $\Delta\bar{x}\Delta b$	Sum
Demographics										
Female	0.000	0.000	0.000	-0.095	0.056	0.151*	0.000	0.000	0.000	0.000
Black	-0.010	0.009	0.019	0.255*	0.024	-0.230	0.002	0.005	-0.004	0.003
Latino	-0.028	0.027	0.055**	0.060	-0.054	-0.115	0.003	0.003	-0.006	0.000
Other race	-0.021	0.021	0.042**	-0.288*	0.006	0.294	-0.006	-0.012*	0.012	-0.006
Education	-0.478	0.475	0.953**	0.002	0.031**	0.028	-0.014	0.002	0.027	0.016
Age	-1.532	1.459	2.991**	-0.008**	-0.013**	-0.005	0.008	-0.025*	-0.015	-0.032**
Age married	-1.511	1.462	2.973**	-0.011	0.001	0.013	-0.019	-0.033	0.037	-0.015
Remarried	-0.027	0.026	0.053**	-0.067	-0.009	0.058	-0.002	-0.004	0.003	-0.002
Premarital cohabitation	-0.124	0.120	0.244**	0.139	0.078	-0.061	0.008	0.034	-0.015	0.027*
Number of children	.050	-0.051	-0.101**	-0.009	0.018	0.027	0.001	0.001	-0.003	-0.001
Any stepchildren	-0.027	0.026	0.053**	0.190	-0.163*	-0.353*	0.010	0.010	-0.019*	0.001
Parental divorce	-0.048	0.047	0.095**	0.109	0.112	0.003	0.000	0.010	0.000	0.011*
Heterogamy index	-0.128	0.123	0.251**	0.104**	0.018	-0.086	0.011	0.026*	-0.021	0.015*
Employment and income										
Husband employed	.011	-0.011	-0.022*	-0.053	0.153	0.206	0.002	0.001	-0.005	-0.001
Husband's hours of work	-0.022	0.025	0.047	-0.001	-0.002	-0.001	0.000	0.000	0.000	0.000
Wife employed	-0.089	0.085	0.174**	0.190	-0.119	-0.309*	0.027*	0.033	-0.054*	0.007
Wife's hours of work	-3.977	3.827	7.804**	-0.001	0.003	0.004	-0.017	-0.009	0.034	0.008
Husband's work demands	-0.011	0.010	0.021	0.024	0.028	0.004	0.000	0.000	0.000	0.001
Wife's work demands	-0.113	0.108	0.213**	0.034	0.027	-0.007	0.001	0.007	-0.001	0.007
Family income	-7.300	7.101	14.401**	0.000	-0.001	-0.002	0.011	0.002	-0.022	-0.008
Use of public assistance	0.019	-0.019	-0.038**	0.217*	0.078	-0.139	-0.003	-0.008*	0.005	-0.006
Economic distress	0.025	-0.024	-0.049**	0.125*	0.212**	0.087	0.002	-0.006	-0.004	-0.008*

	$\bar{x}_1$	$\bar{x}_2$	$\Delta\bar{x}$	b_1	b_2	Δb	$\bar{x}_i\Delta b$	$\Delta\bar{x}\bar{b}_1$	$\Delta\bar{x}\Delta b$	
Gender relations										
Wife's share of income	-0.057	0.054	0.111**	-0.083	-0.113	-0.030	0.002	-0.009	-0.003	-0.011
Traditional gender attitudes	0.182	-0.178	-0.360**	-0.027	-0.004	0.023	0.004	0.010	-0.008	0.006
Husband's share of housework	-0.042	0.041	0.083**	0.123	0.255	0.133	-0.005	0.010	0.011	0.015
Division of labor unfair to husband	-0.016	0.016	0.032**	0.797**	0.441**	-0.356	0.005	0.025*	-0.011	0.019**
Division of labor unfair to wife	-0.007	0.000	0.007	0.468**	0.514**	0.046	0.000	0.003	0.000	0.003
Husband final word sometimes	0.027	-0.027	-0.054**	0.061	0.001	-0.060	-0.002	-0.003	0.003	-0.002
Wife final word sometimes	-0.006	0.005	0.011	0.017	0.026	0.009	0.000	0.000	0.000	0.000
Decision-making equality	-0.076	0.074	0.015**	-0.203**	-0.170**	0.032	-0.003	-0.030**	0.005	-0.028**
Social integration										
No shared friends	-0.017	0.017	0.034**	0.161	0.103	-0.058	0.001	0.005	-0.002	0.005
Some shared friends	-0.033	0.031	0.064**	-0.053	0.088	0.141	-0.005	-0.003	0.009	0.001
All friends shared	0.055	-0.053	-0.108**	-0.227**	-0.032	0.195	0.011	0.024*	-0.021	0.014*
No shared affiliations	0.037	-0.035	-0.072**	0.080	0.062	-0.018	-0.001	-0.006	0.001	-0.005
Some or all affiliations shared	0.025	-0.024	-0.049**	0.123*	0.018	-0.105	-0.003	-0.006	0.005	-0.004
Religiosity	-0.086	0.082	0.168**	0.011	0.007	-0.004	0.000	0.002	-0.001	0.002
Attendance at services	-0.046	0.041	0.087*	-0.044	-0.039	0.005	0.000	-0.004	0.000	-0.004
Support for lifelong marriage	-0.053	0.051	0.104**	-0.148*	-0.097	0.051	-0.003	-0.015*	0.005	-0.013**
Regression constant				0.101	-0.069					
R^2				0.219**	0.182**					
Sum of components							0.028	0.040	-0.055	0.013
Means of marital conflict	0.079	-0.077								

Decomposition of mean difference
$$\bar{x}_2 - \bar{x}_1 = \Delta a + \Sigma\bar{x}_i\Delta b + \Sigma\Delta\bar{x}\bar{b}_1 + \Sigma\Delta\bar{x}\Delta b$$
$$-0.156 = -0.169 + 0.028 + 0.040 + -0.055$$

* $p < .05$ ** $p < .01$

Table 12 Decomposition analysis of 1980 to 2000 change in marital problems with mean-centered explanatory variables

Explanatory variable	x_1 1980	x_2 2000	$\bar{x}_2 - \bar{x}_1$	b_1 1980	b_2 2000	$b_2 - b_1$	Decomposition component			
							Slope $\bar{x}_1 \Delta b$	Level $\Delta \bar{x} b_1$	Joint $\Delta \bar{x} \Delta b$	Sum
Demographics										
Female	0.000	0.000	0.000	0.029	0.034	0.005	0.000	0.000	0.000	0.000
Black	−0.010	0.009	0.019	0.243*	0.115	−0.129	0.001	0.005	−0.002	0.003
Latino	−0.028	0.027	0.055**	0.166	−0.039	−0.205	0.006	0.009	−0.011	0.003
Other race	−0.021	0.021	0.042**	−0.096	−0.161	−0.066	0.001	−0.004	−0.003	−0.005
Education	−0.478	0.475	0.953**	−0.013	−0.009	0.004	−0.002	−0.013	0.005	−0.011
Age	−1.532	1.459	2.991**	−0.004	−0.006	−0.002	0.003	−0.011	−0.005	−0.014*
Age married	−1.511	1.462	2.973**	−0.013*	−0.006	0.007	−0.011	−0.039*	0.022	−0.028**
Remarried	−0.027	0.026	0.053**	0.014	0.078	0.064	−0.002	0.001	0.003	0.002
Premarital cohabitation	−0.124	0.120	0.244**	0.140*	0.118*	−0.023	0.003	0.034*	−0.006	0.032**
Number of children	0.050	−0.051	−0.101**	−0.004	−0.006	−0.003	0.000	0.000	0.000	0.000
Any stepchildren	−0.027	0.026	0.053**	0.057	−0.115	−0.172	0.005	0.003	−0.009	−0.001
Parental divorce	−0.048	0.047	0.095**	0.190**	0.190**	−0.001	0.000	0.018*	0.000	0.018**
Heterogamy index	−0.128	0.123	0.251**	0.076*	0.052*	−0.024	0.003	0.019*	−0.006	0.016**
Employment and income										
Husband employed	0.011	−0.011	−0.022*	−0.249	−0.035	0.214	0.002	0.006	−0.005	0.003
Husband's hours of work	−0.022	0.025	0.047	0.002	0.003	0.001	0.000	0.000	0.000	0.000
Wife employed	−0.089	0.085	0.174**	0.042	−0.220*	−0.262*	0.023	0.007	−0.045*	−0.015
Wife's hours of work	−3.977	3.827	7.804**	0.001	0.003	0.002	−0.009	0.010	0.017	0.018
Husband's work demands	−0.011	0.010	0.021	0.042	0.022	−0.020	0.000	0.001	0.000	0.001
Wife's work demands	−0.113	0.108	0.213**	0.039	0.056*	0.017	−0.002	0.009	0.004	0.010
Family income	−7.300	7.101	14.401**	0.000	0.000	0.000	0.002	0.004	−0.004	0.002
Use of public assistance	0.019	−0.019	−0.038**	0.095	0.287**	0.192	0.004	−0.003	−0.007	−0.007*
Economic distress	0.025	−0.024	−0.049**	0.109	0.470**	0.361**	0.009*	−0.005	−0.018**	−0.014**

Gender relations										
Wife's share of income	−0.057	0.054	0.111**	−0.143	−0.021	0.122	−0.007	−0.016	0.013	−0.009
Traditional gender attitudes	0.182	−0.178	−0.360**	0.070**	0.060*	−0.010	−0.002	−0.025*	0.004**	−0.024**
Husband's share of housework	−0.042	0.041	0.083**	0.094	0.406*	0.313	−0.013	0.008	0.026	0.020*
Division of labor unfair to husband	−0.016	0.016	0.032**	0.600**	0.317**	−0.283	0.004	0.019*	−0.009	0.014**
Division of labor unfair to wife	−0.007	0.000	0.007	0.579**	0.533**	−0.046	0.000	0.004	0.000	0.004
Husband final word sometimes	0.027	−0.027	−0.054**	0.033	−0.062	−0.095	−0.003	−0.002	0.005	0.001
Wife final word sometimes	−0.006	0.005	0.011	0.122	0.153*	0.031	0.000	0.001	0.000	0.002
Decision-making equality	−0.076	0.074	0.015**	−0.139**	−0.224**	−0.085	0.006	−0.021*	−0.013**	−0.027**
Social integration										
No shared friends	−0.017	0.017	0.034**	0.357**	0.222*	−0.135	0.002	0.012*	−0.005	0.010*
Some shared friends	−0.033	0.031	0.064**	0.059	0.021	−0.038	0.001	0.004	−0.002	0.003
All friends shared	0.055	−0.053	−0.108**	−0.054	−0.077	−0.023	−0.001	0.006	0.002	0.007
No shared affiliations	0.037	−0.035	−0.072**	0.066	0.153*	0.087	0.003	−0.005	−0.006	−0.008*
Some or all affiliations shared	0.025	−0.024	−0.049**	0.153**	0.045	−0.109	−0.003	−0.008	0.005	−0.005
Religiosity	−0.086	0.082	0.168**	0.022	0.093**	0.071*	−0.006	0.004	0.012	0.009*
Attendance at services	−0.046	0.041	0.087*	−0.097**	−0.075**	0.022	−0.001	−0.009	0.002	−0.008
Support for lifelong marriage	−0.053	0.051	0.104**	−0.176**	−0.013	0.163	−0.009	−0.018*	0.017	−0.010*
Regression constant				0.050	−0.036					
R^2				0.234**	0.249**					
Sum of components							0.010	0.003	−0.019	−0.006
Means of marital problems	0.047	−0.045								

Decomposition of mean difference

$$\bar{x}_2 - \bar{x}_1 = \Delta a + \Sigma \bar{x}_1 \Delta b + \Sigma \Delta \bar{x} b_1 + \Sigma \Delta \bar{x} \Delta b$$
$$-0.092 = -0.086 + 0.010 + 0.003 + -0.019$$

* $p < .05$ ** $p < .01$

Table 13 Decomposition analysis of 1980 to 2000 change in divorce proneness with mean-centered explanatory variables

Explanatory variable	x̄₁ 1980	x̄₂ 2000	x̄₂ − x̄₁	b₁ 1980	b₂ 2000	b₂ − b₁	Decomposition component			
							Slope $\bar{x}_1 \Delta b$	Level $\Delta \bar{x} b_1$	Joint $\Delta \bar{x} \Delta b$	Sum
Demographics										
Female	0.000	0.000	0.000	0.024	0.069	0.046	0.000	0.000	0.000	0.000
Black	−0.010	0.009	0.019	0.084	0.026	−0.058	0.001	0.001	−0.001	0.001
Latino	−0.028	0.027	0.055**	0.147	−0.003	−0.149	0.004	0.008	−0.008	0.004
Other race	−0.021	0.021	0.042**	−0.191	−0.147	0.044	−0.001	−0.008	0.002	−0.007*
Education	−0.478	0.475	0.953**	0.012	0.016	0.004	−0.002	0.012	0.004	0.014
Age	−1.532	1.459	2.991**	−0.003	−0.005	−0.001	0.002	−0.010	−0.004	−0.012
Age married	−1.511	1.462	2.973**	−0.017**	−0.018**	0.000	0.000	−0.051**	−0.001	−0.052**
Remarried	−0.027	0.026	0.053**	0.023	0.198**	0.174	−0.005	0.001	0.009	0.006
Premarital cohabitation	−0.124	0.120	0.244**	0.234**	0.169**	−0.064	0.008	0.057**	−0.016	0.049**
Number of children	0.050	−0.051	−0.101**	0.031	0.021	−0.010	0.000	−0.003	0.001	−0.003
Any stepchildren	−0.027	0.026	0.053**	0.133	−0.149	−0.282*	0.008	0.007	−0.015	0.000
Parental divorce	−0.048	0.047	0.095**	0.023	0.192**	0.170	−0.008	0.002	0.016	0.010*
Heterogamy index	−0.128	0.123	0.251**	0.116**	0.042	−0.074	0.009	0.029**	−0.018	0.020**
Employment and income										
Husband employed	0.011	−0.011	−0.022*	0.009	0.058	0.049	0.001	0.000	−0.001	−0.001
Husband's hours of work	−0.022	0.025	0.047	−0.001	−0.001	0.001	0.000	0.000	0.000	0.000
Wife employed	−0.089	0.085	0.174**	0.104	−0.007	−0.111	0.010	0.018	−0.019	0.009
Wife's hours of work	−3.977	3.827	7.804**	0.001	0.002	0.001	−0.005	0.009	0.009	0.014
Husband's work demands	−0.011	0.010	0.021	0.021	0.015	−0.006	0.000	0.000	0.000	0.000
Wife's work demands	−0.113	0.108	0.213**	0.032	0.054*	0.022	−0.002	0.007	0.005	0.009
Family income	−7.300	7.101	14.401**	0.001	0.000	−0.001	0.006	0.009	−0.012	0.003
Use of public assistance	0.019	−0.019	−0.038**	0.163*	0.255**	0.092	0.002	−0.006	−0.003	−0.008*
Economic distress	0.025	−0.024	−0.049**	0.146*	0.428**	0.283**	0.007	−0.007	−0.014*	−0.014**

Gender relations

Wife's share of income	−0.057	0.054	0.111**	−0.083	−0.274	−0.190	0.011	−0.009	−0.021	−0.020
Traditional gender attitudes	0.182	−0.178	−0.360**	−0.027	−0.002	0.025	0.005	0.010	−0.009	0.005
Husband's share of housework	−0.042	0.041	0.083**	−0.150	0.283	0.432*	−0.018*	−0.012	0.036*	0.005
Division of labor unfair to husband	−0.016	0.016	0.032**	0.478**	0.349**	−0.129	0.002	0.015*	−0.004	0.013**
Division of labor unfair to wife	−0.007	0.000	0.007	0.404**	0.467**	0.063	0.000	0.003	0.000	0.002
Husband final word sometimes	0.027	−0.027	−0.054**	0.012	−0.086	−0.099	−0.003	−0.001	0.005	0.002
Wife final word sometimes	−0.006	0.005	0.011	0.123*	0.174*	0.051	0.000	0.001	0.001	0.002
Decision-making equality	−0.076	0.074	0.015**	−0.165**	−0.126*	0.039	−0.003	−0.025**	0.006	−0.022**

Social integration

No shared friends	−0.017	0.017	0.034**	0.366**	0.297**	−0.069	0.001	0.012*	−0.002	0.011**
Some shared friends	−0.033	0.031	0.064**	0.133	0.043	−0.090	0.003	0.008	−0.006	0.006
All friends shared	0.055	−0.053	−0.108**	−0.076	−0.007	0.069	0.004	0.008	−0.007	0.005
No shared affiliations	0.037	−0.035	−0.072**	0.085	0.221**	0.135	0.005	−0.006	−0.010	−0.011**
Some or all affiliations shared	0.025	−0.024	−0.049**	0.173**	0.084	−0.089	−0.002	−0.009*	0.004	−0.006*
Religiosity	−0.086	0.082	0.168**	0.015	0.044*	0.029	−0.002	0.003	0.005	0.005
Attendance at services	−0.046	0.041	0.087*	−0.097**	−0.079**	0.019	−0.001	−0.009	0.001	−0.008
Support for lifelong marriage	−0.053	0.051	0.104**	−0.196**	−0.054	0.142	−0.008	−0.020*	0.015	−0.013*
Regression constant				0.032	−0.001					
R^2				0.230**	0.217**					
Sum of components	0.008	−0.006					0.027	0.045	−0.053	0.020

Means of divorce proneness

$$\bar{x}_2 - \bar{x}_1 = \Delta a + \Sigma \bar{x}_i \Delta b + \Sigma \Delta \bar{x} b_1 + \Sigma \Delta \bar{x} \Delta b$$

Decomposition of mean difference

$$-0.014 = -0.033 + 0.027 + 0.045 + -0.053$$

* $p < .05$ ** $p < .01$

References

Acock, Alan. 1997. "Working with Missing Values." *Family Science Review* 10: 76–102.

Allison, Paul D. 2001. *Missing Data.* Thousand Oaks, CA: Sage.

Amato, Paul R. 1989. "Who Cares for Children in Public Places? Naturalistic Observation of Male and Female Caretakers." *Journal of Marriage and the Family* 51: 981–990.

———. 1996. "Explaining the Intergenerational Transmission of Divorce." *Journal of Marriage and the Family* 58: 628–640.

———. 2000. "Consequences of Divorce for Adults and Children." *Journal of Marriage and the Family* 62: 1269–1287.

———. 2001. "Good Enough Marriages, Parental Discord, Divorce, and Children's Well-Being." *Virginia Journal of Social Policy and the Law* 9: 71–94.

Amato, Paul R., and Alan Booth. 1991. "The Consequences of Divorce for Attitudes toward Divorce and Gender Roles." *Journal of Family Issues* 12: 306–322.

———. 1995. "Changes in Gender Role Attitudes and Perceived Marital Quality." *American Sociological Review* 60: 58–66.

———. 1997. *A Generation at Risk: Growing Up in an Era of Family Upheaval.* Cambridge: Harvard University Press.

———. 2001. "The Legacy of Marital Discord: Consequences for Children's Marital Quality." *Journal of Personality and Social Psychology* 81: 627–638.

Amato, Paul R., David R. Johnson, Alan Booth, and Stacy J. Rogers. 2003. "Stability and Change in Marital Quality between 1980 and 2000." *Journal of Marriage and Family* 65: 1–22.

Amato, Paul R., and Denise Previti. 2003. "People's Reasons for Divorcing: Gender, Social Class, the Life Course, and Adjustment." *Journal of Family Issues* 24: 602–626.

Amato, Paul R., and Stacy J. Rogers. 1997. "A Longitudinal Study of Marital Problems and Subsequent Divorce." *Journal of Marriage and the Family* 59: 612–624.

———. 1999. "Do Attitudes toward Divorce Affect Marital Quality?" *Journal of Family Issues* 20: 69–86.

Arabie, Phipps, Lawrence J. Hubert, and Geert De Soete (eds.). 1996. *Clustering and Classification.* River Edge, NJ: World Scientific.

Arbuckle, James L. 1997. *Amos Users' Guide Version 3.6.* Chicago: Smallwaters Corporation.

Arnett, Jeffrey J. 2000. "Emerging Adulthood: A Theory of Development from the Late Teens through the Twenties." *American Psychologist* 55: 469–480.

Axinn, William G., and Arland Thornton. 1992. "The Relationship between Cohabitation and Divorce: Selectivity or Causal Influence?" *Demography* 29: 357–374.

Bachu, Amara. 1999. *Trends in Premarital Childbearing: 1930 to 1994.* Current Population Reports, Series P-23, No. 197. Washington, DC: Government Printing Office.

Bailey, Kenneth D. 1994. *Typologies and Taxonomies: An Introduction to Classification Techniques.* Beverly Hills: Sage.

Barich, Rachel R., and Denise D. Bielby. 1996. "Rethinking Marriage: Change and Stability in Expectations, 1967–1994." *Journal of Family Issues* 17: 139–169.

Bauman, Kurt J., and Nikki L. Graf. 2003. *Educational Attainment: 2000.* Census 2000 Brief. Washington, DC: Government Printing Office.

Becker, Gary S. 1981. *A Treatise on the Family.* Cambridge: Harvard University Press.

Bellah, Robert N., Richard Madsen, William N. Sullivan, Ann Swidler, and Steven N. Tipton. 1985. *Habits of the Heart: Individualism and Commitment in American Life.* Berkeley: University of California Press.

Bengtson, Vern L., Timothy J. Biblarz, and Robert E. L. Roberts. 2002. *How Families Still Matter: A Longitudinal Study of Youths in Two Generations.* New York: Cambridge University Press.

Bennett, Neil G., Ann K. Blanc, and David E. Bloom. 1988. "Commitment and the Modern Union: Assessing the Link between Premarital Cohabitation and Subsequent Marital Quality and Stability." *American Sociological Review* 53: 127–138.

Berardo, Donna H., Constance L. Shehan, and Gerald R. Leslie. 1987. "A Residue of Tradition: Jobs, Careers, and Spouses' Time in Housework." *Journal of Marriage and the Family* 49: 381–390.

Bernard, Jessie. 1982. *The Future of Marriage.* 2nd ed. New Haven: Yale University Press.

Blair, Sampson L., and Michael P. Johnson. 1992. "Wives' Perceptions of the Fairness of the Division of Household Labor: The Intersection of Housework and Ideology." *Journal of Marriage and the Family* 54: 570–581.

Blankenhorn, David. 1990. "American Family Dilemmas." Pp. 3–25 in David Blankenhorn, Steven Bayme, and Jean Bethke Elshtain (eds.), *Rebuilding the Nest: A New Commitment to the American Family.* Milwaukee: Family Service Association.

Blood, Robert O., and Donald M. Wolfe. 1965. *Husbands and Wives: The Dynamics of Married Living.* New York: Free Press.

Blumberg, Rae L., and M. T. Coleman. 1989. "A Theoretical Look at the Gender Balance of Power in the American Couple." *Journal of Family Issues* 10: 225–250.

Blumstein, Philip, and Pepper Schwartz. 1983. *American Couples: Money, Work, Sex.* New York: William Morrow.

Boggs, Carl. 2001. "Social Capital and Political Fantasy: Robert Putnam's *Bowling Alone.*" *Theory and Society* 30: 281–297.

Booth, Alan, and Paul R. Amato. 2001. "Parental Predivorce Relations and Offspring Postdivorce Well-Being." *Journal of Marriage and the Family* 63: 197–212.

Booth, Alan, and John N. Edwards. 1985. "Age at Marriage and Marital Instability." *Journal of Marriage and the Family* 47: 67–75.

———. 1990. "Transmission of Marital and Family Quality over the Generations: The Effects of Parental Divorce and Unhappiness." *Journal of Divorce* 13: 41–58.

———. 1992. "Starting Over: Why Remarriages Are More Unstable." *Journal of Family Issues* 13: 179–194.

Booth, Alan, John Edwards, and David Johnson. 1991. "Social Integration and Divorce." *Social Forces* 70: 207–224.

Booth, Alan, and David Johnson. 1985. "Tracking Respondents in a Telephone Interview Panel Selected by Random Digit Dialing." *Sociological Methods and Research* 14: 53–64.

———. 1988. "Premarital Cohabitation and Marital Success." *Journal of Family Issues* 9: 255–272.

Booth, Alan, David Johnson, A. Branaman, and Alan Sica. 1995. "Belief and Behavior: Does Religion Matter in Today's Marriage?" *Journal of Marriage and the Family* 57: 661–671.

Booth, Alan, David R. Johnson, and John N. Edwards. 1983. "Measuring Marital Instability." *Journal of Marriage and the Family* 45: 387–394.

Booth, Alan, David R. Johnson, Lynn K. White, and John Edwards. 1981. *Female Labor Force Participation and Marital Instability: Methodology Report.* Lincoln: Bureau of Sociological Research, University of Nebraska.

———. 1984. "Women, Outside Employment, and Marital Instability." *American Journal of Sociology* 90: 567–583.

———. 1985. "Predicting Divorce and Permanent Separation." *Journal of Family Issues* 6: 331–346.

Bradbury, Thomas N., Frank D. Fincham, and Steven R. H. Beach. 2000. "Research on the Nature and Determinants of Marital Satisfaction: A Decade in Review." *Journal of Marriage and the Family* 62: 964–980.

Bramlett, Matthew D., and William D. Mosher. 2002. "Cohabitation, Marriage, Divorce, and Remarriage in the United States." *Vital and Health Statistics, Series 23, No. 22.* Hyattsville, MD: National Center for Health Statistics.

Broman, Clifford L. 1993. "Racial Differences in Marital Well-Being." *Journal of Marriage and the Family* 55: 724–732.

Brooks, Clem. 2002. "Religious Influence and the Politics of Family Decline Concern: Trends, Sources, and U.S. Political Behavior." *American Sociological Review* 67: 191–211.

Bryant, Chalandra M., and Rand D. Conger. 1999. "Marital Success and Domains of Social Support in Long-Term Relationships: Does the Influence of Network Members Ever End?" *Journal of Marriage and the Family* 61: 437–451.

Bryant, Chalandra M., Rand D. Conger, and Jennifer M. Meehan. 2001. "The Influence of In-Laws on Change in Marital Success." *Journal of Marriage and the Family* 63: 614–626.

Bryk, Anthony S., and Stephen W. Raudenbush. 1992. *Hierarchical Linear Models: Applications and Data Analysis Methods.* Newbury Park, CA: Sage.

Bumpass, Larry L., Teresa Castro Martin, and James A. Sweet. 1991. "The Impact of Family Background and Early Marital Factors on Marital Disruption." *Journal of Family Issues* 12: 22–44.

Burgess, Ernest W., and Leonard S. Cottrell Jr. 1939. *Predicting Success or Failure in Marriage.* New York: Prentice-Hall.

Burgess, Ernest W., Harvey J. Locke, and Mary M. Thomes. 1963. *The Family: From Institution to Companionship.* New York: American Book Company.

Burgess, Ernest W., and Paul Wallin. 1954. *Courtship, Engagement, and Marriage.* Philadelphia: J. B. Lippincott Company.

Burman, Bonnie, and Gayla Margolin. 1992. "Analysis of the Association between Marital Relationships and Health Problems: An Interactional Perspective." *Psychological Bulletin* 112: 39–63.

Buss, David M., Todd K. Shackelford, Lee A. Kirkpatrick, and Randy J. Larsen. 2001. "A Half Century of Mate Preferences: The Cultural Evolution of Values." *Journal of Marriage and the Family* 63: 491–503.

Capaldi, Deborah M., and Gerald R. Patterson. 1991. "Relations of Parental Transitions to Boys' Adjustment Problems: I. A Linear Hypothesis. II. Mothers at Risk for Transitions and Unskilled Parenting." *Developmental Psychology* 27: 489–504.

Carmines, Edward G., and Richard A. Zeller. 1979. *Reliability and Validity Assessment.* Beverly Hills: Sage.

Casper, Lynne, and Suzanne M. Bianchi. 2002. *Continuity and Change in the American Family.* Thousand Oaks, CA: Sage.

Cherlin, Andrew. 1978. "Remarriage as an Incomplete Institution." *American Journal of Sociology* 84: 634–650.

———. 1992. *Marriage, Divorce, Remarriage.* Rev. ed. Cambridge: Harvard University Press.

———. 2000. "Toward a New Home Socioeconomics of Union Formation." Pp. 126–146 in Linda J. Waite (ed.), *The Ties That Bind: Perspectives on Marriage and Cohabitation.* New York: Aldine de Gruyter.

———. (2004). "The Deinstitutionalization of American Marriage." *Journal of Marriage and Family* 66: 848–861.

Christensen, Kathleen E. 2005. "Achieving Work-Life Balance: Strategies for Dual-Earner Families." Pp. 449–457 in Barbara Schneider and Linda J. Waite (eds.), *Being Together, Working Apart.* New York: Cambridge University Press.

Clydesdale, Timothy T. 1997. "Family Behaviors among Early U.S. Baby Boomers: Exploring the Effects of Religion and Income Change, 1965–1982." *Social Forces* 76: 605–635.

Cohen, Jacob. 1988. *Statistical Power Analysis for the Behavioral Sciences.* 2nd ed. Hillsdale, NJ: Erlbaum.

Coleman, James. 1988. "Social Capital in the Creation of Human Capital." *American Journal of Sociology* 94: 95–120.

Coltrane, Scott. 1996. *Family Man: Fatherhood, Housework, and Gender Equity*. New York: Oxford University Press.

———. 2000. "Research on Household Labor: Modeling and Measuring the Social Embeddedness of Routine Family Work." *Journal of Marriage and the Family* 62: 1208–1233.

Conger, Rand D., and Glen H. Elder. 1994. *Families in Troubled Times: Adapting to Change in Rural America*. New York: Aldine de Gruyter.

Conger, Rand D., Glen H. Elder Jr., Frederick O. Lorenz, Katherine J. Conger, Ronald L. Simons, Les B. Whitbeck, Shirley S. Huck, and Janet N. Melby. 1990. "Linking Economic Hardship to Marital Quality and Instability." *Journal of Marriage and the Family* 52: 643–656.

Coontz, Stephanie. 1992. *The Way We Never Were: American Families and the Nostalgia Trap*. New York: Basic Books.

———. 2000. "Historical Perspectives on Family Diversity." Pp. 15–31 in David H. Demo, Katherine R. Allen, and Mark A. Fine (eds.), *Handbook of Family Diversity*. New York: Oxford University Press.

———. 2005. *Marriage, a History: From Obedience to Intimacy, or How Love Conquered Marriage*. New York: Viking.

Cowan, Carolyn P., and Philip A. Cowan. 1992. *When Partners Become Parents*. New York: Basic Books.

Crouter, Ann C., Maureen Perry-Jenkins, Ted L. Huston, and D. W. Crawford. 1989. "The Influence of Work-Induced Psychological States on Behavior at Home." *Basic and Applied Social Psychology* 10: 273–292.

Curtis, Kristen T., and Christopher G. Ellison. 2002. "Religious Heterogamy and Marital Conflict." *Journal of Family Issues* 23: 551–576.

Danziger, Sheldon, and Peter Gottschalk. 1995. *America Unequal*. Cambridge: Harvard University Press.

Demo, David H. 1992. "Parent-Child Relations: Assessing Recent Changes." *Journal of Marriage and the Family* 54: 104–117.

Deutsch, Francine M. 1999. *Halving It All: How Equally Shared Parenting Works*. Cambridge: Harvard University Press.

Dollahite, David C., Loren D. Marks, and Michael A. Goodman. 2004. "Families and Religious Beliefs, Practices, and Communities." Pp. 411–431 in Marilyn Coleman and Lawrence H. Ganong (eds.), *Handbook of Contemporary Families: Considering the Past, Contemplating the Future*. Thousand Oaks, CA: Sage.

Durkheim, Emile. 1951. *Suicide: A Study in Sociology* (translated by John A. Spaulding and George Simpson). Glencoe, IL: Free Press (first published in 1897).

———. 1984. *The Division of Labor in Society* (translated by W. D. Halls). New York: Free Press (first published in 1933).

Dush, Claire M. Kamp, Catherine L. Cohan, and Paul R. Amato. 2003. "The Relationship between Cohabitation and Marital Quality and Stability: Change across Cohorts?" *Journal of Marriage and Family* 65: 539–549.

Duxbury, Linda E., Christopher Higgins, and Catherine Lee. 1994. "Work-Family Conflict: A Comparison by Gender, Family Type, and Perceived Control." *Journal of Family Issues* 15: 449–466.

Farley, Reynolds. 1996. *The New American Reality*. New York: Russell Sage Foundation.

Felson, Richard B. 2002. *Violence and Gender Reexamined*. Washington, DC: American Psychological Association.

Feng, Du, Roseann Giarrusso, Vern L. Bengtson, and Nancy Frye. 1999. "Inter-generational Transmission of Marital Quality and Marital Instability." *Journal of Marriage and the Family* 61: 451–464.

Ferree, Myra M. 1990. "Beyond Separate Spheres: Feminism and Family Research." *Journal of Marriage and the Family* 52: 866–884.

Fincham, Frank D., and Thomas Bradbury. 1987. "The Assessment of Marital Quality: A Reevaluation." *Journal of Marriage and the Family* 49: 797–809.

Finke, Roger. 1992. "An Unsecular America." Pp. 145–169 in Steve Bruce (ed.), *Religion and Modernization*. Oxford: Clarendon Press.

Firebaugh, Glenn. 1997. *Analyzing Repeated Surveys*. Sage University Papers on Quantitative Applications in the Social Sciences, 07–115. Thousand Oaks, CA: Sage.

Fischer, Claude S. 1982. *To Dwell among Friends: Personal Networks in Town and City*. Chicago: University of Chicago Press.

Fox, Greer Linton, Michael L. Benson, Alfred DeMaris, and Judy Van Wyk. 2002. "Economic Distress and Intimate Violence: Testing Family Stress and Resource Theories." *Journal of Marriage and Family* 64: 793–807.

Fox, Greer Linton, and David Chancey. 1998. "Sources of Economic Distress: Individual and Family Outcomes." *Journal of Family Issues* 19: 725–749.

Furstenberg, Frank F., and Andrew J. Cherlin. 1991. *Divided Families: What Happens to Children When Parents Part*. Cambridge: Harvard University Press.

Glass, Jennifer, and T. Fujimoto. 1994. "Housework, Paid Work, and Depression among Husbands and Wives. *Journal of Health and Social Behavior* 35: 179–191.

Glendon, M. A. 1989. *The Transformation of Family Law: State, Law, and Family in the United States and Western Europe*. Chicago: University of Chicago Press.

Glenn, Norval D. 1987. "Social Trends in the United States: Evidence from Sample Surveys." *Public Opinion Quarterly* 51: 109–126.

———. 1990. "Quantitative Research on Marital Quality in the 1980s: A Critical Review." *Journal of Marriage and the Family* 52: 818–831.

———. 1991. "The Recent Trend in Marital Success in the United States." *Journal of Marriage and the Family* 53: 261–270.

———. 1996. "Values, Attitudes, and the State of American Marriage." Pp. 15–33 in David Popenoe, Jean Bethke Elshtain, and David Blankenhorn (eds.), *Promises to Keep: Decline and Renewal of Marriage in America*. Lanham, MD; Rowman and Littlefield.

———. 1997. *Cohort Analysis*. Sage University Papers on Quantitative Applications in the Social Sciences, 07–005. Beverly Hills: Sage.

———. 1998. "The Course of Marital Success and Failure in Five American 10-year Marriage Cohorts." *Journal of Marriage and the Family* 60: 569–576.

———. 2001. "Is the Current Concern about American Marriage Warranted?" *Virginia Journal of Social Policy and the Law* 9: 5–47.

———. 2004. "Age at First Marriage and Marital Success." Unpublished manuscript.

Glenn, Norval D., and Kathryn B. Kramer. 1987. "The Marriages and Divorces of the Children of Divorce." *Journal of Marriage and the Family* 49: 811–825.

Glenn, Norval D., and Sara McLanahan. 1982. "Children and Marital Happiness: A Further Specification of the Relationship." *Journal of Marriage and the Family* 44: 63–72.

Goldscheider, Francis K., and Linda J. Waite. 1991. *New Families, No Families? The Transformation of the American Home.* Berkeley: University of California Press.

Goode, William J. 1961. "Illegitimacy, Anomie, and Cultural Penetration." *American Sociological Review* 26: 910–925.

———. 1963. *World Revolution and Family Patterns.* New York: Free Press.

———. 1980. "Why Men Resist." *Dissent* 27: 181–193.

Gottman, John M. 1994. *What Predicts Divorce?* Hillsdale, NJ: Lawrence Erlbaum.

Gottman, John M., James Coan, Sybil Carrere, and Catherine Swanson. 1998. "Predicting Marital Happiness and Stability from Newlywed Interactions." *Journal of Marriage and the Family* 60: 5–22.

Gottman, John M., James D. Murray, Catherine C. Swanson, Rebecca Tyson, and Kristin R. Swanson. 2002. *The Mathematics of Marriage: Dynamic Nonlinear Models.* Cambridge: MIT Press.

Gottman, John M., and Clifford I. Notarius. 2000. "Decade Review: Observing Marital Interaction." *Journal of Marriage and the Family* 62: 927–947.

Greeley, Andrew M. 1976. *Religious Change in America.* Cambridge: Harvard University Press.

Greenstein, Theodore N. 1996. "Gender Ideology and Perceptions of the Fairness of the Division of Labor: Effects on Marital Quality." *Social Forces* 74: 1029–1042.

Groves, Ernest R. 1928. *The Marriage Crisis.* New York: Longman, Green and Co.

Hackstaff, Karla B. 1999. *Marriage in a Culture of Divorce.* Philadelphia: Temple University Press.

Hamilton, Gilbert V. 1929. *What is Wrong with Marriage?* New York: A. and C. Boni.

Hareven, Tamara K. 1978. *Transitions: The Family and the Life Course in Historical Perspective.* New York: Academic.

Hartigan, J. A., and M. A. Wong. 1979. "A K-Means Clustering Algorithm." *Applied Statistics* 28: 100–108.

Heaton, Tim B. 2002. "Factors Contributing to Increasing Marital Stability in the United States." *Journal of Family Issues* 23: 392–409.

Heaton, Tim B., and Edith L. Pratt. 1990. "The Effects of Religious Homogamy on Marital Satisfaction and Stability." *Journal of Family Issues* 11: 191–207.

Hernandez, Donald J. 1993. *America's Children: Resources from Family, Government, and the Economy.* New York: Russell Sage Foundation.

Hetherington, E. Mavis, and Kathleen M. Jodl. 1994. "Stepfamilies as Settings for Child Development." Pp. 55–79 in Alan Booth and Judy Dunn (eds.), *Stepfamilies: Who Benefits? Who Does Not?* Hillsdale, NJ: Lawrence Erlbaum.

Hetherington, E. Mavis, and John Kelly. 2002. *For Better or For Worse: Divorce Reconsidered.* New York: W. W. Norton.

Heuveline, Patrick, and Jeffrey M. Timberlake. 2004. "The Role of Cohabitation in Family Formation: The United States in Comparative Perspective." *Journal of Marriage and Family* 66: 1214–1230.

Hill, Charles T., and Letitia A. Peplau. 1999. "Premarital Predictors of Relationship Outcomes: A 15-Year Follow-up of the Boston Couples Study." Pp. 237–278 in Thomas N. Bradbury (ed.), *The Developmental Course of Marital Dysfunction.* New York: Cambridge University Press.

Hill, Martha S. 1988. "Marital Stability and Spouses' Shared Time." *Journal of Family Issues* 9: 427–451.

Hirschl, Thomas A., Joyce Altobelli, and Mark R. Rank. 2003. "Does Marriage Increase the Odds of Affluence? Exploring the Life Course Probabilities." *Journal of Marriage and the Family* 65: 927–938.

Hochschild, Arlie R. 1989. *The Second Shift: Working Parents and the Revolution at Home.* New York: Viking.

———. 1997. *The Time Bind: When Work Becomes Home and Home Becomes Work.* New York: Metropolitan Books.

Homans, George. 1992 [1951]. *The Human Group.* New Brunswick, NJ: Transaction Publishers.

Hood, Jane. 1983. *Becoming a Two-Job Family.* New York: Praeger.

Hughes, Diane, Ellen Galinsky, and Anne Morris. 1992. "The Effects of Job Characteristics on Marital Quality: Specifying Linking Mechanisms." *Journal of Marriage and the Family* 54: 31–42.

Jacobs, Jerry A., and Kathleen Gerson. 2004. *The Time Divide: Work, Family, and Gender Inequality.* Cambridge: Harvard University Press.

Johnson, David R., Teodora Amoloza, and Alan Booth. 1992. "Stability and Developmental Change in Marital Quality: A Three-Wave Panel Analysis." *Journal of Marriage and the Family* 54: 582–594.

Johnson, David R., and Alan Booth. 1998. "Is Marital Quality a Product of the Dyadic Environment or Individual Factors?" *Social Forces* 76: 883–904.

Johnson, David R., Lynn K. White, John N. Edwards, and Alan Booth. 1986. "Dimensions of Marital Quality." *Journal of Family Issues* 7: 31–49.

Johnson, Michael P., John P. Caughlin, and Ted L. Huston. 1999. "The Triparate Nature of Marital Commitment: Personal, Moral, and Structural Reasons to Stay Married." *Journal of Marriage and the Family* 61: 160–177.

Johnson, Michael P., and Janel M. Leone. 2005. "The Differential Effects of Intimate Terrorism and Situational Couple Violence." *Journal of Family Issues* 26: 322–349.

Julien, Danielle, and Howard Markman. 1991. "Social Support and Social Networks as Determinants of Individual and Marital Outcomes." *Journal of Social and Personal Relationships* 8: 549–568.

Julien, Danielle, Howard Markman, S. Leveille, E. Chartrand, and J. Begin. 1994. "Network Support and Interference with Regard to Marriage: Disclosures of Marital Problems to Confidants." *Journal of Family Psychology* 8: 16–31.

Kalmijn, Matthijs. 1999. "Father Involvement in Childrearing and the Perceived Stability of Marriage." *Journal of Marriage and the Family* 61: 409–421.

Kalmijn, Matthijs, and W. Bernasco. 2001. "Separated Lifestyles in Married and Cohabiting Relationships." *Journal of Marriage and the Family* 63: 639–654.

Karney, Benjamin R., and Thomas N. Bradbury. 1995. "The Longitudinal Course of Marital Quality and Stability: A Review of Theory, Method, and Research." *Psychological Bulletin* 118: 3–34.

———. 1997. "Neuroticism, Marital Interaction, and the Trajectory of Marital Satisfaction." *Journal of Personality and Social Psychology* 78: 1075–1092.

Kessler, Ronald C. 1982. "A Disaggregation of the Relationship between Socioeconomic Status and Psychological Distress." *American Sociological Review* 47: 752–764.

Kiecolt-Glaser, Janice K., and T. L. Newton. 2001. "Marriage and Health: His and Hers." *Psychological Bulletin* 127: 472–503.

Kiernan, Kathleen. 2002. "Cohabitation in Western Europe: Trends, Issues, and Implications." Pp. 3–31 in Alan Booth and Ann Crouter (eds.), *Just Living Together: Implications of Cohabitation for Families, Children, and Social Policy.* Mahwah, NJ: Lawrence Erlbaum.

Kitson, Gay. 1992. *Portrait of Divorce: Adjustment to Marital Breakdown.* New York: Guilford Press.

Kreider, Rose M., and Jason M. Fields. 2002. *Number, Timing, and Duration of Marriages and Divorces: Fall 1996.* Current Population Reports, P70–80. Washington, DC: U.S. Census Bureau.

Kurdek, Lawrence. 2002. "Predicting the Timing of Separation and Marital Satisfaction: An Eight-Year Prospective Longitudinal Study." *Journal of Marriage and Family* 64: 163–180.

Lamanna, Mary Ann. 2002. *Emile Durkheim on the Family.* Thousand Oaks, CA: Sage.

Lareau, Annette. 2003. *Unequal Childhoods: Class, Race, and Childhood.* Berkeley: University of California Press.

Larsen, G. S., and David Olson. 1989. "Predicting Marital Satisfaction Using Prepare: A Replication Study." *Journal of Marital and Family Therapy* 15: 311–322.

Laub, John, D. Nagin, and Robert Sampson. 1998. "Trajectories of Change in Criminal Offending: Good Marriages and the Desistance Process." *American Sociological Review* 63: 225–238.

Laub, John H., and Robert Sampson. 2002. "Sheldon and Eleanor Glueck's Unraveling Juvenile Delinquency Study: The Lives of 1,000 Boston Men in the Twentieth Century." Pp. 87–115 in Erin Phelps, Frank F. Furstenbert Jr., and Anne Colby (eds.), *Looking at Lives: American Longitudinal Studies of the Twentieth Century.* New York: Russell Sage Foundation.

Lee, Yun-Suk. 2005. "Measuring the Gender Gap in Household Labor: Accurately Estimating Wives' and Husbands' Contributions." Pp. 229–247 in Barbara Schneider and Linda J. Waite (eds.), *Being Together, Working Apart.* New York: Cambridge University Press.

Lehrer, Evelyn L. 1998. "Religious Intermarriage in the United States: Determinants and Trends." *Social Science Research* 27: 245–263.

———. 2003. "The Economics of Divorce." Pp. 55–74 in Shoshana A. Grossbard-Shechtman (ed.), *Marriage and the Economy: Theory and Evidence from Advanced Industrial Societies.* New York: Cambridge University Press.

Lesthaeghe, Ron. 1995. "The Second Demographic Transition in Western Countries: An Interpretation." Pp. 17–62 in Karen Oppenheim Mason and An-Magritt Jensen (eds.), *Gender and Family Change in Industrialized Countries.* Oxford: Clarendon.

Lesthaeghe, R., and K. Neels. 2002. "From the First to the Second Demographic Transition: An Interpretation of the Spacial Continuity of Demographic Innovation in France, Belgium, and Switzerland." *European Journal of Population* 18: 325–360.

Levinger, George. 1976. "A Socio-psychological Perspective on Marital Dissolution." *Journal of Social Issues* 52: 21–47.

Levy, Frank. 1995. "Incomes and Income Inequality." Pp. 1–57 in Reynolds Farley (ed.), *State of the Union: America in the 1990s.* Vol. 1, *Economic Trends.* New York: Russell Sage Foundation.

Lewis, Robert A., and Graham B. Spanier. 1979. "Theorizing about the Quality and Stability of Marriage." Pp. 268–294 in Wesley R. Burr, Reuben Hill, F. Ivan Nye, and Ira L. Reiss (eds.), *Contemporary Theories about the Family.* Vol. 1, *Research Based Theories.* New York: Free Press.

Locke, H., and K. Wallace. 1959. "Short Marital Adjustment and Prediction Tests: Their Reliability and Validity." *Marriage and Family Living* 21: 251–255.

Lund, M. 1985. "The Development of Investment and Commitment Scales for Predicting Continuity of Personal Relationships." *Journal of Social and Personal Relationships* 2: 3–23.

Mahoney, Annette, Kenneth I. Pargament, Nalini Tarakeshwar, and Aaron B. Swank. 2001. "Religion in the Home in the 1980s and 1990s: A Meta-Analytic Reviewe and Conceptual Analysis of Links between Religion, Marriage, and Parenting." *Journal of Family Psychology* 15: 559–596.

Manning, Wendy, and Pamela J. Smock. 1995. "Why Marry? Race and the Transition to Marriage among Cohabitors." *Demography* 32: 509–520.

Marks, Nadine F., and James K. Lambert. 1998. "Marital Status Continuity and Change among Young and Midlife Adults: Longitudinal Effects on Psychological Well-Being." *Journal of Family Issues* 19: 652–687.

Mason, Mary Ann, Mark A. Fine, and Sarah Carnochan. 2004. "Family Law for Changing Families in the New Millennium." Pp. 432–450 in Marilyn Coleman and Lawrence H. Ganong (eds.), *Handbook of Contemporary Families: Considering the Past, Contemplating the Future.* Thousand Oaks, CA: Sage.

Mattingly, Marybeth J., and Suzanne M. Bianchi. 2003. "Gender Differences in the Quantity and Quality of Free Time: The U.S. Experience." *Social Forces* 81: 999–1030.

McGraw, Lori A., and Alexis J. Walker. 2004. "Gendered Family Relations: The More Things Change, the More They Stay the Same." Pp. 174–191 in Marilyn Coleman and Lawrence H. Ganong (eds.), *Handbook of Contemporary Families: Considering the Past, Contemplating the Future.* Thousand Oaks, CA: Sage.

McGue, Matt, and David T. Lykken. 1992. "Genetic Influence on Risk of Divorce." *Psychological Science* 3: 368–373.

McLanahan, Sara S., and Gary Sandefur. 1994. *Growing Up with a Single Parent: What Helps? What Hurts?* Cambridge: Harvard University Press.

McLeod, Jane D. 1991. "Childhood Parental Loss and Adult Depression." *Journal of Health and Social Behavior* 32: 205–220.

McLeod, Jane, and Karen Kaiser. 2004. "Child Emotional and Behavioral Problems and Educational Attainment." *American Sociological Review* 78: 636–658.

McLoyd, Vonnie C., Ana Mari Cauce, David Takeuchi, and Leon Wilson. 2000. "Marital Processes and Parental Socialization in Families of Color: A Decade Review of Research." *Journal of Marriage and the Family* 62: 1070–1093.

Milardo, Robert M. 1987. "Changes in Social Networks following Divorce: A Review." *Journal of Family Issues* 8: 78–96.

Mintz, Steven, and Susan Kellogg. 1988. *Domestic Revolutions: A Social History of American Family Life.* New York: Free Press.

Mirowsky, John, and Catherine E. Ross. 2003. *Social Causes of Psychological Distress.* 2nd ed. New York: Aldine de Gruyter.

Mizan, A. N. 1994. "Family Power Studies: Some Major Methodological Issues." *International Journal of Sociology of the Family* 24: 85–91.

Mowrer, Ernest R. 1927. *Family Disorganization*. Chicago: University of Chicago Press.

Myers, Scott M., and Alan Booth. 1999. "Marital Strains and Marital Quality: The Role of High and Low Locus of Control." *Journal of Marriage and the Family* 61: 423–436.

Nock, Steven. 1998. *Marriage in Men's Lives*. New York: Oxford University Press.

Nomaguchi, Kei M., Melissa A. Milkie, and Suzanne M. Bianchi. 2005. "Time Strains and Psychological Well-Being." *Journal of Family Issues* 26: 756–792.

Norton, R. 1983. "Measuring Marital Quality: A Critical Look at the Dependent Variable." *Journal of Marriage and the Family* 45: 141–151.

Oliker, Stacey J. 1989. *Best Friends and Marriage*. Berkeley: University of California Press.

Ooms, Theodora. 2002. "The Role of the Federal Government in Strengthening Marriage." *Virginia Journal of Social Policy and the Law* 9: 163–191.

Oppenheimer, Valerie K. 1997. "Women's Employment and the Gain to Marriage: The Specialization and Trading Model." *Annual Review of Sociology* 23: 431–453.

Oropesa, R. S., and Bridget K. Gorman. 2000. "Ethnicity, Immigration, and Beliefs about Marriage as a Tie That Binds." Pp. 188–211 in Linda J. Waite (ed.), *The Ties That Bind: Perspectives on Marriage and Cohabitation*. New York: Aldine de Gruyter.

Overall, J. E., B. W. Henry, and A. Woodward. 1974. "Dependence of Marital Problems on Parental Family History." *Journal of Abnormal Psychology* 83: 446–450.

Parke, Mary, and Theodora Ooms. 2002. "More Than a Dating Service: State Activities Designed to Strengthen and Promote Marriage." *Policy Brief*. Publication No. 02–64. Washington, DC: Center for Law and Social Policy.

Parsons, Talcott, and Robert F. Bales. 1955. *Family, Socialization and Interaction Process*. Glencoe, IL: Free Press.

Pasch, L. A., T. N. Bradbury, and J. Davila. 1997. "Gender, Negative Affectivity, and Observed Social Support in Marital Interaction." *Personal Relationships* 4: 361–378.

Perry-Jenkins, Maureen, and Karen Folk. 1994. "Class, Couples, and Conflict: Effects of the Division of Labor on Assessments of Marriage in Dual-Earner Families." *Journal of Marriage and the Family* 56: 165–180.

Perry-Jenkins, Maureen, Rena L. Repetti, and Ann C. Crouter. 2000. "Work and Family in the 1990s." *Journal of Marriage and the Family* 62: 981–998.

Pina, Darlene L., and Vern L. Bengtson. 1993. "The Division of Household Labor and Wives' Happiness: Ideology, Employment, and Perceptions of Support." *Journal of Marriage and the Family* 55: 901–912.

Pleck, Joseph, and Brian P. Masciadrelli. 2004. "Paternal Involvement by U.S. Residential Fathers: Levels, Sources, and Consequences." Pp. 222–271 in Michael E. Lamb (ed.), *The Role of the Father in Child Development*. 4th edition.

Popenoe, David. 1988. *Disturbing the Nest: Family Change and Decline in Modern Societies*. New York: Aldine De Gruyter.

———. 1993. "American Family Decline: 1960–1990: A Review and Appraisal." *Journal of Marriage and the Family* 55: 527–556.

———. 1996. *Life without Father*. New York: Martin Kessler.

Presser, Harriet. 1994. "Employment Schedules among Dual-Earner Spouses and the Division of Household Labor by Gender." *American Sociological Review* 59: 348–364.

———. 2000. "Nonstandard Work Schedules and Marital Instability." *Journal of Marriage and the Family* 62: 93–110.

———. 2003. *Working in a 24/7 Economy: Challenges for American Families.* New York: Russell Sage Foundation.

Putnam, Robert D. 2000. *Bowling Alone: The Collapse and Revival of American Community.* New York: Simon and Schuster.

Raley, R. Kelly. 2000. "Recent Trends and Differentials in Marriage and Cohabitation: The United States." Pp. 19–39 in Linda J. Waite (ed.), *The Ties That Bind: Perspectives on Marriage and Cohabitation.* New York: Aldine de Gruyter.

Rennison, Callie Marie. 2001. *Intimate Partner Violence and Age of Victim, 1993–1999.* Washington, DC: U.S. Department of Justice.

Repetti, Rena L. 1989. "Effects of Daily Workload on Subsequent Behavior during Marital Interaction: The Roles of Social Withdrawal and Spouse Support." *Journal of Personality and Social Psychology* 57: 651–659.

———. 1994. "Short-Term and Long-Term Processes Linking Job Stressors to Father-Child Interaction." *Social Development* 3: 1–15.

Reynolds, Jeremy. 2003. "You Can't Always Get the Hours You Want: Mismatches between Actual and Preferred Work Hours in the U.S." *Social Forces* 81: 1171–1199.

Risman, Barbara J., and D. Johnson-Sumerford. 1998. "Doing It Fairly: A Study of Postgender Marriages." *Journal of Marriage and the Family* 60: 23–40.

Roberts, Nicole A., and Robert W. Levenson. 2001. "The Remains of the Workday: Impact of Job Stress and Exhaustion on Marital Interaction in Police Couples." *Journal of Marriage and the Family* 63: 1052–1067.

Robinson, John P. 1993. "As We Like It." *American Demographics* 15: 44–48.

Robinson, John P., and Geoffrey Godbey. 1997. *Time for Life: The Surprising Ways Americans Use Their Time.* University Park: Pennsylvania State University Press.

Rogers, Stacy J. 1999. "Wives' Income and Marital Quality: Are There Reciprocal Effects?" *Journal of Marriage and the Family* 61: 123–132.

———. 2004. "Dollars, Dependency, and Divorce: Four Perspectives on the Role of Wives' Income." *Journal of Marriage and Family* 66: 59–74.

Rogers, Stacy J., and Paul R. Amato. 2000. "Have Changes in Gender Relations Affected Marital Quality?" *Social Forces* 79: 731–753.

Rogers, Stacy J., and Danielle D. DeBoer. 2001. "Changes in Wives' Income: Effects on Marital Happiness, Psychological Well-Being, and the Risk of Divorce." *Journal of Marriage and the Family* 63: 458–472.

Rogers, Stacy J., and Dee C. May. 2003. "Spillover between Marital Quality and Job Satisfaction: Long-Term Patterns and Gender Differences." *Journal of Marriage and Family* 65: 482–495.

Rogge, Ronald D., and Thomas N. Bradbury. 1999. "Recent Advances in the Prediction of Marital Outcomes." Pp. 331–360 in Rony Berger and Mo Therese Hannah (eds.), *Preventive Approaches in Couples Therapy.* New York: Brunner/Mazel.

Rosenfeld, Michael J. 2002. "Measures of Assimilation in the Marriage Market:

Mexican Americans 1970–1990." *Journal of Marriage and the Family* 64: 152–162.

Rosenfeld, Michael J., and Brung-Soo Kim. 2005. "The Independence of Young Adults and the Rise of Interracial and Same-Sex Unions." *American Sociological Review* 70: 541–642.

Rosenthal, Robert. 1994. "Parametric Measures of Effect Size." Pp. 231–244 in Harris Cooper and Larry V. Hedges (eds.), *The Handbook of Research Synthesis.* New York: Russell Sage Foundation.

Ross, Catherine E., and Chia-ling Wu. 1995. "The Links between Education and Health." *American Sociological Review* 60: 719–745.

Rothstein, B. 2002. Marital Strife: Do the Voters Really Care? *The Hill,* April 10 (http://www.hillnews.com).

Rubin, Donald B. 1987. *Multiple Imputation for Nonresponse in Surveys.* New York: John Wiley.

Rubin, Lillian B. 1983. *Intimate Strangers: Men and Women Together.* New York: Harper and Row.

———. 1985. *Just Friends: The Role of Friendship in Our Lives.* New York: Harper and Row.

Rusbult, Caryl E., Victor L. Bissonnette, Ximena B. Arriaga, and Chante L. Cox. 1998. "Accommodation Processes during the Early Years of Marriage." Pp. 74–113 in Thomas N. Bradbury (ed.), *The Developmental Course of Marital Dysfunction.* Cambridge, UK: Cambridge University Press.

Sabatelli, Ronald M., and Karen Ripoll. 2004. "Variations in Marriage over Time: An Ecological/Exchange Perspective." Pp. 79–95 in Marilyn Coleman and Lawrence H. Ganong (eds.), *Handbook of Contemporary Families: Considering the Past, Contemplating the Future.* Thousand Oaks, CA: Sage.

Sanchez, Laura. 1994. "Gender, Labor Allocations, and the Psychology of Entitlement within the Home." *Social Forces* 73: 533–554.

Sanchez, Laura, Steven L. Nock, James D. Wright, and Constance T. Gager. 2002. "Setting the Clock Forward or Back? Covenant Marriage and the Divorce Revolution." *Journal of Family Issues* 23: 91–120.

Sandberg, J. F., and Sandra L. Hofferth. 2001. "Changes in Children's Time with Parents: United States, 1981–1997." *Demography* 38: 423–436.

Scanzoni, John. 1978. *Sex Roles, Women's Work, and Marital Conflict: A Study of Family Change.* Lexington, MA: Heath.

———. 2001. "From the Normal Family to Alternate Families to the Quest for Diversity with Interdependence." *Journal of Family Issues* 22: 688–710.

Schafer, John L. 1999. *NORM: Multiple Imputation of Incomplete Multivariate Data under a Normal Model, Version 2.* Software for Windows 95/98/NT, available from http://www.stat.psu.edu/~jls/misoftwa.html.

Schoenborn, Charlotte A. 2004. "Marital Status and Health: United States, 1999–2002." *Advanced Data from Vital and Health Statistics,* no. 351. Hyattsville, MD: National Center for Health Statistics.

Schumm, Walter R., Lois A. Paff-Bergen, Ruth C. Hatch, Felix C. Obiorah, Janette M. Copeland, Lori F. Meens, and Margaret A. Bugaighis. 1986. "Concurrent and Discriminant Validity of the Kansas Marital Satisfaction Scale." *Journal of Marriage and the Family* 48: 381–387.

Shelton, Beth Anne. 2000. "Understanding the Distribution of Housework between Husbands and Wives." Pp. 353–365 in Linda J. Waite (ed.), *The Ties That Bind: Perspectives on Marriage and Cohabitation.* New York: Aldine de Gruyter.

Shelton, Beth Anne, and Daphne John. 1996. "The Division of Household Labor." *Annual Review of Sociology* 22: 299–322.

Sherkat, Darren E., and Christopher G. Ellison. 1999. "Recent Developments and Current Controversies in the Sociology of Religion." *Annual Review of Sociology* 25: 363–394.

Skolnick, Arlene S. 1991. *Embattled Paradise: The American Family in an Age of Uncertainty.* New York: Basic Books.

Spain, Daphne, and Suzanne Bianchi. 1996. *Balancing Act: Motherhood, Marriage, and Employment among American Women.* New York: Russell Sage Foundation.

Spanier, Graham. 1976. "Measuring Dyadic Adjustment: New Scales for Assessing the Quality of Marriage and Similar Dyads." *Journal of Marriage and the Family* 38: 15–27.

Stacey, Judith. 1990. *Brave New Families: Stories of Domestic Upheaval in Late Twentieth Century America.* New York: Basic Books.

———. 1996. *In the Name of the Family: Rethinking Family Values in the Postmodern Age.* Boston: Beacon Press.

Stack, Steven, and J. Ross Eshleman. 1998. "Marital Status and Happiness: A 17-Nation Study." *Journal of Marriage and the Family* 60: 527–536.

Stanley, Scott M., and Howard J. Markman. 1992. "Assessing Commitment in Personal Relationships." *Journal of Marriage and the Family* 54: 595–608.

StataCorp. 1999. *Stata Statistical Software: Release 6.0.* College Station, TX: Stata Corporation.

Stekel, Wilhelm. 1931. *Marriage at the Crossroads.* New York: W. Godwin.

Steverink, Nardi, Gerben J. Westerhof, Christina Bode, and Freya Dittmann-Kohli. 2001. "The Personal Experience of Aging, Individual Resources, and Subjective Well-Being." *Journals of Gerontology: Series B: Psychological Sciences and Social Sciences* 56: 364–373.

Sweeney, Megan M. 2002. "Two Decades of Family Change: The Shifting Economic Foundations of Marriage." *American Sociological Review* 67: 132–147.

Sweet, James A., and Larry L. Bumpass. 1987. *American Families and Households.* New York: Russell Sage Foundation.

Tallman, Irving, L. N. Gray, V. Kullberg, and D. Henderson. 1999. "The Intergenerational Transmission of Marital Conflict: Testing a Process Model." *Social Psychology Quarterly* 62: 219–239.

Teachman, Jay. 2002. "Stability across Cohorts in Divorce Risk Factors." *Demography* 65: 507–524.

Teachman, Jay, and Karen Polonko. 1990. "Cohabitation and Marital Stability in the United States." *Social Forces* 69: 207–220.

Terman, L. M. 1938. *Psychological Factors in Marital Happiness.* New York: McGraw-Hill.

Thompson, Linda. 1991. "Family Work: Women's Sense of Fairness." *Journal of Family Issues* 12: 181–196.

———. 1993. "Conceptualizing Gender in Marriage: The Case of Marital Care." *Journal of Marriage and the Family* 55: 557–570.

Thompson, Linda, and Alexis J. Walker. 1991. "Gender in Families: Women and

Men in Marriage, Work, and Parenthood." Pp. 76–102 in Alan Booth (ed.), *Contemporary Families: Looking Forward, Looking Back.* Minneapolis: National Council on Family Relations.

Thornton, Arland. 1996. "Comparative and Historical Perspectives on Marriage, Divorce, and Family Life." Pp. 69–87 in David Popenoe, Jean Bethke Elshtain, and David Blankenhorn (eds.), *Promises to Keep: Decline and Renewal of Marriage in America.* Lanham, MD: Rowman and Littlefield.

Thornton, Arland, William G. Axinn, and Daniel H. Hill. 1992. "Reciprocal Effects of Religiosity, Cohabitation, and Marriage." *American Journal of Sociology* 98: 628–651.

Thornton, Arland, and Linda Young-DeMarco. 2001. "Four Decades of Trends in Attitudes toward Family Issues in the United States: The 1960s through the 1990s." *Journal of Marriage and the Family* 63: 1009–1037.

Timmer, Susan G., and Joseph Veroff. 2000. "Family Ties and the Discontinuity of Divorce in Black and White Newlywed Couples." *Journal of Marriage and the Family* 62: 349–361.

Touliatos, John. 2001. *Handbook of Family Measurement Techniques.* Thousand Oaks, CA: Sage.

Tucker, M. Belinda. 2000. "Marital Values and Expectations in Context: Results from a 21-City Survey." Pp. 187–197 in Linda J. Waite (ed.), *The Ties That Bind: Perspectives on Marriage and Cohabitation.* New York: Aldine de Gruyter.

Umberson, Debra. 1987. "Family Status and Health Behaviors: Social Control as a Dimension of Social Integration." *Journal of Health and Social Behavior* 28: 306–319.

U.S. Census Bureau. 1998. *Marital Status and Living Arrangements.* Current Population Reports, Series P20–514. Washington, D.C.: Government Printing Office.

———. 2000. *Statistical Abstract of the United States: 2000.* Washington D.C.: Government Printing Office.

———. 2001. *Statistical Abstract of the United States: 2001.* Washington D.C.: Government Printing Office.

———. 2002. *Statistical Abstract of the United States: 2002.* Washington, D.C.: Government Printing Office.

———. 2003. *Statistical Abstract of the United States: 2003.* Washington D.C.: Government Printing Office.

VanLaningham, Jody, David R. Johnson, and Paul R. Amato. 2001. "Marital Happiness, Marital Duration, and the U-Shaped Curve: Evidence from a Five-Wave Panel Study." *Social Forces* 78: 1313–1341.

Vemer, Elizabeth, Marilyn Coleman, Larry Ganong, and Harris Cooper. 1989. "Marital Satisfaction and Remarriage: A Meta-Analysis." *Journal of Marriage and the Family* 51: 713–725.

Voydanoff, Patricia. 1988. "Work Role Characteristics, Family Structure Demands, and Work/Family Conflict." *Journal of Marriage and the Family* 50: 749–761.

Waite, Linda J. 1995. "Does Marriage Matter?" *Demography* 32: 483–507.

———. 2000. "Trends in Men's and Women's Well-Being in Marriage." Pp. 368–392 in Linda J. Waite (ed.), *The Ties That Bind: Perspectives on Marriage and Cohabitation.* New York: Aldine de Gruyter.

Waite, Linda J., and Maggie Gallagher. 2000. *The Case for Marriage: Why Married People Are Happier, Healthier, and Better Off Financially.* New York: Doubleday.

White, Lynn K. 1983. "Determinants of Spousal Interaction: Marital Structure or Marital Happiness?" *Journal of Marriage and the Family* 45: 511–519.

———. 1990. "Determinants of Divorce: A Review of Research in the Eighties." *Journal of Marriage and the Family* 52: 904–912.

White, Lynn K., and Alan Booth. 1985. "The Quality and Stability of Remarriages: The Role of Stepchildren." *American Sociological Review* 50: 689–698.

White, Lynn K., Alan Booth, and John N. Edwards. 1986. "Children and Marital Happiness: Why the Negative Correlation?" *Journal of Family Issues* 7: 131–147.

White, Lynn K., and Bruce Keith. 1990. "The Effect of Shift Work on the Quality and Stability of Marital Relations." *Journal of Marriage and the Family* 52: 453–462.

White, Lynn K., and Stacy J. Rogers. 2000. "Economic Circumstances and Family Outcomes: A Review of the 1990s." *Journal of Marriage and the Family* 62: 1035–1051.

Whitehead, Barbara D. 1993. "Dan Quayle Was Right." *Atlantic Monthly*, April, pp. 47–84.

———. 1996. "The Decline of Marriage as the Social Basis of Childrearing." Pp. 3–14 in David Popenoe, Jean Bethke Elshtain, and David Blankenhorn (eds.), *Promises to Keep: Decline and Renewal of Marriage in America.* Lanham, MD: Rowman and Littlefield.

Wilcox, W. Bradford. 2002. "Religion, Convention and Paternal Involvement." *Journal of Marriage and the Family* 64: 780–792.

Williams, Kristi. 2003. "Has the Future of Marriage Arrived? A Contemporary Examination of Gender, Marriage, and Psychological Well-Being." *Journal of Health and Social Behavior* 44: 470–487.

Wilson, James Q. 2002. *The Marriage Problem: How Our Culture Has Weakened Families.* New York: HarperCollins.

Winslow, Sarah. 2005. "Work-Family Conflict, Gender, and Parenthood, 1977–1997." *Journal of Family Issues* 26: 727–755.

Wolfinger, Nicholas. 1999. "Trends in the Intergenerational Transmission of Divorce." *Demography* 33: 415–420.

Wu, Lawrence L., Larry L. Bumpass, and Kelly Musick. 2001. "Historical and Life Course Trajectories of Nonmarital Childbearing." Pp. 3–47 in Lawrence L. Wu and Barbara Wolfe (eds.), *Out of Wedlock: Causes and Consequences of Nonmarital Fertility.* New York: Russell Sage Foundation.

Zinn, Maxine Baca, and Barbara Wells. 2000. "Diversity within Latino Families: New Lessons for Family Social Science." Pp. 203–232 in David H. Demo, Katherine Allen, and Mark A. Fine (eds.), *Handbook of Family Diversity.* New York: Oxford University Press.

Zuo, Ji-Ping. 1992. "The Reciprocal Relationship between Marital Interaction and Marital Happiness—A 3-Wave Study." *Journal of Marriage and the Family* 54: 870–878.

Index

Accommodative behavior, 252–253, 255
Acock, Alan, 269
Affluent couples, 126, 162, 226–227, 228, 231, 232
Age at first marriage: increase in, 1, 17, 20, 22, 31, 70, 76–79, 93, 184, 205, 207, 215, 216, 218, 219, 241; and marital quality, 20, 40, 70, 71, 77–79, 93, 94–95, 96, 208, 215, 216, 218, 219, 222, 255, 260; teenage marriage, 66, 76, 78; wives vs. husbands, 76; and education, 76, 79; and premarital cohabitation, 76–77; and economic security, 77, 79; and marital interaction, 78, 79, 96, 216, 238; and heterogamy, 89; and relations with in-laws, 184–185; in cluster analysis, 226, 227, 228
Age of spouses: as heterogamous, 70, 87, 88, 90, 91, 95; and marital quality, 84, 93, 96, 216, 217, 218, 219–220, 238, 270; wives vs. husbands, 87; and flattening of affect, 93; and labor-force participation, 102, 106; and number of friends, 180–181; and religion, 192; and attitudes toward lifelong marriage, 199, 200; in cluster analysis, 225–226, 227, 232; and marital interaction, 236–237
Aging effects, 61, 62, 63, 65, 147, 181, 183
Allison, Paul D., 269
Altobelli, Joyce, 2

Amoloza, Teodora, 48
Arabie, Phipps, 225, 271
Arbuckle, James L., 49
Arnett, Jeffrey J., 77
Arriaga, Ximena B., 252, 253
Assistance to Families with Dependent Children (AFDC), 245
Attitudes toward marriage, general, 1–2, 32, 33, 65, 224; in racial and ethnic groups, 2, 19; as social obligation, 4–5; as path to self-fulfillment, 4–5, 13–18, 30–31, 70, 71, 77, 80, 94, 95, 237, 240, 242, 262; expectations for marriage, 8–9, 10–11, 12–16, 17–18, 27–28, 31, 51, 71, 80, 94, 95, 108, 122–123, 167, 236, 237, 240, 257, 258–259; wives vs. husbands, 15–16, 53, 60, 68, 199, 200, 207; and subjective evaluation perspective, 38, 40–41; regarding involvement in family life, 108, 122–123, 136; and marital quality, 200–201, 202, 203, 208, 215, 217, 218, 219, 238, 254, 257–258, 260, 263; sexual fidelity, 244. *See also* Attitudes toward marriage as lifelong; Marital-decline perspective; Marital-resilience perspective
Attitudes toward marriage as lifelong: and religion, 29–30, 35, 199, 218; and divorce proneness, 30, 81, 200, 201, 202, 219; and premarital cohabitation, 74; and remarriage, 81, 200; increase in support,